D1323492

T

09

# Genres across the Disciplines

07/03/2015

# THE CAMBRIDGE APPLIED LINGUISTICS SERIES

The authority on cutting-edge Applied Linguistics research

Series Editors     2007–present: Carol A. Chapelle and Susan Hunston
                           1988–2007: Michael H. Long and Jack C. Richards

For a complete list of titles please visit: http://www.cambridge.org/elt/cal

*Recent titles in this series*:

# Genres across the Disciplines
## Student writing in higher education

*Hilary Nesi*
Coventry University

and
*Sheena Gardner*
Coventry University

JUBILEE CAMPUS LRC

CAMBRIDGE
UNIVERSITY PRESS

CAMBRIDGE UNIVERSITY PRESS
Cambridge, New York, Melbourne, Madrid, Cape Town,
Singapore, São Paulo, Delhi, Tokyo, Mexico City

Cambridge University Press
The Edinburgh Building, Cambridge CB2 8RU, UK

Published in the United States of America by Cambridge University Press,
New York

www.cambridge.org
Information on this title: www.cambridge.org/9780521149594

© Cambridge University Press 2012

This publication is in copyright. Subject to statutory exception
and to the provisions of relevant collective licensing agreements,
no reproduction of any part may take place without the written
permission of Cambridge University Press.

First published 2012

Printed in the United Kingdom at the University Press, Cambridge

*A catalogue record for this publication is available from the British Library*

*Library of Congress Cataloguing in Publication data*

Nesi, Hilary.
  Genres across the disciplines : student writing in higher education /
Hilary Nesi and Sheena Gardner.
     p. cm.
  Includes bibliographical references and index.
  ISBN 978-0-521-14959-4 (pbk.) -- ISBN 978-0-521-76746-0 (hardback)
  1. English language--Rhetoric--Study and teaching (Higher) 2. Report
writing--Study and teaching (Higher) I. Gardner, Sheena. II. Title.
  PE1404.N47 2012
  808'.0420711--dc23

  1006912026

  2011039520

ISBN 978-0-521-14959-4 Paperback
ISBN 978-0-521-76746-0 Hardback

Cambridge University Press has no responsibility for the persistence or
accuracy of URLs for external or third-party internet websites referred to in
this publication, and does not guarantee that any content on such websites is,
or will remain, accurate or appropriate.

# Contents

# Series editors' preface

This study of writing by undergraduate students in the UK draws on one of the largest collections of student essays ever made: the British Academic Written English (BAWE) corpus. It introduces the surprising variety of genres used by students today, from the traditional essay or lab report to more exploratory genres, such as the reflective essay or the personal narrative. Comparisons are made between disciplines, including Sciences, Engineering, Humanities and Social Sciences, and between students at different stages in their study.

Professor Nesi and Dr Gardner use a variety of methods in investigating their corpus, so that the book is a demonstration of how to proceed with such an investigation as well as a report of its outcome. Methods include the identification of moves in a genre, the comparison of frequencies of a variety of language features, and more detailed investigations of individual words and phrases. The book demonstrates how these methods work together to provide a picture of writing practices.

Each chapter of the book considers a 'family' of genres, each of which is linked to a social function. These are: 'demonstrating knowledge and understanding'; 'critical evaluation and developing arguments'; 'developing research skills'; 'preparing for professional practice'; and 'writing for oneself and others'. These functions map on to stages in the student's university life, from understanding new concepts to undertaking independent research and preparing to enter the world of work.

The book has many purposes. On the one hand it provides documentation on the range of writing produced by students in one educational system. It will inform courses and materials that prepare students who are entering that system to succeed in the tasks they are set. It will assist teachers and assessment specialists by providing information about assessment task outcomes: put simply, does the task produce the kind of writing, and the evidence of thought, that the assessors expect? On the other hand, it provides an example of how research of this kind might be undertaken, demonstrating the congruence of qualitative and quantitative methodologies, including the classification of thousands of individual texts and the comparative analysis of multiple sub-corpora. The book meets the needs of two kinds of Applied Linguists: the practitioner (what is it that university students in each year of their study need to know how to do?) and the researcher (how do I extract meaningful information from a multidimensional collection of texts?). It is a valuable addition to the *Cambridge Applied Linguistics Series*.

Carol A. Chapelle and Susan Hunston

# Abbreviations

| | |
|---|---|
| AH | – Arts and Humanities |
| BAAL | – The British Association for Applied Linguistics |
| BASE | – British Academic Spoken English |
| BAWE | – British Academic Written English |
| CALS | – Centre for Applied Language Studies |
| CELTE | – Centre for English Language Teacher Education |
| CLAWS | – Constituent Likelihood Automatic Word-tagging System |
| EAP | – English for Academic Purposes |
| ELC | – Engineering Lecture Corpus |
| ELFA | – English as a Lingua Franca in Academic Settings |
| ETS | – Educational Testing Service |
| GP | – General Practitioner, physician in the UK |
| HTLM | – Hospitality, Leisure and Tourism Management |
| IELTS | – International English Language Testing System |
| IMRD | – Introduction, Methods, Results, Discussion |
| IPCAC | – Issue, Principle, Case, Application, Conclusion |
| L2 | – Second Language |
| LS | – Life Sciences |
| MICASE | – Michigan Corpus of Academic Spoken English |
| MICUSP | – Michigan Corpus of Upper-level Student Papers |
| NVQ | – National Vocational Qualification |
| PDP | – Personal Development Planning |
| PS | – Physical Sciences |
| PSRB | – Professional, Statutory and Regulatory Body |
| QAA | – Quality Assurance Agency |
| RAPRIOP | – Reassurance and explanation; Advice; Prescription / other medical intervention; Referral and team working; Investigation; Observation; Prevention |
| SFL | – Systemic Functional Linguistics |
| SS | – Social Sciences |

T2K SWAL    – TOEFL 2000 Spoken and Written Academic
            Language
TOEFL       – Test of English as a Foreign Language
UCREL       – University Centre for Computer Corpus Research
            on Language
USAS        – UCREL Semantic Analysis System
VESPA       – Varieties of English for Specific Purposes database
WRiSE       – Write Reports in Science and Engineering

# *Acknowledgements*

The British Academic Written English (BAWE) corpus was developed at the Universities of Warwick, Reading and Oxford Brookes by Hilary Nesi, Sheena Gardner, Paul Thompson and Paul Wickens as part of the project *An investigation of genres of assessed writing in British Higher Education* which was funded by the Economic and Social Research Council (project number RES-000–23–0800) from 2004 to 2008. This book is dedicated to the laughter and professional expertise of those in CELTE who created the conditions for this project to develop and grow.

In addition, we wish to acknowledge the contributions of others who worked with us on the project: Douglas Biber at Northern Arizona University, Martin Wynn at the Oxford Text Archive, as well as Alois Heuboeck, Richard Forsyth, Jasper Holmes, Dawn Hindle, Sian Alsop, Elaine Roberts, Signe Ebeling, Maria Leedham, Lisa Ganobcsik-Williams, Mary Deane and Laura Powell, whose contribution of interview data from students was funded by the Warwick Undergraduate Research Scholarship Scheme. Most importantly, we acknowledge the contributions of university staff who were generous with their time in answering our questions, and the hundreds of university students who contributed their written work, without which there would have been no project.

The production of this volume benefitted enormously from the editorial feedback and the careful attention to detail by Susan Hunston, Jane Walsh, Anna Linthe, Joanna Garbutt, Sylvia Goulding and Kathleen Corley.

Sheena Gardner and Hilary Nesi

# PART I:
# INVESTIGATING STUDENT WRITING: FROM CORPUS TO GENRE FAMILY

# 1 *Investigating student writing with the BAWE corpus*

The book draws on the findings of a four-year study to investigate genres of student writing in higher education[1]. It provides an overview of the kind of writing British university students produce, showing the similarities and differences between writing assignments at different levels and across a range of disciplines. This information will be useful to researchers analysing the discourse of academic writing, to academics concerned with developing writing tasks at university level and to teachers who provide academic writing support to students, whether this is within the context of English for Academic Purposes (EAP) or in writing centres which largely cater for native speakers of English.

The book proposes a system of describing and distinguishing between different types of tertiary-level writing task. We identify and describe thirteen major types of assignment, each of which has a unique purpose and structure, but which is also subject to some variation in response to disciplinary requirements. Readers who devise academic writing tasks can use our descriptions of these assignment types as templates or as a stimulus for thought about the purpose and structure of the writing they expect their students to produce. Our descriptions may help them to distinguish between the different requirements of different writing tasks, and may also help them to make these distinctions clear to their students. Additionally, the descriptions can serve as a reference for writing teachers who are guiding their students towards more appropriate stylistic and organisational choices. The book describes the discourse features of successful assignments in terms of their underlying communicative purpose; successful assignments are those which achieve the intended purpose of the writing task, with due acknowledgement of disciplinary norms and expectations.

## 1.1 The educational context of university student writing

This book is written at a time of massive expansion in higher education. According to UNESCO (2008) about 138 million students were enrolled in tertiary education in 2005, an increase of 45 million university students worldwide since 1999. This rise has been partly due to population growth, and partly due to widening participation policies. Some countries have made great efforts to attract into higher education young people who have been academically disadvantaged, and to this end have encouraged universities to accept students without traditional university entry qualifications. In some countries a state university place is now guaranteed to all young people who have successfully completed secondary school.

Alongside widening participation there has been a huge rise in student mobility. Wächter (2008) cites UNESCO data indicating that the number of international students globally grew more than fourfold between 1975 and 2005, from 600,000 to 2.7 million. Most mobile students want to be taught in English, a language which they already know from their school studies, and which the international labour market requires. Countries where English is spoken as a first language are popular destinations for these students, but other countries have also gained a share of the international student market by adopting English as an educational lingua franca, for example Malaysia and Singapore (Sugimura, 2008), and non-English-speaking European countries (Wächter and Maiworm, 2008).

Thus, university students around the world are increasingly likely to be using English for their studies, although in many cases their pre-degree preparation will not have included extensive writing practice in English in the relevant genres. These students need to learn how to write well, because writing is the means by which they will construct disciplinary knowledge, the main means by which they will demonstrate their attainment for assessment purposes, and, in many cases, also the means by which they will communicate with professional colleagues in years to come.

However, although writing is probably the single most important skill necessary for academic success, and although we cannot assume that students will have acquired this skill before they begin their university studies, there is considerable confusion amongst students and writing instructors regarding the kinds of writing students are required to produce across disciplines and levels of study. Subject lecturers[2] often fail to make explicit the thinking behind the writing assignments they set, as Haggis (2006) points out, because traditionally student knowledge about genres has been acquired implicitly over time, via a process described by Turner as 'the pedagogy of osmosis' (2011: 21).

Moreover, academic writing programmes often proceed in ignorance of disciplinary genres, as Wardle (2009) discovered when she examined the 'pseudotransactional' assignments set in first year US university composition classes. Wardle rightly concludes that writing classes need to teach students about genres of student writing, and writing teachers need to be able to discern what the key features of these genres are.

## 1.2 What this book aims to do

This book is divided into two parts. Part I provides the context for our research, by explaining our methodologies and introducing the concepts of genre and genre family that are fundamental to our approach. This first chapter will describe the context in which our research took place, our data sources and our research methods. Chapter 2 explains how the genre classification was developed and introduces the thirteen genre families through their purpose, stages, genre networks, examples, characterisation in terms of multidimensional analysis, and distribution across levels of study and disciplinary groups.

Part II examines the social functions of university student writing, and the ways in which student writers develop and display various abilities through their writing. Genres and genre families are discussed individually, and Chapters 3, 4, 5 and 6 also each focus on a larger genre set by grouping together genre families which demonstrate similar educational purposes. These larger groupings help to distinguish some of the fundamental purposes of student writing, such as the ability to explain disciplinary concepts, to critically evaluate, to build sustained arguments, to carry out independent research projects and to prepare for professional practice. They also highlight writing requirements which are occasionally in conflict. Chapter 7 examines further functions of university student writing in those genres which enable writers to monitor their own personal development, and to practise writing for a readership outside their own specialism. The final chapter (Chapter 8) provides an overview of networks across genres and disciplines, and discusses the concept of academic register in relation to student writing. In this chapter we also suggest areas for further research, and provide details of how to access the BAWE corpus and other related resources.

## 1.3 Our starting point

The genres of student writing that we investigate in this book are those represented in the British Academic Written English (BAWE) corpus[3]. This collection presents a broad picture of British university student writing at the beginning of the 21st century, thus providing insights into the prevailing teaching and learning practices, the priorities of departments, and the demands of disciplines and professional bodies.

We founded our investigation on the following assumptions, derived from our experience as teachers of academic writing, the findings of prior studies in the field and discussions with academic staff in many university departments in the UK and internationally.

1 *University students are required to produce a range of different genres of assessed written work, reflecting a range of different communicative purposes.*
We knew of a number of studies that had described writing tasks set at university level, or had analysed the written work produced by specified groups of university students, but we wanted to explore further the relationships between assignments produced for different disciplines and levels of study, and to compare and contrast different types of student writing on a much larger scale.

2 *The nomenclature used within university departments to specify different assignment types goes some way towards identifying and distinguishing these genres.*
We already knew that students produced assignments labelled as 'book reviews', 'business plans', 'case studies', 'film commentaries', 'lab reports' and so on. These titles are given to the students by their lecturers, and we assumed that they encapsulated information about the purpose of the assignment and its linguistic features, format and structure. On the other hand we were aware that some descriptors such as 'essay' or 'project' were used very loosely, and that different names were sometimes given to very similar assignments, whilst other dissimilar assignment types were sometimes known by the same name. Whilst drawing what insights we could from departmental usage, we wanted to identify more robust categories of assignment genres.

3 *Within broad discipline areas certain genres are favoured and others are produced only rarely, if at all.*
We were aware that it would be impossible to prove that a genre was completely absent from an academic discipline. This is because lecturers vary the assignments they set from year to year, and in some contexts they are encouraged to invent alternatives to old, familiar assignment types. We wanted, however, to create a clearer picture of the distribution of assignment types across the disciplines.

4 *The types of writing that university students are required to produce change as they progress through their course of study. Students are expected to conform increasingly to the norms of favoured genres, and may also be given generically different writing tasks at different stages of study.*

It seemed reasonable to assume that students would gain more and more technical expertise in their field, and that their writing might approximate more and more closely to published academic or professional workplace writing. In one way or another, we anticipated different expectations placed upon students in their first year at university and in subsequent years, and we wanted to see how these expectations affected the writing students produced.

5 *An overview of student writing in English at the beginning of the 21st century would not only reflect the educational context in which it was produced, but also resonate with accounts of university student writing internationally, produced in different contexts.*

This is to suggest that with the globalisation and internationalisation of higher education there is value in describing and explaining the genres of writing in one context, to inform any future comparisons and developments with other contexts that are removed in time or place.

We tested these assumptions, and tried to answer the questions we associated with them, by analysing assignment registers and genres in the light of discourse community perspectives. Central to our investigations was the creation of the BAWE corpus.

## 1.4 The contents of the BAWE corpus

A rationale for the creation of the BAWE corpus is presented in Nesi et al. (2005), and the process of its development is described in Alsop and Nesi (2009). Briefly, the corpus was designed so that roughly equal numbers of assignments could be collected from four levels of study (first year undergraduate to taught Masters level) and four disciplinary groupings. These groupings (Arts and Humanities, Life Sciences, Physical Sciences and Social Sciences) were intended to facilitate comparison with two influential corpora of academic spoken English: the Michigan Corpus of Spoken Academic English (MICASE) and the British Academic Spoken English (BASE) corpus. We only collected assignments that had already been positively assessed by subject tutors, because we wanted to ensure that they conformed to departmental expectations. When they were writing their assignments the students would not have known that their work was going to become part of the corpus; at that time their only priority would have been to fulfil the task requirements and gain the best possible grade.

Assignments came from four different universities in England, which ensured access to a broad range of disciplines. Different departments operated rather different grading systems, but the pass mark in most was 40 per cent or above, and we only accepted assignments with grades of at least 60 per cent (or equivalent). The quality of these assignments was consistent with the award of an upper-second-class (2:1) or first class honours degree, and could be described in terms of 'merit' and 'distinction'.[4]

As far as possible, we collected equal numbers of assignments in each of the main disciplines we targeted, at each level of study. This ideal was difficult to achieve in practice, however, because of the much smaller numbers of students studying at Masters level in the Arts and Humanities, for example, and because of our requirement that all assignments should have reached a certain standard of proficiency. To facilitate data processing, only word-processed assignments were accepted for the corpus, excluding handwritten examination scripts, handwritten lab notebooks, assignments consisting solely of mathematical calculations and PowerPoint presentations assessed through oral delivery. As one assignment might include several essays or several lab reports (that is, several texts), a distinction was made between assignments which were submitted as one piece of work and texts which were analysed as genres. The final make-up of the corpus is illustrated in Table 1.1.

In addition to the assignments themselves, we collected information about the title of each assignment and its corresponding module, the department that set the assignment, and the grade that it had been given. At the end of the project some of this information was conflated, for example the assignment file headers identifying disciplinary rather than departmental provenance, as in some cases assignments from departments at more than one university contributed to the corpus holdings for a single discipline. Similarly, because of variation in the way assignments were graded, we simply divided them into those which had received a grade of between 60 per cent and 69 per cent, or its equivalent (a 'merit' grade, 'M') and those which had received a grade of 70 per cent or over, or its equivalent (a 'distinction' grade, 'D'). This distinction grade is comparable to an 'A' grade in the U.S. university system, while the merit grade is comparable to a 'B' grade, although the proportion of grades in each division varies.[5] The corpus contains almost equal numbers of distinction assignments (1,251) and merit assignments (1,402).

Table 1.1  Overview of BAWE corpus holdings

| | | Level 1 | Level 2 | Level 3 | Level 4 | Total |
|---|---|---|---|---|---|---|
| **Arts and Humanities (AH)** | assignments | 239 | 228 | 160 | 78 | 705 |
| Archaeology; Classics; Comparative | texts | 255 | 229 | 160 | 80 | 724 |
| American Studies; English; History; | words | 468,353 | 583,617 | 427,942 | 234,206 | 1,714,118 |
| Linguistics / English Language Studies; Philosophy; others | | | | | | |
| **Life Sciences (LS)** | assignments | 180 | 193 | 113 | 197 | 683 |
| Agriculture; Biological Science; Food | texts | 183 | 206 | 120 | 205 | 719 |
| Science; Health; Medicine; Psychology | words | 299,370 | 408,070 | 263,668 | 441,283 | 1,412,391 |
| **Physical Sciences (PS)** | assignments | 181 | 149 | 156 | 110 | 596 |
| Architecture; Chemistry; Computer | texts | 181 | 154 | 156 | 133 | 624 |
| Science; Cybernetics / Electronic | words | 300,989 | 314,331 | 426,431 | 339,605 | 1,381,356 |
| Engineering; Engineering; Mathematics; Meteorology; Physics; Planning | | | | | | |
| **Social Sciences (SS)** | assignments | 207 | 197 | 166 | 207 | 777 |
| Anthropology; Business; Economics; | texts | 216 | 198 | 170 | 207 | 791 |
| Hospitality, Leisure and Tourism; | words | 371,473 | 475,668 | 447,950 | 704,039 | 1,999,130 |
| Management; Law; Politics; Publishing; Sociology | | | | | | |
| **Total students** | | 333 | 302 | 235 | 169 | 1039 |
| **Total assignments** | | 807 | 767 | 595 | 592 | 2761 |
| **Total texts** | | 840 | 787 | 606 | 625 | 2858 |
| **Total words** | | 1,440,185 | 1,781,686 | 1,565,991 | 1,719,133 | 6,506,995 |

The discipline, level and grade of each assignment were important factors influencing our collection policy; we set a limit on the number of assignments at each level in each discipline, and we rejected assignments that had not achieved the required grade. However we also gathered other types of contextual information which did not affect our decision about whether or not to include an assignment in the corpus, such as the gender, year of birth and native speaker status of the contributor, and the number of years of UK secondary education he or she had received. Corpus findings concerning these factors must be treated with caution, because contributor features are not distributed equally across the corpus holdings. For example, anyone wishing to analyse the corpus from the perspective of gender should bear in mind that there are more female than male contributors, and their assignments are not entirely comparable in terms of discipline and disciplinary groupings. Likewise, anyone wishing to compare native and non-native speaker writing in the corpus should bear in mind that assignments contributed by speakers of languages other than English tend to be concentrated in the Social Sciences and at Masters level. Further details of the corpus contents in terms of the contributors' gender and first language are provided in Appendix 1.1.

## 1.5 Other sources of data

Throughout this book we will be drawing on corpus evidence as well as contextual data of various kinds gathered in connection with the project. This information was also considered when categorising assignments into genres and groups of similar genres, or genre families.

During the process of corpus compilation the students' own perceptions about the type of assignment they were submitting were recorded. We asked, for example, whether they thought their assignment was an essay, a lab report, a case study or some other kind of text. Students' responses were later compared with the way they had described their assignments within the text itself, and the way other contributors had described the same or similar tasks.

Although we did not have a prolonged engagement with each department, we were influenced by the ethnographic approach of Prior (1998), who used departmental documents and tutor representations of tasks to build a 'thick'[6] description of the contexts and processes of student writing. We referred to module descriptions from each of the target departments and explored departmental environments both informally and through semi-structured interviews with teaching staff and students.

Staff were selected for interviews because they were involved in teaching and in the assessment of student assignments. The interviews, described in Nesi and Gardner (2006) and mentioned again in Chapter 2, centred on the following questions, adapted from a similar but smaller-scale investigation by Woodward-Kron (2002: 125):

- What role does assignment writing play in your department?
- What genres do you require your students to write?
- What are you looking for when you assess written work in different genres?
- How do your expectations of students' writing change during the course of the degree?

These methods were subsequently replicated by an undergraduate student researcher who interviewed 36 undergraduate students (Gardner and Powell, 2006). In this case the fact that the interviewer was a student encouraged the interviewees to respond more freely, and provided us with insights that we would not have obtained from talking to staff alone. The distribution of student interviews is reproduced in Appendix 1.2.

This contextual information was triangulated with textual information to inform our decisions regarding the classification of corpus holdings. The process of grouping similar genres together is described in Chapter 2; ultimately all texts in the corpus were assigned to one and only one genre family, making the description of large numbers of texts more manageable and facilitating comparisons across disciplines.

The distribution of the thirteen genre families across levels is shown in Table 1.2. The levels correspond essentially to first year, second

Table 1.2    Distribution of genre families by level

|  | Level 1 | Level 2 | Level 3 | Level 4 | Total |
|---|---|---|---|---|---|
| Case Study | 26 | 30 | 35 | 103 | 194 |
| Critique | 78 | 79 | 68 | 97 | 322 |
| Design Specification | 24 | 19 | 35 | 15 | 93 |
| Empathy Writing | 10 | 3 | 18 | 5 | 36 |
| Essay | 416 | 360 | 267 | 194 | 1237 |
| Exercise | 28 | 28 | 31 | 27 | 114 |
| Explanation | 81 | 62 | 34 | 37 | 214 |
| Literature Survey | 10 | 6 | 9 | 10 | 35 |
| Methodology Recount | 120 | 127 | 49 | 65 | 361 |
| Narrative Recount | 18 | 19 | 21 | 17 | 75 |
| Problem Question | 12 | 19 | 6 | 3 | 40 |
| Proposal | 10 | 19 | 11 | 36 | 76 |
| Research Report | 7 | 16 | 22 | 16 | 61 |
| Total | 840 | 787 | 606 | 625 | 2858 |

year, third (or final) year and taught Masters level, although it should be noted that Masters level dissertations were not included in the corpus. Further tables throughout this book will show distribution in greater detail, in terms of disciplines and genres.

## 1.6 Methods of analysis

Throughout the book we refer to a variety of research techniques, choosing whichever method best reveals the character of a genre, or best distinguishes one genre family from another.     *genre analysis*

Our genre family classification system draws on the work of the Sydney School, which has been particularly influential in using Systemic Functional Linguistics (SFL) to identify and explain genres of secondary and primary school texts. Genre is widely regarded as 'the system of staged goal-oriented social processes through which social subjects in a given culture live their lives' (Martin, 1997: 13). We identify the educational purposes and stages that typify and distinguish genre families, for example Essays and Critiques (Chapter 4) and Research Reports and Literature Surveys (Chapter 5)[7]. Our genre families are different from those in the Sydney School classifications, however, partly because we aimed to develop them by grouping similar assignments, rather than imposing a classification developed for other contexts, and partly because we were also influenced by research on academic genres by Swales (1990) and in the field of academic literacies (Lea and Street, 2000).

Our examination of the linguistic features associated with the stages of genres draws on Systemic Functional Linguistics (Halliday and Matthiessen, 2004) to explore the prosodic nature of evaluation, and the functions of hyperNews (Martin, 1992) to make claims which help build an argument (Chapter 4). We also use the appraisal system developed by Martin (2000) and Martin and White (2005) to analyse evaluative resources in texts (Chapter 7). All these methods of analysis will be explained more fully in the relevant chapters.

We use the results of multidimensional analysis to help us characterise the genre families we describe. This analysis was conducted by Biber at the University of Northern Arizona, using five dimensions he identified (Biber, 1988). The BAWE corpus was tagged for 67 linguistic features, grouped into 16 grammatical / functional categories:

| | |
|---|---|
| 1 tense and aspect markers | 5 nominal forms |
| 2 place and time adverbials | 6 passives |
| 3 pronouns and pro-verbs | 7 stative forms |
| 4 questions | 8 subordination features |

(cont.)

9 prepositional phrases,
  adjectives and adverbs
10 lexical specificity (type–
  token ration and mean word
  length)
11 lexical classes such as
  downtoners, hedges,
  amplifiers and emphatics
12 modals

13 specialised verb classes such
  as 'public', 'private' and
  'suasive' verbs
14 reduced forms and
  dispreferred structures such
  as split infinitives
15 coordination
16 negation

So, for example, place adverbials include *above* and *beside*, and time adverbials include *early, instantly* and *soon*. 'Public' verbs include *say, tell* and *explain*, 'private' verbs include *believe, think* and *know*, and 'suasive' verbs include *command, insist* and *propose*.

The texts in the corpus were compared across genre families, disciplinary groupings and levels of study, and scores along each dimension were allocated to each corpus subgroup. These scores characterise the register of the subgroup, and indicate tendencies towards information density, chronologically ordered narrative, deictic references to time and place, and so on. A summary of linguistic features in relation to the five dimensions is provided in Appendix 1.3, adapted from Biber et al. (2002). The dimensions are explained more fully below, with reference to Biber (1988) (also summarised in Conrad and Biber, 2001).

## DIMENSION 1: *Involved versus informational*

This contrasts verbal and nominal styles. Biber found conversation to be extremely involved, with a score of 35, with high frequencies of present tense verbs, private verbs, first and second person pronouns, and contractions. At the opposite end of the scale general academic prose (published research in journals, books and reports from the Lancaster–Oslo/Bergen, or LOB, corpus) had a score of -15.

## DIMENSION 2: *Narrative versus non-narrative*

This dimension is associated with past time narration. Biber found romance fiction to be heavily narrative, with a score of 7, because it contains many third person pronouns, past tense verbs, perfect aspect verbs, and public verbs such as *say* and *tell*. Academic prose, official documents and radio broadcasts were positioned at the opposite end of the scale, with scores below -2.

## DIMENSION 3: *Elaborated versus situation-dependent*

Elaborated texts can be understood in contexts that are distant in time and place from the context in which they were originally produced. They identify referents explicitly, through features such as relative clause constructions, nominalisations, and time and place adverbials for temporal and locative reference. The official documents in Biber's study scored more than 7 on this dimension. Conversations and broadcasts, on the other hand, scored -4 or less, because when we listen to these sorts of texts we interpret what is being said in terms of where the speaker is, and what is happening at the time.

## DIMENSION 4: *Persuasive*

This dimension identifies overtly argumentative texts, and is characterised by infinitives, suasive verbs such as *agree, ask, insist* and *recommend*, conditional subordination, split auxiliaries, and modals expressing prediction, necessity and possibility. The editorials and professional letters analysed by Biber scored 3 or more, while radio broadcasts scored below -4.

## DIMENSION 5: *Non-impersonal versus abstract and impersonal*

Impersonal texts are characterised by passive constructions, conjuncts such as *thus* and *however*, and adverbial and postnominal clauses. Such features are typical of written as opposed to spoken texts. Biber found that general academic prose from the LOB corpus had high scores on this dimension (more than 5). Conversations had low scores (less than -3).

Tables 1.3 and 1.4 show scores for BAWE corpus texts across the four levels of study and across the four disciplinary groups. The entirely negative scores on the involved and narrative dimensions

Table 1.3   Dimension scores by level

| Level | Involved | Narrative | Elaborated | Persuasive | Abstract and impersonal |
|---|---|---|---|---|---|
| 1 | −12.7 | −2.7 | 5.1 | −1.4 | 5.9 |
| 2 | −13.9 | −2.8 | 5.6 | −1.4 | 6.2 |
| 3 | −14.7 | −3.0 | 5.7 | −1.5 | 6.4 |
| 4 | −17.2 | −3.2 | 6.3 | −2.0 | 5.5 |

Table 1.4    Dimension scores by disciplinary group

|     | Involved | Narrative | Elaborated | Persuasive | Abstract and impersonal |
|-----|----------|-----------|------------|------------|-------------------------|
| AH  | –13.4    | –2.1      | 5.7        | –2.3       | 5.5                     |
| LS  | –15.6    | –3.0      | 5.7        | –1.5       | 5.7                     |
| PS  | –13.4    | –3.7      | 4.4        | –1.2       | 6.5                     |
| SS  | –15.3    | –3.0      | 6.5        | –1.3       | 6.2                     |

indicate a high informational focus and a low level of narration overall, but students' writing also becomes increasingly informational and elaborated as they progress through their degree programmes, and has progressively fewer narrative and persuasive features. Abstract impersonal features increase until Masters level; their decline at Level 4 has not yet been fully explained, but may be associated with the fact that Masters students contributed a greater number of case studies and proposals to the corpus, and these are some of the least abstract genre families (see Chapters 2 and 6).

Table 1.4 shows that texts in the Life Sciences (LS) are the most informational (that is, the least involved), and those in the Arts and Humanities (AH) have the greatest amount of narrative features. Physical Sciences (PS) have the fewest narrative features and are the most impersonal and persuasive. Texts in the Social Sciences (SS) are the most elaborated.

Dimension scores for the thirteen genre families are presented in Chapter 2, and the competing effects of disciplinary group and genre family are discussed in Chapter 9.

In addition to the results of multidimensional analysis, we refer throughout the book to data generated through the use of WordSmith Tools (Scott, 2010), and Sketch Engine (Kilgarriff et al., 2004). Details of the functions of Sketch Engine with special reference to the BAWE corpus are provided in Nesi and Thompson (2011).

WordSmith Tools and Sketch Engine were both used to create concordance lines. These provide contexts for corpus words and phrases throughout the book. Subcorpora of genres and genre families were manually prepared for use with WordSmith Tools. Sketch Engine enabled us to filter the corpus so that we could view concordance output from selected levels, genres and disciplines.

WordSmith and Sketch Engine were also used to create lists of keywords and lemmas, calculated by comparing their relative frequencies in a study corpus (all or part of the BAWE corpus) with those of a larger reference corpus (the British National Corpus or the entire

BAWE corpus). A word or lemma is considered positively key if its frequency in the study corpus is unusually high. WordSmith provides a 'keyness' score, measured by cross-tabulation and chi-square significance test (Scott, 2010). Sketch Engine provides a 'keyword score', using a statistic based on 'word W is N times as frequent in corpus X versus corpus Y'[8]. The keywords and lemmas listed in this book have very high scores, and the probability of the keyness being accidental is very low. The table in Appendix 1.4 shows the top key lemmas in the BAWE corpus compared with the British National Corpus, calculated using Sketch Engine.

Common word combinations, or 'clusters', were identified using WordSmith Tools Version 5. Clusters often reveal common underlying concepts and functions shared by groups of texts. Some writers use the term 'cluster' to refer to recognisable multi-word units which are identified by searching for strings containing a given 'seed term'. For example, a cluster search based on the seed term *of* might find multi-word units such as *in terms of, on account of, the context of* and so on. In this book, however, the term cluster is used for any frequent string of words; there is no seed term, and the only parameters are the length of the string and the minimum frequency. Thus, for us, the term is synonymous with 'n-gram' (see, for example, Gries, Newman and Shaoul, 2011) and 'lexical bundle' (see, for example, Biber, 2007).

All the words in the BAWE corpus have been annotated for part of speech, using the Constituent Likelihood Automatic Word-tagging System (CLAWS). The version we used identifies 137 part-of-speech categories and subcategories, for example singular and plural common, locative and temporal nouns, singular and plural proper nouns, and singular and plural units of measurement. The words in the BAWE corpus have also been annotated for semantic category, using the UCREL[9] Semantic Analysis System (USAS). This system groups words in terms of 21 thesaurus-style categories, developed on the basis of those in the *Longman Lexicon of Contemporary English* (McArthur, 1981). Details of the CLAWS system are provided in Garside and Smith (1997), and details of the USAS system are given in Archer et al. (2002).

Frequencies of words in some of the main USAS categories are provided in Appendix 1.5. Instructions on how to search for these features in Sketch Engine are provided in Nesi and Thompson (2011). Semantic analysis is used in Chapter 6, with reference to Case Studies, Design Specifications, Proposals and Problem Questions.

Basic statistics, such as the average word length of assignments, the average number of sentences per assignment and the average sentence length, were calculated from an Excel spreadsheet of the corpus

Table 1.5    BAWE corpus statistics

| Average \ Level | 1 | 2 | 3 | 4 |
|---|---|---|---|---|
| words per assignment | 1782 | 2323 | 2637 | 2903 |
| sentences per assignment | 75 | 95 | 108 | 122 |
| paragraphs per assignment | 21 | 29 | 34 | 40 |
| words per sentence | 24.8 | 25.6 | 25.5 | 24.6 |
| sentences per paragraph | 4.8 | 4.6 | 4.5 | 3.7 |
| tables | 0.6 | 0.7 | 1.0 | 1.0 |
| figures | 1.0 | 1.2 | 2.1 | 2.0 |
| block quotes | 0.5 | 1.1 | 0.8 | 0.7 |
| formulae | 2.0 | 5.2 | 7.3 | 1.8 |
| lists | 0.4 | 0.5 | 0.6 | 1.6 |

holdings. Table 1.5 provides statistics for each level of study produced by this means. These statistics clearly show how the average word length of assignments increases from Level 1 to 4, although average sentence and paragraph lengths do not increase. Assignments written at later levels of study contain more tables, figures and lists. The averages for formulae must be interpreted with caution, because there is very wide variation in their use. The range of formulae per assignment is 1–70 at Level 1 and 1–51 at Level 4, but at Levels 2 and 3 there are 13 assignments containing more than 100 formulae, and three containing more than 800.

Basic statistics for each genre family will be discussed in the appropriate chapters, where we will see meaningful differences between, for instance, Essays and Critiques, in terms of block quotes versus figures. These statistics help us characterise the genres and point to features that analyses of individual texts can miss.

## 1.7 Insights from the analysis of our data

In this book we recognise that there are tensions between the demands of various participants in the student writing process. While all probably subscribe to the view that the act of writing is a means of developing skills and constructing knowledge, many students are equally if not more concerned to satisfy their course demands and gain the grades they need in order to graduate. They may also seek self-expression and personal development through their writing. Departments, on the other hand, will view student writing as a form of quality control, visible to internal and / or external assessors during institutional, departmental and course reviews, and a key element in the external examining system. Additionally, employers and professional bodies have their own requirements for student writing (see Chapters 6 and 7) which departments are usually keen to accommodate to improve the employability of their students.

We have also noted a possible conflict between the different requirements of different types of intended reader in some less traditional genres of student writing (see Chapters 6 and 7). Students may be expected to write ostensibly for a professional colleague or a non-expert, whilst at the same time meeting the academic assessment criteria of the department which assigns the grade, and addressing their own personal learning and self-development needs.

However, whilst acknowledging possible tension between these demands, our data does not suggest that there is conflict between the various participants in the communicative process. By and large employers, staff and students work together to enable each other's demands to be met. The very wide range of genres we have identified in use across the disciplines, and the enthusiasm of lecturers to innovate, bear testimony to a genuine desire on the part of staff to accommodate the needs of students, the discipline, the professions and industry. It seems to us that any problems with the assessment process are less likely to arise because of intransigence on the part of participants, and more likely to be due to failure to adequately explain the nature of the relevant assignment genres.

In this book we therefore aim to promote a better understanding of the diverse nature of writing in English university degree programmes. Our corpus does not represent every university discipline, and we do not provide detailed studies of every individual genre, but we do develop a framework for future researchers who might wish to make more detailed studies, using the BAWE corpus, another collection of student writing, or a combination of the two. We also hope that our genre family descriptions will be useful to those who teach academic writing for university study, especially by drawing attention to similarities and differences within families that have been obscured by departmental naming practices and were neglected in previous studies that have not been able to draw on such a large collection of textual evidence.

## Notes

1. 'An investigation of genres of assessed writing in British higher education', funded by the UK Economic and Social Research Council, 2004–2008 (RES-000–23–0800) under the directorship of Hilary Nesi and Sheena Gardner (formerly of the Centre for Applied Linguistics [previously called CELTE],

University of Warwick), Paul Thompson (formerly of the Department of Applied Linguistics, University of Reading) and Paul Wickens (Westminster Institute of Education, Oxford Brookes University).

2. Throughout this book the terms 'lecturer' and 'tutor' are used broadly to include professors, readers, teaching fellows and other academic tutors who set assignments for students.

3. One outcome of the project 'An investigation of genres of assessed writing in British higher education', see Note 1.

4. Although all the assignments in the BAWE corpus were given high marks, the writers were students, not experts, and the assignments were not edited to publication standard. For this reason the corpus does contain a few spelling and grammar mistakes.

5. In 2009/10, 14 per cent of all undergraduate degrees awarded in the UK were first class, i.e., included a majority of distinction grades (Higher Education Statistics Agency, 2011).

6. In ethnography, a 'thick' description is a description not only of people's behaviour, but also of its underlying meanings within their own culture.

7. We use lower case to refer to concepts in general (e.g., explanation) and upper case to refer to genre families (e.g. Explanation genres, Essay genres).

8. For an explanation of the statistic used to generate the score see http://trac. sketchengine.co.uk/wiki/SimpleMaths

9. UCREL is the University Centre for Computer Corpus Research on Language, a research centre at Lancaster University in the UK.

## References

Alsop, S., & Nesi, H. (2009). Issues in the development of the British Academic Written English (BAWE) corpus. *Corpora*, 4(1), 71–83.

Archer, D., Wilson, A., & Rayson, P. (2002). *Introduction to the USAS category system*. University Centre for Computer Corpus Research on Language, Lancaster University, UK. See http://ucrel.lancs.ac.uk/usas/usas%20guide. pdf.

Biber, D. (1988). *Variation across speech and writing*. Cambridge: Cambridge University Press.

Biber, D. (2007). Lexical bundles in university spoken and written registers. *English for Specific Purposes*, 26(3), 263–86.

Biber, D., Conrad, S., Reppen, R., Byrd, P., & Helt, M. (2002). Speaking and writing in the university: A multidimensional analysis. *TESOL Quarterly*, 36(1), 9–49.

Conrad, S., & Biber, D. (2001). Multi-dimensional methodology and the dimensions of register variation in English. In S. Conrad & D. Biber (Eds.), *Variation in English: Multi-dimensional studies*. Harlow, Essex: Pearson Education.

Gardner, S., & Powell, L. (2006). An investigation of genres of assessed writing in British higher education: A Warwick–Reading–Oxford Brookes project.

Paper presented at the seminar 'Research, scholarship and practice in the area of Academic Literacies', University of Westminster, 30 June.

Garside, R., & Smith, N. (1997). A hybrid grammatical tagger: CLAWS4. In R. Garside, G. Leech, & A. McEnery (Eds.), *Corpus annotation: Linguistic information from computer text corpora.* Longman, London, 102–21.

Gries, S. T., Newman, J., & Shaoul, C. (2011). N-grams and the clustering of registers. *Empirical Language Research*, 5(1).

Haggis, T. (2006). Pedagogies for diversity: Retaining critical challenge amidst fears of 'dumbing down'. *Studies in Higher Education 31(5)*, 521–35.

Halliday, M. A. K., & Matthiessen, C. M. I. M. (2004). *An introduction to functional grammar* (3rd edition). London: Arnold.

Higher Education Statistics Agency. (2011). *Product: SFR 153 higher education student enrolments and qualifications obtained at higher education institutions in the United Kingdom for the academic year 2009/10.* www.hesa.ac.uk.

Kilgarriff, A., Rychly, P., Smrz, P., & Tugwell, T. (2004). The Sketch Engine. In G. Williams & S. Vessier (Eds.), *Proceedings of Eleventh EURALEX International Congress.* Lorient, France: Université de Bretagne-Sud.

Lea, M., & Street, B. (2000). Student writing and staff feedback in higher education: An academic literacies approach. In M. Lea and B. Stierer (Eds.), *Student writing in higher education: New contexts.* Buckingham: The Society for Research into Higher Education and Open University Press.

Martin, J. R. (1992). *English text: System and structure.* Amsterdam: Benjamins.

Martin, J. R. (1997). Analysing genre: Functional parameters. In F. Christie & J. R. Martin (Eds.), *Genres and institutions: Social processes in the workplace and school.* London: Continuum.

Martin, J. R. (2000). Beyond exchange: APPRAISAL systems in English. In S. Hunston & G. Thompson (Eds.), *Evaluation in text.* Oxford: Oxford University Press, 142–75.

Martin, J. R., & White, P. R. (2005). *The language of evaluation: Appraisal in English.* Basingstoke: Palgrave Macmillan.

McArthur, T. (1981). *Longman lexicon of contemporary English.* Harlow: Longman.

Nesi, H., & Gardner, S. (2006). Variation in disciplinary culture: University tutors' views on assessed writing tasks. In R. Kiely, G. Clibbon, P. Rea-Dickins, & H. Woodfield (Eds.), *Language, culture and identity in applied linguistics* (British Studies in Applied Linguistics, vol 21). London: Equinox Publishing, 99–117.

Nesi, H., Gardner, S., Forsyth, R., Hindle, D., Wickens, P., Ebeling, S., Leedham, M., Thompson, P., & Heuboeck, A. (2005). Towards the compilation of a corpus of assessed student writing: An account of work in progress. In P. Danielsson & M. Wagenmakers (Eds.), *Proceedings from the corpus linguistics conference series.* Birmingham: University of Birmingham.

Nesi, H., & Thompson, P. (2011). *Using Sketch Engine with BAWE.* Available online at http://trac.sketchengine.co.uk/wiki/SharedResources.

Prior, P. (1998). *Writing / disciplinarity: A sociohistoric account of literate activity in the academy.* Mahwah, NJ: Lawrence Erlbaum.

Scott, M. (2010). *WordSmith Tools Version 5*. Oxford: Oxford University Press.

Sugimura, M. (2008). International student mobility and Asian higher education: Framework for global network. Paper presented at the Asia-Pacific Sub-regional Preparatory Conference for the 2009 World Conference on Higher Education, September 24–26, 2008, Macau, PR China. Available online at www.unescobkk.org/fileadmin/user_upload/apeid/workshops/macao08/papers/1-d-3.pdf.

Swales, J. M. (1990). *Genre analysis. English in academic and research settings*. Cambridge: Cambridge University Press.

Turner, J. (2011). *Language in the academy: Cultural reflexivity and intercultural dynamics*. Bristol: Multilingual Matters.

UNESCO (2008). *Education for all. Global Monitoring Report 2008*. United Nations Education Scientific and Cultural Organisation. www.efareport.unesco.org.

Wächter, B. (2008). Teaching in English on the rise in European higher education. *International Higher Education, 52*(3).

Wächter, B., & Maiworm, F. (2008). *English-taught programmes in European higher education: The picture in 2007*. Bonn: Lemmens.

Wardle, E. (2009). 'Mutt Genres' and the goal of FYC: Can we help students write the genres of the university? *College Composition and Communication, 60*(4), 765–89.

Woodward-Kron, R. (2002). Critical analysis versus description? Examining the relationship in successful student writing. *Journal of English for Academic Purposes, 1*(2), 121–43.

# 2 Families of genres of assessed writing

/ Genres are abstract, socially recognised ways of using language.
(Hyland, 2002a: 114)

Hyland's definition of genres as 'abstract, socially recognised ways of using language' is general enough to be widely acceptable, but as such it masks significant differences in how genres are more specifically defined and operationalised in research and teaching contexts. This chapter explains what we mean by academic genres, and how we classify genres of assessed student writing into groups of similar genres, called genre families.

We begin with a fabricated scenario which raises some of the methodological issues involved in investigating student writing. This is followed by an overview of distinctions and concepts needed to conduct such a study (assignments, texts, genres, academic writing, genre family, social purpose, staging and register).

Our thirteen genre families with their purposes and stages are presented in Section 2.2. They are grouped according to five broad social functions of student writing, each of which is explored in more detail in a subsequent chapter (Chapters 3 to 7).

Differences in register are highlighted in Section 2.3 through the typical clusters of lexical and grammatical features identified by the multidimensional analysis for each of the thirteen genre families. For example, the language of Proposal genres is more persuasive than the language of Literature Survey genres, but both have highly informational registers when compared to argumentative Essay genres.

Section 2.4 maps out the distribution of the genre families across the four university levels (first year to taught Masters) and across four disciplinary groups of study. This provides a broad picture of assignment genres across the academy.

## 2.1　Investigating student writing: A scenario

If you ask a student in Sociology, or in Engineering, what is involved in writing assignments in their discipline, they will soon start to explain that there are different types of writing – essays, research proposals, reports, projects and more – and that each of these has a different function; each relates differently to research or practical work being done and to reading and lectures in the discipline; and so each is organised differently. You will also begin to realise that when a Sociology student talks about a 'report' or a 'project' or a 'case study', they may well be describing a rather different type of assignment than that referred to by an Engineering student who uses the same labels. This line of investigation (interviews) will only get you so far in understanding the nature of academic writing, however, and eventually you will ask to see some examples of each type of assignment, and ask the students to explain to you how the text fulfils the purpose of the assignment, what they think is going on in different parts of the text, and how this meets disciplinary expectations. This will lead to some kind of rationale or discussion about the point of the initial stages such as abstracts, executive summaries or introductions; of medial stages such as literature reviews or methods or costings; and of final stages such as conclusions or recommendations. In turn, this allows you to compare more easily across disciplines, and you can begin to develop your own classification, identifying assignments that have similar stages and giving them your own labels. You will also begin to understand how these assignments fit into the degree programme – how a Sociology research proposal is part of a sequence of assignments leading to a dissertation, or how an Engineering assignment may be designed to replicate a professional engineering activity and thus to prepare students for working as an engineer. To obtain a more rounded view of what the students say, you would want to ask tutors, look at course documentation and find out about university and national expectations of student writing. The more you learn about different types of university writing and about the nature of knowledge and research in different disciplines, the easier this will be. As this scenario suggests, in order to reach a university-wide classification of student assignment texts it will be necessary to consult a range of sources, to interpret these in their disciplinary and university-wide contexts, and to develop categories that are essentially abstractions from specific assignments in specific contexts. Before we present our genre classification, we explain key distinctions and terms used.

## Tasks, assignments, texts and genres

One fruitful line of enquiry has developed classifications of academic writing by studying the tasks set in university courses (Carter, 2007; Hale et al., 1996; Melzer, 2009; Moore and Morton, 2005; Rosenfeld et al., 2004). In contrast, our investigation focuses on classifying the written assignment papers themselves.

Broadly, student assignments are written for a particular module in response to a prompt. They are read by academics who generally comment on how well the assignment has met the expectations of the course and award a grade which contributes to the student's degree progression. The format is highly conventional: front matter (such as module name), student ID number, date, word count and plagiarism declaration, followed by the body of the assignment which is typically realised by a genre such as a lab report, discussion essay or book review. Thus most assignments instantiate specific, conventionally recognised genres, partly because they are high-stakes texts – failing an assignment can mean failing a degree which can be costly in academic, social and financial terms. This assessment context not only imposes constraints on the nature of student writing, but also means that students, tutors and those involved in developing academic programmes nationally and internationally are all motivated to understand the socially recognised expectations and the relative value placed on features of the assignments.

One broad social purpose of assignment writing is therefore for accreditation. This can explain how the academic writing in student assignments is different in nature from that in textbooks or published academic journal articles, which have different social purposes.

It is also important to point out that while most assignments are realised by one text that realises a single genre, there are some assignments with what we can call a 'compound macrostructure'. Thus, work that is submitted and assessed as one assignment may be realised as one front matter plus three texts (e.g., three lab reports). This explains why there are more texts in our corpus than assignments. While it is possible to develop a classification of *assignments* with different types of simple, complex and compound macrostructure (Gardner and Holmes, 2010), in the rest of this chapter we concentrate on our classification of student coursework *genres* which are realised by texts that occur in the body of assessed student assignments.

## Genres and academic writing

The concept of 'genre' is central to research on academic writing. It is employed across approaches, from academic literacies to corpus linguistics, from linguistic ethnography to critical discourse analysis (Hyland, 2002b). Research on academic writing focuses on genres such as academic journal research articles, academic textbooks, doctoral theses or undergraduate student coursework. Such broad genre categories correspond to everyday categories and are therefore socially recognised and relatively unproblematic. Nevertheless, 'genre' is a contested term, hard to define and pin down precisely, and different traditions of genre analysis have developed (see for example Hyland, 2002a; Johns, 2002).

Genres are abstractions – so they are not the written texts themselves, but conventional ways of doing things, realised through the written texts. Swales suggests that a genre is 'a class of communicative events' (1990: 45), where communicative events 'compris[e] not only the discourse itself and its participants, but also the role of that discourse and the environment of its production and reception, including its historical and cultural associations' (1990: 46). In a similar vein, though from a different school of genre analysis, Martin describes genres as a 'system of staged goal-oriented social processes through which social subjects in a given culture live their lives' (Martin, 1997: 13).

These social and cultural perspectives are important. It means that if someone writes an essay to give to his grandmother as a gift for her to keep, this will be a different communicative event / social process than if a student writes an essay to be assessed as part of a university course. It has a different type of audience, the writer is writing as a grandchild not as a student, the writing has a different social purpose, and its effect on how they live their lives will be different. (In our experience writing essays for grandparents as gifts to keep is not part of the way we live our lives, so this is not an authentic, recognisable genre, i.e., not part of our culture!) Equally if a student writes an essay on a general topic in a university admissions test, this is ultimately a different social (educational) process from the essays we are interested in, which are written in university departments to be assessed as part of a university degree course, and we would expect these differences to be evident in the language used. In a study of university entrance English proficiency examination scripts, Coffin and Hewings (2004) point to a range of contextual factors to explain a relatively high use of the language of hearsay (e.g., *some people think that*) and pronounce (e.g., *I believe that*) compared with their use in other types of academic writing. Thus, while differences in purpose, audience, writer role and context are crucial in identifying genres, we also expect that these will shape the ways the texts unfold and be reflected in the language (lexico-grammar) used.

## From genre to genre family

If we continue to narrow this contextual lens, we will find differences in assignments written in the Chemistry department and the Classics department; or written by Level 1 students and more experienced Level 3 students; we may also be able to detect differences according to the type of secondary school education, or ultimately features associated with individual students. As our aim is to identify a class of communicative events or a system of social processes from which we can generalise about assessed student writing across disciplines and levels of study, we sought to identify assignment purposes found across the academy. This involved identifying genres and grouping them into genre families. For instance, when students write a 'book review', they are expected to describe features of the book and evaluate its impact from a disciplinary perspective. This is similar to the purpose of a 'product evaluation' in Engineering where students describe features of a product and evaluate its effectiveness from a disciplinary perspective. These two genres have a similar purpose (to demonstrate / develop understanding of the object of study and the ability to evaluate and / or assess the significance of the object of study) and similar stages (identify or describe the object of study, then evaluate specific features). In our classification they are grouped with book reports, website evaluations and other members of what we call the Critique genre family. In a similar way, a catering plan and a research proposal share the purpose of developing plans for future activity, and are grouped in what we call the Proposal genre family.

The term 'family' is used about genres by Swales and about groups of genres by Martin. Swales (1990: 49ff), drawing on Wittgenstein, discusses family resemblance among members of a genre, and their variation in prototypicality. Equally, in our classification, there is variation in the prototypicality of members of a genre family. For Martin, genres may belong to different families in that they may share a central function, or they may have evolved in the same disciplinary context. For example, his 'report family' includes descriptive reports, classifying reports and compositional reports, which all have different staging but share a classifying and describing function (Martin and Rose, 2008: 142ff). In contrast, the discourses of history, having 'evolved within the institutional contexts of recording, explaining and debating the past' (Martin and Rose, 2008: 99), give rise to a family of history genres which includes recounts, explanations and discussions.

As our aim is to compare academic writing across disciplines, we have created genre families whose members *share* central functions or social purposes and key stages. These functions and stages are not given a priori, but developed from an examination of the assignment texts in our corpus, with due attention to the wider university and disciplinary contexts. Thus the labels of our genre families are specific to this purpose of classifying university student writing across disciplines, though inspired by labels from the disciplinary discourse communities as well as from the literature on written academic genres. Because labels such as report and case study are used in different ways across disciplines, we have identified central functions and stages to define them. For instance, because many of the assignments called case studies in the disciplines include recommendations, and this recommendation stage was highlighted in interviews as crucial in the assessment of the assignment, and because being able to analyse specialist material and make recommendations is one expected social outcome of a university education, we have identified recommendations for future practice as an essential stage in our Case Study genre family. Within genre families we can explore variation according to level of study or academic discipline. Chapter 6 illustrates how, for instance, medical Case Studies and business Case Studies differ.

## Social purposes of genres of assessed student writing

Student assignments have complex formative and summative purposes, where formative purposes relate to developing skills and expertise, while summative purposes relate more to achievement levels, assessment criteria and grades. Assignments not only provide opportunities for students to develop knowledge, understanding and expertise, but also expect students to display these in writing. Their purpose is not solely to explain or argue a point, for example, but also to demonstrate that they can explain or argue that point in writing, in accordance with the expectations of the discipline, of the lecturer(s) and of the academic department which set the assignment. Students undoubtedly do learn and benefit from writing assignments, but the multiple audiences and functions give university assignments a somewhat unreal or hybrid quality as polished texts whose main transactional value is to earn a grade which accumulates as educational capital towards a university degree.

In our interviews with lecturers (Nesi and Gardner, 2006) and students (Gardner and Powell, 2006), we investigated expectations of the communicative and educational purposes of assignments, and their multiple audiences (academic and non-academic) or discourse communities. For lecturers setting assignments and guiding student performance, there seems to be tension between developing disciplinary knowledge and meeting the requirements of the wider academic and professional communities (Gardner, 2004). Just how these wider expectations are met is not always clear; the lecturers in our interviews revealed different understandings of academic expectations, particularly around issues of knowledge transfer. Some decried the pressure to deliver 'vocational' training and relevance, some aimed to make their vocational courses more academic through a research emphasis, while others argued in favour of the rigorous demands of professional assignments in terms of 'real world constraints' such as the legally binding nature of recommendations in engineering student projects, or the customer satisfaction requirement in computer systems development projects.

Despite these differences expressed by individual lecturers, as we increased our familiarity with the assignments, courses and wider social context of university writing nationally and internationally (see Section 1.1), we were able to identify three broad purposes for student assignment writing: to demonstrate disciplinary knowledge and understanding; to produce new disciplinary knowledge or research; and to prepare for professional practice following graduation (Nesi and Gardner, 2006). A comparison of the specific stages of writing in student assignments enabled us to develop this initial classification further and thus to understand more fully the social functions that university assessment serves. The five broad functions identified are (1) demonstrating knowledge and understanding; (2) developing powers of independent reasoning; (3) building research skills; (4) preparing for professional practice; and (5) writing for oneself and others.

## Genres and staging

While the communicative or social purpose may be primary in identifying genres, most genre analysis also relies heavily on the identification of moves in the communicative event (Swales, 1990), or stages in the unfolding of the social process (Martin, 1992). Thus while an important purpose of writing a laboratory report is recording what happened during a particular experiment, there are conventional ways of doing this which involve first introducing the experiment, then describing the methods used, followed by presenting the results and discussing the findings. These stages – Introduction, Methods, Results, Discussion (IMRD) – represent the conventional structure of a lab report (Dudley-Evans, 1985). In Systemic Functional Linguistic conventions, the sequence of the stages is represented by a carat sign (^) which means 'is followed by':

Introduction^Methods^Results^Discussion

Laboratory reports often have section headings which indicate the purpose of each stage, and the language in each section is also conventional and recognisable as such, as this extract from a lab report in Biochemistry suggests:

*... The aim of the experiment was to understand these concepts and methods of bacterial genetics by exchanging pieces of E. coli chromosome between different strains by the process of conjugation and using a non-quantitative method to establish the order of some genes relating to amino acid metabolism and sugar catabolism.*

Method
*The experiment was carried out as laid out in the lab manual with the following detail.*
*The donor strain used was E. coli KL14 (thi-1 Hfr KL14).*
*The bacteria donor and recipient strains were allowed to grow in the shaking water bath at 37°C for 120 minutes before being mixed together.*

Results
*From the results it is clear that the bacteria could grow earlier on some plates than others. In this case the sample selective media lacking threonine (Plate 6) grew first at time 0 minutes (but also had growth on the recipient strain area), then on both plates lacking arginine (plate 1) and with xylose as the sugar (plate 7) at 15 minutes. The sample on plate 3, lacking ...*
(Level 1 Biochemistry)

Of all the student writing genres we describe, the lab report is one of the most predictable in terms of its staging. This makes it an excellent choice for the development of interactive teaching materials, as in the online 'Write Reports in Science and Engineering' (WRiSE) project (Drury, 2010). Within this genre there can still be considerable variation across levels and across disciplines (see Section 5.3). It is therefore important to recognise that genres are abstractions; they generalise from a set of instances. This means that while there will be prototypical instances of genres, there will also be instances of genres that are less typical. Moreover, as genres reflect the contexts in which they are produced, and the social and educational contexts are changing all the time, genres too change over time.

Similar IMRD stages are also found in Research Reports, and in Chapter 5 we explain how we differentiate research reports from lab reports according to differences in their social purpose and key stages.

In other words, if an assignment is divided into four main parts called introduction, methods, results and discussion, it will probably be a lab report, but we need to find out more about the assignment through reading it and investigating what was 'given' to the students and what they developed themselves in order to identify its social purpose and classify it as an instance of a particular genre.

## Genres and disciplines

In our discussion above of variation within genres, we have indicated that genres also vary across disciplines. Thus lab reports in Physics have 'experimental details' rather than 'methods', while lab reports in Food Sciences regularly include 'calculation' as a distinct section, as can be seen in Table 2.1.

Table 2.1   Typical IMRD Lab Report headings in two disciplines

| | |
|---|---|
| **Physics** | introduction, experimental details, results, discussion |
| **Food Sciences** | objective, introduction, method, results, calculation, discussion |

If the general social purpose is the same, and the same key stages are evidenced, then further differences often reflect the disciplinary context. In a similar way, a book review in English may demonstrate disciplinary differences from a book review in Psychology or Sociology, even where the same book is reviewed. At a cross-disciplinary level, however, the purpose and key stages of a book review genre will be evidenced.

As our aim is to understand the nature of assessed writing across the academy, our classification proposes genre families at a level of delicacy that groups similar genres across disciplines. This enables us to compare genres across disciplines. For example, a comparison of Engineering, Sociology and History shows the diversity of writing purposes in Engineering compared with History where students develop argumentative essay writing skills in more depth.

If we then look at how populated each genre family is, we find that most assignments in History and in Sociology are members of the Essay genre family, whereas assignments in Engineering are distributed across all thirteen genre families.

As the title of Table 2.2 suggests, this is not an exhaustive list, but a list designed to show the relationship between genres and genre families. It may be, for instance, that case studies are frequent in some modules in History and Sociology but for some reason these did not find their way into our corpus. Studies such as Gillett and Hammond

Table 2.2    Main genre families and genres found in undergraduate (Levels 1–3) History, Sociology and Engineering assignments

| Genre families | Genres in History | Genres in Sociology | Genres in Engineering |
|---|---|---|---|
| Case Study | | | company report<br>accident report |
| Critique | book review | evaluation of research methods<br>book review | evaluations of products, techniques, performance, systems, tools and buildings |
| Design Specification | | | design plan |
| Essay | exposition<br>discussion<br>challenge<br>factorial | exposition<br>discussion | exposition<br>discussion |
| Exercise | | | calculations<br>short answer |
| Explanation | | | industry overview<br>system overview |
| Methodology Recount | | | lab report<br>design report |
| Narrative Recount | | urban ethnography<br>library search | reflection on team work |
| Proposal | | research proposal | design proposal |
| Research Report | long essay | dissertation | project |

(2009) or Melzer (2009), which look at all assignment questions set in a particular course, can provide more accurate information about the spread of assignment tasks over departments. They do not, however, examine the actual assignments written, as we do.

## Genres and registers    ⟨X⟩ *definition of register*

In Systemic Functional Linguistics, the term register 'refers to the fact that the language we speak or write varies according to the type of situation' (Halliday, 2009: 439). This goes beyond notions of genres

*the tenor of sth: (formal) the general character or meaning of sth*

as described above to consider notions of field, tenor and mode. Thus
for student writing, we expect the language of an Explanation genre
in Biology to be similar to an Explanation genre in Physics because
they both aim to explain a scientific phenomenon, but we also expect
it to be different in register, in ways that reflect the type of situation:
who is writing it (tenor); what is being explained (field); and the role
language plays (mode). Within genre families, we can explore differences in tenor by comparing first and final year writing, we can
explore differences in field by exploring writing across different disciplines, and we can explore differences in mode by considering the
role that features such as tables, figures and graphs play alongside
writing in student assignments. Halliday's theory of register points
us to particular linguistic features that may be relevant: the nature of
the activity (field) will be reflected in the ideas or participants, processes and circumstances[1] represented, the role relationships (tenor)
help to determine the expressions of certainty, hedging, evaluation
and other interpersonal features, and the symbolic organisation of the
text (mode) influences choices in areas such as cohesion and reference
(Halliday, 2009: 55).

There is no general consensus about the meanings of the terms
'genre' and 'register', however, as Biber and Conrad (2009: 21) point
out. Biber's 1988 study refers to 'genre' rather than 'register', but
later studies (Biber, 1995; Biber et al., 1999) refer exclusively to
'register' and Biber and Conrad (2009) use both terms, but in rather
different ways from Halliday (2009) and from Martin (1992). Like
Martin (1992), Biber and Conrad regard rhetorical organisation
(staging) as a defining characteristic of genre (2009: 16), but they also
count formatting and the use of specialised expressions as generic
features, whereas for SFL these are more often indicative of mode and
field. The features Biber and Conrad associate with genre are difficult
to quantify, and are not considered during the process of multidimensional analysis. Register is described by Biber and Conrad not
only in terms of lexico-grammatical features (see Appendix 1.3), but
also in terms of situational context and communicative purpose. It is
assumed that linguistic features occur because they suit the context
and the purpose of the register, and that 'linguistic features are always
functional when considered from a register perspective' (Biber and
Conrad, 2009: 6). *definition of register*

Halliday, Martin and Biber may differ significantly in their methodology, but all are concerned with identifying lexico-grammatical
features that occur in specific social situations. This too is our perspective on register. Following Martin (1992), we can separate decisions about genre (based on social purpose and staging) and cultural

ways of doing things from decisions about register (based on the specific situation) where our focus in particular is on the experience of the writer and the disciplinary context.

## 2.2 Thirteen genre families identified

Having introduced the key concepts used in developing our classification, we now explain the procedure followed and present the thirteen genre families grouped under the five broad social functions identified.

### *Starting from disciplinary contexts*

Our grouping of texts into genres and genre families started not with the texts themselves, but with their disciplinary contexts. We knew that if we simply read the texts, we would bring to bear our own interpretations of their functions and purposes, of what was important and what was less significant. This bias in reading has been shown to apply across disciplines; for example, English teachers trained in the Humanities interpret writing differently from business persons (Forey, 2004).

Although we have worked for decades with tutors and students from many disciplinary backgrounds, and had a general awareness of disciplinary differences from earlier research and readings, for this study we interviewed students (Gardner and Powell, 2006) and lecturers (Nesi and Gardner, 2006), and examined course handbooks and assignment briefs from across the disciplines, as well as university and national documentation on assessment criteria and benchmarking in higher education. This enabled us to understand participants' views about what is deemed important in a piece of writing, what makes a good assignment, why certain stages or features are significant, what is mandated, what is provided by the tutor in various ways (readings, laboratory experiment objectives, demonstrations), and where students are expected or encouraged to show their own initiative. Through this process we deepened our insights into disciplinary perspectives on student writing.

We became aware, for instance, that although assignments from different levels of study in Physics might look similar, the proportion of work done by the students without guidance increases as they progress through the levels. We learned that the rationale for 'self-assessment' components to assignments is quite varied across disciplines. We realised, not surprisingly perhaps, that lecturers from the same department value different, and in some cases contradictory, features in student writing – the role of signposting is a typical example where some feel strongly that this is a positive feature and others prefer texts with very little metatext. Perhaps most importantly for our study, we began to understand the values associated in different disciplines with the metalanguage of assessment, with terms such as 'argument', 'critical perspective', 'explanation' and 'evidence'. These understandings were related not only to specific texts and assignments, but also to trends in the broader educational and disciplinary contexts.

The second major reason for starting from disciplinary context was to inform the composition of the corpus. We first interviewed a department's director of studies, or someone recommended as having an interest and breadth of experience in teaching in the department. We asked not only about the assignments and what was valued in them, but also about the spread of modules and assignments across each level, which modules set out-of-class written assignments as opposed to tests, final exams or other practical exams, and the typical progression routes through the department courses. From these consultations and course literature we developed a plan to target a balance of core and optional modules for each level. University degree structures in England are still relatively standard, with students tending to major in one or two subjects, and with most students following a similar path towards graduation within each department.

## Grouping similar texts

Once the corpus was compiled, we read all the assignments and began the process of grouping those that were similar. Our classification is grounded in 2,761 assignments set by tutors in around 1,000 modules from 300 degree courses (the BAWE corpus). As an abstraction, it provides an account of the nature of student writing across disciplines and across levels of study.

The grouping was essentially a bottom-up process, starting with assignments which responded to the same type of brief or title and were organised in a similar way. The more specific the assignment type, the easier it was to create a group. Assignments with a highly conventionalised structure, such as the patient portfolio case reports produced by students in the Medical School, were quickly sorted, initially leaving large groups of what looked like essays and reports that required greater differentiation.

Whilst reading and re-reading the assignments, we looked for statements of assignment purpose which might be found in abstracts, or in introductions and conclusions; headings and subheadings were useful in extracting assignment skeletons or macrostructures (Gardner and

Holmes, 2010) to inform the grouping process. The first and last sentences of each section and paragraph gave a rough idea of the content of that section / paragraph and could be quickly skim-read, and reading and rereading the texts enabled us to determine the purpose and stages of what had been written, and to recognise it in other texts.

Through discussion and the posing of questions about function, stages and purpose, we grouped assignments and were able to identify critical features that differentiated one set from another. Thirteen distinct groups were ultimately identified through this process (see list) and given labels. We refer to these as genre families, where each text is assigned exclusively to one of the 13 families. As with genres, there are clear prototypical examples, as well as more marginal examples, some of which may seem to be on the border between two genre families. In marginal cases we made decisions about which functions and purposes were dominant, or which components obligatory, and here in particular reference to contextual information was helpful.

Our classification of genre families is thus grounded in our corpus of texts. The extent to which our findings are generalisable will emerge in future applications.

**The thirteen genre families**
1  Case Study
2  Critique
3  Design Specification
4  Empathy Writing
5  Essay
6  Exercise
7  Explanation
8  Literature Survey
9  Methodology Recount
10 Narrative Recount
11 Problem Question
12 Proposal
13 Research Report

The 13 genre families differ in social purpose, in generic stages, and in the networks they form with other professional and / or academic genres. Examples of genres within each family are included here for information, and described in more detail in subsequent chapters.

As explained earlier, the social purpose of university assignments is a complex notion. It would therefore be possible to group the genre families in different ways. For example, it would be possible to distinguish assignments that involve planning future activity from those that involve reporting on past activity. Thus genres in the Proposal and Design Specification families share a future orientation; where most genres in the Research Report, Methodology Recount and Narrative Recount families share an orientation of retelling what has been achieved.

Other genre families focus less on activity and more on theories and concepts. Thus we can distinguish assignments which involve explaining or summarising important ideas or bodies of literature such as Explanations and Literature Surveys, from those that involve analysing and evaluating entities, such as Case Studies, Critiques and Problem Questions, and from those whose main focus is the development of a thesis or an original piece of research, such as Essays and Research Reports.

These rhetorical perspectives suggest a logical progression where summary, explanation and evaluation of the work of others inform independent original work; and where planning a project logically precedes reporting on it. Such patterns can be seen in some departments, but most courses do not follow this sequence consistently.

In this book we have grouped the genre families according to the broader social and educational purposes they serve as part of a university education. These reflect expectations that universities will produce graduates who are (1) knowledgeable in specific disciplines; (2) who can make informed judgements; (3) who can design and conduct independent research; (4) who are prepared for graduate employment; and (5) who are able to critically reflect on their learning and personal development.

These five broad social functions of university education are reflected in national education guidelines, as we shall see in subsequent chapters. Universities not only prepare students to enter specific professions, or to pursue further research or training, but more generally, they also prepare graduates who are expected to contribute to the world of work and to an educated society.

Within these five broad categories, each genre family has its own distinctive social purpose, where the typical unfolding stages of each genre family are also core defining characteristics. In addition, genre networks provide information about the connections between genre families, suggesting how specific genres in each family may relate to other professional or academic genres. Tables 2.4–2.8 indicate the social purpose, stages and networks, with examples of each genre family. Readers are encouraged to read these tables, as our intention here is to introduce the genre families, then to more fully describe them in subsequent chapters as indicated in the right hand column of Table 2.3.

Table 2.3    Thirteen genre families grouped by social function

5 *broader*

| Social function | Genre families | *see* |
|---|---|---|
| 1. demonstrating knowledge and understanding | Explanation, Exercise | Chapter 3 |
| 2. developing powers of independent reasoning | Critique, Essay | Chapter 4 |
| 3. building research skills | Literature Survey, Methodology Recount, Research Report | Chapter 5 |
| 4. preparing for professional practice | Case Study, Design Specification, Problem Question, Proposal | Chapter 6 |
| 5. writing for oneself and others | Narrative Recount, Empathy Writing | Chapter 7 |

## Demonstrating knowledge and understanding

Two genre families have as a central purpose the demonstration of knowledge and detailed understanding: Exercises and Explanations.

Exercise genres give students opportunities to demonstrate understanding, generally of basic skills and concepts. Exercise genres tend to be easy to identify from their layout: they are typically short, numbered responses to questions that are not included in the student texts. The responses may be calculations with minimal explanation, or short answers such as definitions of key terms. Writing such assignments allows students and lecturers to check that students have mastered basic skills and concepts, and ensures that they are prepared to move on to perform calculations and use central ideas appropriately in future assignments. Exercises are set as formative and summative assignments, by which we mean that if marks are given, they do not necessarily contribute towards the degree classification. The Exercises in the BAWE corpus, like all assignments in the corpus, were all formally graded as very good or excellent (see Section 1.4).

Explanation genres also require students to demonstrate knowledge and understanding, and to answer questions, such as 'What is x?', but they are generally longer than Exercises, and additionally expect students to explain how something works or functions. Explanations are common in Biology, Chemistry, Engineering and other sciences where students may be asked to explain the nature of phenomena such as stem cells, organophosphates, road vehicle drag or code-switching. Writing an explanation may involve consulting

Table 2.4   Exercises and Explanations

| Genre family | Exercise | Explanation |
|---|---|---|
| Social purpose | to provide practice in key skills (e.g., the ability to interrogate a database, perform complex calculations or explain technical terms or procedures), and to consolidate knowledge of key concepts | to demonstrate / develop understanding of the object of study and the ability to describe and / or account for its significance |
| Stages | data analysis or a series of responses to questions | includes descriptive account and explanation |
| Networks | may correspond to part of a Methodology Recount, Design Specification or Research Report | may correspond to a published Explanation, or to part of a Critique or Research Report |
| Examples | calculations data analysis mixed (e.g., calculations + short answers) short answers statistics exercise | business explanation concept / job / legislation overview instrument description methodology explanation organism / disease account site / environment report species / breed description account of natural phenomenon system / process explanation |

several sources and synthesising what they say, but the explanations themselves are intended to demonstrate current shared knowledge and understanding.

## Developing independent reasoning

Particularly at lower undergraduate levels, the underlying educational function of Explanations, Critiques and Essays is very similar in encouraging students to make sense of central phenomena and claims in their discipline, yet the stages of the assignment genres differ, as does the way sense making is expressed. In Explanations students are expected to put forward a shared view generally with certainty to answer the question, 'What is x and how does it work?'; in Critiques

Table 2.5    Critiques and Essays

| Genre family | Critique | Essay |
|---|---|---|
| Social purpose | to demonstrate / develop understanding of the object of study and the ability to evaluate and / or assess the significance of the object of study | to demonstrate / develop the ability to construct a coherent argument and employ critical thinking skills |
| Stages | includes descriptive account with optional explanation, and evaluation with optional tests | introduction, series of arguments, conclusion |
| Networks | may correspond to part of a Research Report or Design Specification, or to an expert evaluation such as a book review | may correspond to a published academic / specialist paper |
| Examples | academic paper review<br>approach evaluation<br>business environment analysis<br>business / organisation evaluation<br>financial report evaluation<br>interpretation of results<br>legislation evaluation<br>(legal) case report<br>policy evaluation<br>product / building evaluation<br>programme evaluation<br>project evaluation<br>review of a book / film / play / website<br>system evaluation<br>teaching evaluation | challenge<br>commentary<br>consequential<br>discussion<br>exposition<br>factorial |

they are expected to also evaluate the phenomenon or theory and to answer the more open question, 'What is the value of x?', while in Essays students are expected to develop ideas, make connections between arguments and evidence, and develop an individualised thesis.

Essays form the bulk of assignments in History, English, Philosophy, Archaeology and Classics, where the evidence to support an argument has to be sought, and is more open to interpretation. Most Essays are written in response to questions given by tutors, such as 'Is it worthwhile to test intelligence?' These expect students to gather evidence and form their own thesis in response. In Chapter 4 we shall see how the core stages of introduction, series of arguments and conclusion are realised in the different Essay genres such as challenge, discussion and exposition.

## Building research skills

Although it could be argued that other genres, for example Explanations, contribute towards building research skills in students, when we look at final year projects as an example of Research Reports, we see the main thing that differentiates them from a lab report conducted earlier in the course is the inclusion of a substantial literature review, a member of the Literature Survey genre family.

Many of the Literature Surveys in our corpus are annotated bibliographies, summaries of articles and literature reviews that students write as a first step towards conducting research. In this sense they are preparatory, and allow lecturers to assess progress in the research process.

The most frequent and most uniformly structured genre family in this group is the Methodology Recount, of which laboratory reports are prototypical. These correspond to the well-documented IMRD experimental report texts. There is variation across disciplines in the specifics, labels used and lengths of each stage (Gardner and Holmes, 2009), but the general format is easily recognisable. The main purpose of the genre is to present an account of the procedures followed and the findings of an experimental study.

The third genre family here is Research Report. These are generally the longest student assignments in the discipline and are designed to demonstrate an ability to conduct a complete piece of research, as in a final year project or undergraduate dissertation.[2]

## Preparing for professional practice

Case Studies, Design Specifications, Problem Questions and Proposals share the objective of making recommendations for future practice, and an orientation to professional activity outside the university.

In Problem Questions a situation is described and students have to analyse it from a professional perspective to produce recommendations that conform to guidelines such as legal rules and precedents. In Case Studies students focus on a particular instance of a more general case in order to describe it from a range of perspectives and conclude with recommendations intended to improve the 'case'. As the names suggest, Design Specifications are concentrated in areas of manufacturing and computing, while Proposals, which include

Table 2.6    Literature Surveys, Methodology Recounts, Research Reports

| Genre family | Literature Survey | Methodology Recount | Research Report |
|---|---|---|---|
| Social purpose | to demonstrate / develop familiarity with literature relevant to the focus of study | to demonstrate / develop familiarity with disciplinary procedures, methods and conventions for recording experimental findings | to demonstrate / develop ability to undertake a complete piece of research including research design, and an appreciation of its significance in the field |
| Stages | includes summary of literature relevant to the focus of study and varying degrees of critical evaluation | describes procedures undertaken by writer and may include IMRD sections | includes student's research aim / question, investigation and relevance to other research in the field |
| Networks | may correspond to part of a Research Report or to a published review article or to an anthology | may correspond to part of a Research Report or published research article | may correspond to a published experimental research article or topic-based research paper |
| Examples | analytical bibliography annotated bibliography anthology literature overview literature review research methods review review article | computer analysis data analysis report development report experimental report field report forensic report lab report materials selection report (program) | research article student research project topic-based dissertation |

research proposals, are found across disciplines. Both genre families are forward looking and expect students to produce plans that are detailed and realistic.

Problem Questions occur most frequently in the Social Sciences such as Law, Accounting and Economics, while Case Studies are common in Health and Business areas.

Table 2.7  Case Studies, Design Specifications, Problem Questions, Proposals

| Genre family | Case Study | Design Specification | Problem Question | Proposal |
|---|---|---|---|---|
| **Social purpose** | to demonstrate / develop an understanding of professional practice through the analysis of a single exemplar | to demonstrate / develop the ability to design a product or procedure that could be manufactured or implemented | to provide practice in applying specific methods in response to professional problems | to demonstrate / develop ability to make a case for future action |
| Stages | description of a particular case, often multifaceted, with recommendations for future action | typically includes purpose, design development and testing of design | problem scenario (may not be stated in assignment), application of relevant arguments or development of possible solution(s) | includes purpose, detailed plan and persuasive argumentation |
| Networks | typically corresponds to professional genres (e.g., in business, medicine and engineering) | may correspond to a professional design specification or to part of a Proposal or Research Report | problems or situations resemble or are based on real legal, engineering, accounting or other professional cases | may correspond to professional or academic proposals |
| Examples | business start-up company report organisation analysis patient report single issue | application design building design database design game design label design product design system design website design | business scenario law problem logistics simulation question | book proposal building proposal business plan catering plan legislation reform marketing plan policy proposal procedural plan research proposal |

## Writing for oneself and others

The construction of audience in academic writing is complex. All assessed writing is written to some degree for the tutor, and for other internal and external moderators, and therefore has to address explicit assessment criteria. This can be challenging when non-traditional genres are assigned, as is the case with Empathy Writing and reflective Narrative Recounts.

Empathy Writing, a term coined by Lea and Street (2000: 39), here refers to assignments that involve communicating disciplinary knowledge in forms such as newspaper articles or information leaflets and in registers suitable for 'general' rather than academic audiences. As assignments, they challenge writers to understand disciplinary knowledge and express it using transferable, 'non-academic' writing skills that are intended to prove useful in the world of work.

Table 2.8    Empathy Writing and Narrative Recount

| Genre family | Empathy Writing | Narrative Recount |
|---|---|---|
| Social purpose | to demonstrate / develop understanding and appreciation of the relevance of academic ideas by translating them into a non-academic register, to communicate to a nonspecialist readership | to demonstrate / develop awareness of motives and / or behaviour in individuals (including self) or organisations |
| Structure | may be formatted as a letter, newspaper article or similar non-academic genre | fictional or factual recount of events, with optional comments |
| Network | may correspond to private genres as in personal letters, or to publically available genres as in information leaflets | may correspond to published literature, or be part of a Research Report |
| Examples | expert information for journalist<br>expert advice to industry<br>expert advice to layperson<br>information leaflet<br>job application<br>letter (e.g., reflective letter to a friend, business correspondence)<br>newspaper article | accident report<br>account of literature search<br>account of website search<br>biography<br>character outline<br>creative writing: short story<br>plot synopsis<br>reflective recount<br>report on disease outbreak<br>urban ethnography |

Empathy Writing genres are common in the Sciences where students may be asked to write a letter to a mathematician or to develop a nutritional advice leaflet for the general public.

Narrative Recounts include personal accounts of website or literature searches and reports on events such as accidents or disease outbreaks. The chronological presentation enables students to review the events and understand how they fit together. As these are personal, they can assume a reflective angle which is intended to enable student writers to consider the processes of their personal and professional development. In this sense, they are writing 'for themselves'.

While the thirteen genre families are characterised in Tables 2.4–2.8 in terms of their social purposes and their stages, it follows that members of genre families also share patterns of linguistic features. The multidimensional analysis of these genre families conducted by Biber (1988) at the University of Northern Arizona allows us to show relationships between these genres, as characterised by their lexico-grammatical features.

## 2.3 Plotting the genre families along five register dimensions

Multidimensional analysis, as described in Biber (1988) and explained in Section 1.6, allows us to plot the distribution of genre families along five dimensions which suggest how informational, narrative, situation dependent, persuasive and impersonal the writing is (Biber et al., 2002: 18). While readers should be able to predict the position of Recount versus Proposal genres, for instance, on certain dimensions, the multidimensional analysis provides evidence from linguistic features in support of our classification of genre families. The distribution of genre families shows, for instance, how two genre families can be similar on one dimension, and different on others, and thus enhances our understanding of the genre families classification.

### *Highly informational*

The first dimension analysis shows that student writing has 'high informational density and precise informational content' (Biber et al., 2002: 17), with relatively many nouns, prepositions, long words and a high type–token ratio[3]. All our student writing is on the informational end of the dimension, comparable with general academic (published) prose[4] at −15 (Biber, 1988) and with university textbooks[5] at −16 (Biber et al., 2002: 25) and in contrast with the interactive, personal

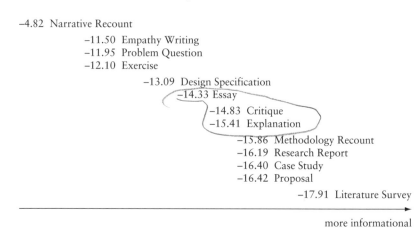

Figure 2.1    The involved versus informational dimension

and highly involved register of classroom teaching (+28) or university service encounters (+57) (ibid.). Among genre families, the Literature Survey register is significantly more informational at just less than −18 while the Narrative Recount register is significantly[6] less informational at just less than −5.

The similarity of Empathy Writing, Problem Question and Exercise at about −12 on this dimension differentiates them from the more densely informational style of Research Reports or Case Studies. Literature Surveys are significantly the most informational, which is consistent with their purpose of summarising information. This dimension also suggests that where Narrative Recounts tend to have a relatively low type–token ratio reflecting the repetition typical of narrative (see Narrative Recount extract on page 48), Literature Surveys have a relatively high type–token ratio as they involve summarising information from a range of different sources.

## Non-narrative

As might be predicted, Narrative Recounts are also significantly higher on this dimension than all other genre families, suggesting they have more past tense verbs, third person pronouns and perfect aspect verbs. However in comparison with non-academic texts such as general fiction which scored +6, or romantic fiction which scored +7 (Biber, 1988) they are still very much on the negative or 'academic' end of the scale, and again close to general academic writing (Biber, 1988) and the T2K-SWAL (TOEFL 2000 Spoken and Written Academic Language corpus) textbooks which scored −3 (Biber et al., 2002: 29).

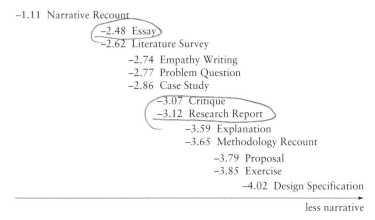

Figure 2.2    The narrative versus non-narrative dimension

Interesting here is the position of Essays as second, which can be explained if we consider the predominance of Essays in disciplines such as History and Classics, where we might expect narration. The position of Methodology Recounts at −3.65 towards the least narrative end is perhaps surprising, given the central role that reporting past events plays in this genre family, but it serves to remind us that Methodology Recounts are more than records of what was done; they have four stages (IMRD), only one of which, albeit the key defining stage, involves recounting what happened. As Proposals and Design Specifications involve future plans, their position as least narrative makes sense if we remember that narrative is interpreted through *past* tense and *third* person grammatical features as well as public verbs such as 'explained' and 'said'. The span of this dimension between Essays and Design Specifications is also relatively small (−2 to −4), suggesting there is less difference in register between all the genre families on this dimension than might be thought.

## Elaborated reference

The third dimension reflects a polarity from situation-dependent reference, with frequent use of time and place adverbials, to elaborated reference, including frequent use of *wh*-relative clauses, phrasal coordination and nominalisations (Biber et al., 2002: 30). Student writing clusters at the elaborated end of the dimension alongside general academic writing (Biber, 1988) and the T2K-SWAL textbooks which scored −6.[7]

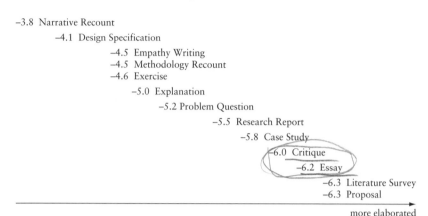

−3.8 Narrative Recount
    −4.1 Design Specification
        −4.5 Empathy Writing
        −4.5 Methodology Recount
        −4.6 Exercise
            −5.0 Explanation
                −5.2 Problem Question
                    −5.5 Research Report
                      −5.8 Case Study
                        −6.0 Critique
                          −6.2 Essay
                            −6.3 Literature Survey
                            −6.3 Proposal

more elaborated

Figure 2.3   The elaborated versus situation-dependent dimension

In contrast to Dimension 2 (the narrative versus non-narrative dimension), this dimension places Design Specifications and Methodology Recounts closer to Narrative Recounts. This highlights their shared attention to specific circumstantial details, in contrast to Essays and Proposals where reference is more elaborated.

## *The persuasive dimension*

Overt expressions of persuasion or argument are seen at the positive end of this dimension where infinitives (*hope to go*), prediction modals (*will, would, shall*), suasive verbs (*command, insist, propose*), conditional subordination (*if you want*) and necessity modals (*must, should, have to*) are significant. Again student writing is similar to textbooks in the T2K-SWAL corpus at −1.8 (Biber et al., 2002: 34), but interestingly most genre families appear to have fewer persuasive features than general academic writing texts, which in Biber's (1988) study were unmarked for this dimension at 0. In other words, in this dimension much student writing is more similar to textbooks in its absence of persuasive features than to published research where some persuasive features are found. Unusually BAWE student writing is in the middle of this dimension which extends from newspaper editorials at 3 to radio broadcasts at −4.

Persuasive register features are most salient in Problem Questions, which involve giving advice or recommendations. They are also found in Proposals and Design Specifications which involve making a case for future action. Although the purpose of Essays is to make

1.6  Problem Question
    1.3  Proposal
        0.8  Empathy Writing
        0.7  Design Specification
            –0.5  Case Study
            –0.7  Narrative Recount
                –1.3  Exercise
                –1.6  Critique
                –1.8  Essay
                    –2.3  Explanation
                    –2.4  Research Report
                    –2.5  Methodology Recount
                        –3.4  Literature Survey

less persuasive

Figure 2.4    The persuasive dimension

a case or develop an argument, as we shall see in Chapter 4, they do not typically use this type of persuasive language to do so. It is important to remember that these descriptions are based on multidimensional analysis of grammatical features in the data as a mass of text, not functional or genre analysis of whole texts. This dimension groups the more 'factual' genre families of Explanation, Methodology Recount and Literature Survey together in their lack of interpersonal, future-oriented and persuasive grammatical features.

## The non-impersonal versus abstract and impersonal dimension

The genre family registers on the fifth dimension are identified as abstract and impersonal through their use of conjuncts (*thus, however*) and passive structures including agentless passives, past participial adverbial and post-nominal clauses (Biber et al., 2002). Interestingly this is the only dimension where the T2K-SWAL corpus textbook register at –3.9 is at one end rather than around the middle of the BAWE corpus genre families. This suggests that textbooks with attention to their pedagogic function are less impersonal than student assignments.

It is not surprising that Methodology Recounts, most of which are in the sciences, use many agentless passives and that this genre family is the most abstract and impersonal in this sense. What is perhaps more surprising is the extent to which all student writing is characterised as abstract and impersonal, even Empathy Writing and Narrative Recounts.

```
-4.0 Narrative Recount
        -4.5 Case Study
        -4.5 Empathy Writing
              -4.8 Proposal
              -5.0 Literature Survey
                           -5.7 Exercise
                           -5.8 Explanation
                           -5.9 Essay
                                  -6.4 Critique
                                  -6.4 Problem Question
                                         -6.8 Design Specification
                                                -7.2 Research Report
                                                -7.3 Methodology Recount
```

more abstract and impersonal

Figure 2.5   The abstract impersonal dimension

## Registers across genre families

The mapping of genre families along the register dimensions identifies the Narrative Recount genre family as an outlier on four of the five dimensions, and statistically significantly different from the others on two. As the following extract suggests, the language used in Narrative Recounts is not typical of academic writing:

> *We carried out an assigned task to discuss 'what we were like in a team' and it became apparent that we all wished to work towards a similar outcome and had roughly the same attitude towards teamwork. This involved everyone taking their fair share of work, commitment to deadlines and to the team. Initially I was quite worried about working within a team, as this was a method of working I had not been exposed to at university in previous terms. I felt quite relieved and enthusiastic once I had discovered members of my group had similar team objectives; however we were all unwilling to express strong opinions at this point.*

(Narrative Recount)

This extract includes many of the features of 'involved' rather than 'informational' texts in Dimension 1 not usually associated with academic writing: first person (*I, we*), private verbs or mental processes (*wished, worried, felt relieved and enthusiastic, unwilling*), general hedges (*roughly, quite*). This is still far from conversational language, and there are also features more typically associated with academic writing, such as lack of contractions and nominalisation (*task, outcome, teamwork, objectives, opinions*).

The other twelve genre families share different features across the range. For example, Essays are similar to Literature Surveys on narrative and situation dependent dimensions, but different on the informational and persuasive dimensions; Methodology Recounts are similar to Research Reports on most dimensions, but differ in situation dependence. Proposals and Design Specifications differ on most dimensions but are similar in persuasion.

A comparison of two Proposals from different disciplines shows differences in field (zoos and chimpanzees versus deals, clients and solutions) and in tenor (the writer's role as indicated through the presence versus absence of first person '*I*').

Preliminary investigations at four other locations
*I plan to spend a minimum of three days at each of the other four zoos before beginning my two-week observation period at each location, starting in May 2006. During preliminary visits to the zoos I will take digital photographs of each of the chimpanzees, and in the presence of the caregivers write down the names, ages and sexes of those individuals. I will then be able to compile an identification sheet for each chimpanzee, and I will spend the days of my preliminary unrecorded observations recognising the group members.*

(Anthropology Proposal)

1   *When a deal is struck between SI and the client, a series of meetings can be held at either of the offices regarding the details of the needs of the client vis-à-vis exact solutions that SI can provide. If some need of the client is out of the SI expertise domain it can look for other companies that can carry out the service required efficiently.*
2   *After the initial round of meetings, an exact timeline could be mapped out detailing delivery, installation & training of the softwares.*
3   *Depending on the length of the project a series of review meetings could be planned which are weekly (for small tasks), monthly (for intermediate tasks) and bi-monthly (for overview of the project).*
4   *Finally after successful completion of the project, after completion checks could be carried out whereby hassle free running of the software is ensured.*

(Engineering Proposal)

Despite the contrasting registers, both these extracts explicitly *plan* and show their future orientation predominantly through modals of prediction (*I will*) or of possibility (*can, could*), alongside other overtly persuasive features such as conditional subordination (*when..., if...*).

These similarities will become clearer in later chapters where examples of the genre families are discussed, but the potential for applications to teaching should be immediately evident from the mapping of salient grammatical features onto genre families. More importantly for this chapter, the multidimensional analysis provides empirical evidence which makes sense in support of the distinct genre family categories. It also shows how similar student writing registers are to those of general academic writing and of the textbooks in the T2K-SWAL corpus.

Broadly speaking, the registers of student writing are characterised as highly informational, non-narrative, elaborated, lacking overt features of persuasion, and highly impersonal. The next questions to ask are whether they become increasingly so as students progress from Level 1 to Level 4 (i.e., from first year undergraduate through to final year and taught Masters courses), and how genres and registers vary across disciplinary groups.

## 2.4 Progression over levels of study and disciplinary group

### Distribution of genre families over disciplinary groups

The 13 genre families are well distributed across the four disciplinary groups of Arts and Humanities (AH), Life Sciences (LS), Physical Sciences (PS) and Social Sciences (SS) in our corpus as shown in Table 2.9, where the genre families are arranged by frequency (Nesi et al., 2008). As expected, the Essay is the most populous genre family, but the least populated genre families of Literature Survey and Empathy Writing also occur across all four disciplinary groups.

The range shows the distribution across the 24 main collection departments, that is those from where we have at least 50 assignments. Essays and Critiques are found in all 24 departments; most

Table 2.9    Distribution of genre families across disciplinary groups

| | Essay | Method. Recount | Critique | Explanation | Case Study | Exercise | Design Spec. | Proposal | Narrative Recount | Research Report | Problem Question | Empathy Writing | Literature Survey |
|---|---|---|---|---|---|---|---|---|---|---|---|---|---|
| AH | ✓ | ✓ | ✓ | ✓ | X | ✓ | ✓ | ✓ | ✓ | ✓ | X | ✓ | ✓ |
| LS | ✓ | ✓ | ✓ | ✓ | ✓ | ✓ | ✓ | ✓ | ✓ | ✓ | ✓ | ✓ | ✓ |
| PS | ✓ | ✓ | ✓ | ✓ | ✓ | ✓ | ✓ | ✓ | ✓ | ✓ | ✓ | ✓ | ✓ |
| SS | ✓ | ✓ | ✓ | ✓ | ✓ | ✓ | ✓ | ✓ | ✓ | ✓ | ✓ | ✓ | ✓ |
| Frequency | 1237 | 361 | 322 | 214 | 194 | 114 | 93 | 76 | 75 | 61 | 40 | 36 | 35 |
| Range / 24 | 24 | 15 | 24 | 15 | 12 | 15 | 7 | 15 | 14 | 17 | 7 | 11 | 11 |

genre families occur in between 11 and 15 departments; while Design Specifications and Problem Questions are the most specialised, occurring in seven of the main 24 departments in our corpus.

Thus most departments use a range of genres, and all thirteen genre families appear in at least seven of our major collection departments. As the genre family classification was developed after data collection was complete, and as we collected across modules and assignment types (e.g., what departments called essays, reports or case studies) rather than across genres, it is possible that the genre families are distributed even more widely.

We would not expect the genre families to be evenly distributed, however. For example, Essays represent over 90 per cent of the Level 1 Arts and Humanities (AH1) assignments collected and fewer than 10 per cent of the Level 4 Physical Science (PS4) assignments. The distribution across levels and disciplinary groups will now be explored further.

## Distribution of genre families over disciplines and levels of study

In our description of genre families we have pointed out that some, like Exercises, are intended to develop lower level skills, while others, like Research Reports, are intended to be a culmination of earlier work in a substantial project. It will be no surprise then to learn that the distribution of genre families over levels of study in the BAWE corpus reflects this. In Figure 2.6 we display the distribution of genre families by level and disciplinary group, where the Levels 1 to 4 represent first year, second year and final year undergraduate work, and postgraduate work. The data are found in Appendix 2.

This graph shows the dominance of Essays in Arts and Humanities as well as Social Sciences, at more than 50 per cent of all assignments, in comparison to the range of genres in Life Sciences and Physical Sciences, where Explanations and Methodology Recounts are more frequent.

For Arts and Humanities, we note that as the proportion of Essays decreases with level of study from Level 1 (AH1) at 91 per cent to Level 4 (AH4) at 61 per cent, the proportion of Critiques increases from 4 per cent to 20 per cent. This also reflects the general finding that a greater diversity of genres is required with each level of study, particularly at undergraduate level.

In Social Sciences the proportion of Case Studies increases from 4 per cent (SS1) to 11 per cent (SS3) while the proportion of Problem Questions fluctuates from 5 per cent (SS1) through 7 per cent (SS2) to

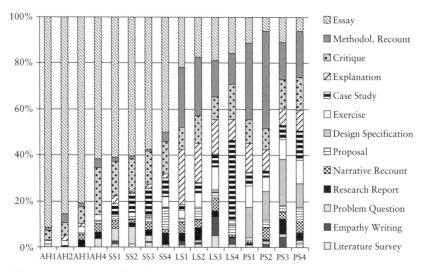

Figure 2.6    Genre family proportions by disciplinary level

2 per cent (SS3). Most Problem Questions are found here in SS1 and SS2 modules.

In contrast, most Explanations are found in the Life Sciences, where their proportion decreases significantly from 25 per cent in LS1 to 9 per cent in LS4 as the proportion of Empathy Writing increases towards 8 per cent in LS3 and graduation. The significant proportion of Case Studies in LS4 (35 per cent) reflects the large number of medical case studies produced across modules in postgraduate training.

Methodology Recounts are found in large proportions in the early years of the Physical Sciences with 33 per cent at Level 1 rising to 46 per cent at Level 2. There is then a notable switch to a more balanced range of activity including Design Specifications (20 per cent), Research Reports (6 per cent) and Empathy Writing (4 per cent) in Level 3.

The proportions[8] of genre families at each disciplinary level are presented here to extend our earlier account (Section 2.2) of the functions of the different genres, and how students are expected to progress through their degree pathways from, for instance, typical Level 2 genres of Problem Questions in Social Sciences, Explanations in Life Sciences and Methodology Recounts in Physical Sciences, to genres that allow for more student originality such as Research Reports that build on these understandings, and to Empathy genres that anticipate the workplace.

## 2.5  Conclusion

This chapter has explained how and why we classified the texts in the BAWE corpus into genre families. It has provided an overview of the thirteen genre families, grouped according to their broad social functions. The development of our classification started in discussions with lecturers and students which informed our careful reading of all texts in the corpus, with particular attention to their purposes and staging. Our descriptions of these thirteen genre families are enhanced by brief accounts of the genre networks and examples of genre members from across the disciplines. We then described the registers of the thirteen genre families along five dimensions which help explain some of the differences between the genre families. Our account of genre families across disciplinary groups and levels of study helps to locate the genre families across the academy, while the account of register variation across levels of study underscores the similarity between student writing and other written academic genres.

We now turn our focus to the broader social functions of university student writing which we identify as demonstrating knowledge and understanding (Chapter 3), developing independent reasoning (Chapter 4), building research skills (Chapter 5), preparing for professional practice (Chapter 6) and writing for oneself and others (Chapter 7). The development of each of these chapters moves from discussion of the broad social functions of student writing in context through a description of those genre families and their members that most centrally realise the functions, to disciplinary differences across these genres and registers, and an examination of specific linguistic features.

## Notes

1. Those not familiar with the linguistic features linked here to field, tenor and mode may wish to consult an accessible introduction to Systemic Functional Linguistics, such as Bloor and Bloor (2004).
2. Note that Masters dissertations are not included in the corpus.
3. The type–token ratio is the ratio between the number of different words in a text (the 'types') and the total number of words in the text (the 'tokens'). For the full list of features and their salience in the dimensions, see Biber (1988). A summary of these is given in Biber et al. (2002: 15–16) and in our Appendix 1.3.
4. The academic prose in the 1988 study is from the scientific and learned component of the LOB corpus which includes published research from journals, books and reports from across broad disciplinary groups (Johansson, Leech and Goodluck, 1978).

5. The 176 university textbooks form a subcorpus of the TOEFL 2000 Spoken and Written Academic Language (T2K-SWAL) corpus. They are from lower and upper undergraduate courses and graduate courses from across the disciplines.
6. Duncan's multiple-range test was used to identify genres with means that are not statistically different.
7. Following Biber et al. (2002), we reverse the polarity of Dimensions 3 and 5 in this chapter for easier comparisons across the dimensions of academic writing.
8. As we did not compile statistical data on how many assignments students write in total, these figures should not be interpreted as representing the proportion of student writing in each genre. For example, if a student contributor had written ten lab reports in one module and one product evaluation in another module, we would probably have collected just one lab report and one product evaluation from that student for those two modules.

# References

Biber, D. (1988). *Variation across speech and writing*. Cambridge: Cambridge University Press.

Biber, D. (1995). *Dimensions of register variation: A cross-linguistic comparison*. Cambridge: Cambridge University Press.

Biber, D., & Conrad, S. (2009). *Register, genre, and style*. Cambridge: Cambridge University Press.

Biber, D., Conrad, S., Reppen, R., Byrd, P., & Helt, M. (2002). Speaking and writing in the university: a multidimensional comparison. *TESOL Quarterly*, 36(1), 9–48.

Biber, D., Johansson, S., Leech, G., Conrad, S., & Finegan, E. (1999). *Longman grammar of spoken and written English*. Harlow, Essex: Pearson Education.

Bloor, T., & Bloor, M. (2004). *The functional analysis of English: A Hallidayan approach* (2nd edition). London: Arnold.

Carter, M. (2007). Ways of knowing, doing and writing in the disciplines. *College Composition and Communication*, 58, 385–418.

Coffin, C., & Hewings, A. (2004). IELTS as preparation for tertiary writing: Distinctive interpersonal and textual strategies. In L. Ravelli & R. Ellis (Eds.), *Analysing academic writing: Contextualized frameworks*. London: Continuum, 153–71.

Conrad, S., & Biber, D. (2001). Multi-dimensional methodology and the dimensions of register variation in English. In S. Conrad & D. Biber (Eds.), *Variation in English: Multi-dimensional studies*. Harlow, Essex: Pearson Education.

Drury, H. (2010). The challenge of teaching academic writing online: developing report writing programmes for science and engineering. Paper presented at the 37th International Systemic Functional Linguistic conference, Vancouver, July 2010. See also www.usyd.edu.au/learningcentre/wrise.

Dudley-Evans, T. (1985). *Writing laboratory reports*. Thomas Nelson: Melbourne.

Forey, G. (2004). Workplace texts: Do they mean the same for teachers and business people? *English for Specific Purposes*, 23, 447–69.

Gardner, S. (2004). Knock-on effects of mode change on academic discourse. *Journal of English for Academic Purposes*, 3, 23–38.

Gardner, S., & Holmes, J. (2009). 'Can I use headings in my essay?' Section headings, macrostructures and genre families in the BAWE corpus of student writing. In M. Charles, S. Hunston & D. Pecorari (Eds.), *Academic writing: At the interface of corpus and discourse*, London: Continuum, 251–71.

Gardner, S., & Holmes, J. (2010). From section headings to assignment macrostructure in undergraduate student writing. In E. Swain (Ed.), *Thresholds and potentialities of systemic functional linguistics: Applications to other disciplines, specialised discourses and languages other than English*. Trieste: Edizioni Universitarie Trieste, 254–76.

Gardner, S., & Powell, L. (2006). An investigation of genres of assessed writing in British higher education: A Warwick–Reading–Oxford Brookes project. Paper presented at the seminar "Research, scholarship and practice in the area of Academic Literacies", University of Westminster, 30 June.

Gillett, A., & Hammond, A. (2009). 'Mapping the maze of assessment: An investigation into practice.' *Active Learning in Higher Education*, 10, 120–37.

Hale, G., Taylor, C., Bridgeman, B., Carson, J., Kroll, B., & Kantor, R. (1996). A study of writing tasks assigned in academic degree programs. Research Report 54. Princeton, NJ: ETS.

Halliday, M.A.K. (2009). *The essential Halliday*. J.J.Webster (Ed.). London: Continuum.

Hyland, K. (2002a). Genre: Language, context and literacy. *Annual Review of Applied Linguistics*, 22, 113–35.

Hyland, K. (2002b). *Teaching and researching writing*. Harlow: Longman.

Johansson, S., Leech, G., & Goodluck, H. (1978). *Manual of information to accompany the Lancaster–Oslo/Bergen Corpus of British English, for use with digital computers*. Oslo: University of Oslo.

Johns, A. (Ed.) (2002). *Genre in the classroom: Multiple perspectives*. Mahwah, NJ: Lawrence Erlbaum.

Lea, M., & Street, B. (2000). Student writing and staff feedback in higher education: An academic literacies approach. In M. Lea & B. Stierer (Eds.), *Student writing in higher education: New contexts*. Buckingham: The Society for Research into Higher Education and Open University Press.

Martin, J.R. (1992). *English text: System and structure*. Amsterdam: Benjamins.

Martin, J.R. (1997). Analysing genre: Functional parameters. In F. Christie & J.R. Martin (Eds.), *Genres and institutions: Social processes in the workplace and school*. London: Continuum.

Martin, J.R., & Rose, D. (2008). *Genre relations: Mapping culture*. London: Equinox.

Melzer, D. (2009). Writing assignments across the curriculum: A national study of college writing. *College Composition and Communication*, 61(2), W240–61.

Moore, T., & Morton, J. (2005). Dimensions of difference: A comparison of university writing and IELTS writing. *Journal of English for Academic Purposes* 4(1),43–66.

Nesi, H., & Gardner, S. (2006). Variation in disciplinary culture: university tutors' views on assessed writing tasks. In R. Kiely, G. Clibbon, P. Rea-Dickins, & H. Woodfield (Eds.), *Language, culture and identity in applied linguistics* (British Studies in Applied Linguistics, vol 21) London: Equinox Publishing, 99–117.

Nesi, H., Gardner, S., Thompson, P., Wickens, P., Forsyth, R., Heuboeck, A., Holmes, J., Hindle, D., Ebeling, S., Leedham, M., & Alsop, S. (2008). 'An Investigation of Genres of Assessed Writing in British Higher Education'. Final ESRC Report for Project No. RES-000–23–0800. March 2008.

Rosenfeld, M., Courtney, R., & Fowles, M. (2004). *Identifying the writing tasks important for academic success at the undergraduate and graduate levels.* GRE Board Research Report No. 4, Princeton, NJ: Educational Testing Service.

Swales, J. M. (1990). *Genre analysis. English in academic and research settings.* Cambridge: Cambridge University Press.

# PART II:
# SOCIAL FUNCTIONS OF UNIVERSITY STUDENT WRITING

# 3  *Demonstrating knowledge and understanding*

{ Explaination
  exercise

A ... graduate will have developed an understanding of a
complex body of knowledge ...
(Quality Assurance Agency 2001: Executive Summary)

One central function of university education is to enable students
to develop current and specialised academic knowledge in particular disciplines. This chapter begins by exploring what this means
for assessed writing (3.1) and continues with an examination of the
two genre families which foreground this function of demonstrating knowledge and understanding: Explanations and Exercises (3.2).
The Explanation and Exercise genres are described in more detail
as they vary across disciplines and levels of study in Sections 3.3
and 3.4 respectively. As developing knowledge and understanding
is an important concern across much academic writing beyond the
Explanation and Exercise genre families considered here, Section
3.5 previews the role developing knowledge and understanding
plays in other genre families. The chapter concludes with an analysis of keywords and word clusters used in Explanations in student
assignment writing.

## 3.1  Developing coherent and detailed knowledge

A fundamental criterion for any university degree relates to the expectation that students will demonstrate 'a systematic understanding of
key aspects of their field of study, including acquisition of coherent
and detailed knowledge, at least some of which is at, or informed by,
the forefront of defined aspects of a discipline' (Quality Assurance
Agency [QAA], 2001: Annex 1). This is the first criterion listed in
the framework for higher education qualifications in England, Wales
and Northern Ireland (QAA, 2001; 2008), and similar criteria are
found internationally. Students demonstrate such current and specialised understanding and knowledge in most if not all assignments, but

this demonstration is the central purpose of assignment texts in the Explanation genre family.

Our interviews with lecturers point to the role explanation holds in student writing:

*An 'essay' [in Biology] is written to a title, for example: 'How is the vertebrate limb patterned?' It is an exercise in learning about a certain area of science. The student must understand the current state of knowledge and how it was acquired, and be able to explain it. In year 1 you can find everything you need to know from the textbook.*

(Biology lecturer)

In this quotation, which is typical of how lecturers described one type of assignment they set, we see that Explanation genres may be referred to as 'essays', but their central purpose is not for students to develop an argument, but for them to demonstrate knowledge and understanding, through presenting information that may be found in textbooks, and explaining whatever concept, process, entity or idea is given by the lecturer in the title of the assignment. Such understanding may be demonstrated through an Exercise which comprises a number of questions requiring calculations or short paragraph answers, or may be demonstrated through a more extended Explanation.

Despite the fact that the necessary information tends to be readily available, demonstrating knowledge and understanding in an Explanation presents its own writing challenge:

*I didn't have to write a scientific essay before. That's quite different purely because you get no personal detail or personal information in these scientific essays. That's hard, it's purely factual. And one of the hardest things with a scientific essay is that you're not allowed to plagiarise ... So in order to try and translate academic people who have written articles in journals and you haven't a clue [about] half of the words, you have to paraphrase it yourself. It's quite difficult. Does that make sense?*

(Level 2 Chemistry student)

As this student points out, the task of explaining in science involves not only understanding highly technical academic written language, but also translating this knowledge into a student assignment text. Thus one of the functions of academic writing is for students to develop an understanding of and proficient, confident use of the technical language of their discipline. This may also involve translating between modes, as explanation in student assignments often includes figures, tables, formulae and photographs which are then described by the students in the process of explaining. This entails using their 'own words' in the sense of their own 'wording', that is, their own construals of existing concepts using the technical words of the discipline.

As we saw in Chapter 2, Explanation genres are concentrated in the Life Sciences, but the importance of the function of explaining is found across disciplines:

*Maths is difficult but students must learn to explain it.*

(Mathematics lecturer)

*How do determiners differ from other pre-head modifiers within the English Noun Phrase structure?*

(Linguistics assignment title)

Guidance may be given about audience so that students do not explain very basic terms, but are able to concentrate on explaining complex bodies of current knowledge:

*Undergraduates should aim at a non-specialist audience: they should think of explaining the essence of a debate to a fellow student in the hall of residence who isn't doing philosophy. If they can do that, they clearly have understood what they have read.*

(Philosophy lecturer)

*[In our chemistry essay] we were told to target someone who has an A Level in chemistry. So the level is slightly below us. The idea is that they should understand most of it so you don't have to define every single scientific term – they know what most of them are.*

(Level 2 Chemistry student)

For students coming to university who have studied A levels[1], these decisions about what should and need not be explained will be easier than for students from other educational systems.

In addition to using their own wording, and writing for an appropriate audience, a third challenge in demonstrating knowledge and understanding lies in deciding what to include and what to omit in that demonstration. The appropriate use of certain 'keywords' signals whether the student is thinking along the right track.

*If they concentrate on explaining the minutiae of a thoroughly irrelevant aspect ..., you know that they've not really understood the main thrust.*

(BioSciences lecturer)

It is worth pointing out here that demonstrating knowledge and understanding of a complex body of information is internationally seen as a central purpose of university student writing, and that demonstrating knowledge and understanding is generally differentiated from argumentation. For instance, in Hale et al.'s classification of student writing tasks at American universities, demonstration of knowledge and understanding would fall within the rhetorical task of exposition, which they define as entailing:

...( the expression of ideas, opinions, and explanations, ... intended to inform or promote understanding of a particular piece of knowledge or fact. ... [In contrast] Argument was characterised as a particular form of exposition that included persuasion. )

(Hale et al., 1996: 23)

Interestingly, in their examination of student tasks, Hale et al. infer that 'Exposition was involved in all assignments, ... Narration or Description were involved in zero percent ... Argument was present only to a modest degree.' (1996: 49) A detailed comparison of this classification system and resulting findings with ours is not possible because of the rather different categories established, but the implication that developing knowledge and understanding is common to all assignments is one that we share (see Section 3.5).

## 3.2  The Explanation and Exercise genre families

While most assignments can lay some claim to developing know-ledge and understanding, two genre families in our classification (see Table 2.4) foreground demonstrating knowledge and understanding as their central purpose: Explanations are set to develop students' understanding of an object of study, and their ability to describe it and account for its significance, whereas Exercises are intended to give students practice in key skills and consolidate knowledge of key concepts. Both may be realised as written texts or as multimodal texts with diagrams and formulae.

### *Fewer words...*

Aside from sharing a common focus on developing knowledge and understanding, Explanations and Exercises both tend to be shorter than average in terms of the total number of words and sentences (Table 3.1). The Explanation average is around 2,000 words long and the Exercise average is around 1,500 words long, compared to the corpus average of over 2,300 words. Exercises and Explanations in the corpus range from around 500 to 6,000 words in length with most Exercises between 500 and 2,500 words, while most Explanations are between 1,000 and 4,000 words. Despite being shorter, their sentence lengths in words (w/s) and paragraph lengths in sentences (s/p) are similar to the average (Table 3.1). In fact, Explanations are identical to the corpus average with an average sentence length of 25 words and average paragraph length of four sentences. So although the assignments themselves are shorter than average there is no reason

Table 3.1    Length of Explanations and Exercises[2]

| | words | s-units | p-units | w/s | s/p | block quotes | tables | formulae | figures | lists |
|---|---|---|---|---|---|---|---|---|---|---|
| Average | 2,357 | 98 | 30 | 25 | 4 | 1 | 1 | 4 | 1 | 0.7 |
| Explanations | 2,075 | 87 | 26 | 25 | 4 | 0 | 1 | 2 | 3 | 0.4 |
| Exercises | 1,568 | 80 | 40 | 21 | 3 | 0 | 2 | 12 | 4 | 1.1 |

to suppose that the quality of writing in Explanations is less. This average sentence length of 25 words is shorter than results Bloor (1999) reports for published research article methods sections, but in line with an average of 27.6 w/s in Barber's corpus of scientific prose, and 23.8 w/s in the Brown corpus' scientific section (Huddleson, 1971; cited in Bloor, 1999: 97).

Exercises almost by definition are shorter than most assignments, but there are also short Explanations set. For example, so called 'mini essays' (1,000–1,500 words) in Economics involve 'reading technical texts and demonstrating understanding in writing' (Economics lecturer); in Philosophy there are 'short pieces of work connecting several concepts – just trying to explain concepts rather than making a claim' (Philosophy lecturer).

The prevalence of short tasks similar to Exercises is also noted in the American Educational Testing Service study where they occurred in around 20 per cent of all modules (Hale et al., 1996: 35). '[Short] tasks called for writing more than one or two sentences and up to one-half page in response to a given question or other stimulus. Such tasks might consist, for example, of questions on a test or a problem set.' (1996: 46). An in-depth analysis of one type of short answer genre from a Level 1 Biology module in Australia is found in Drury (2001), which highlights the preparatory role they can play in a degree course towards longer assignments. In the ETS study, short tasks occurred in all disciplines at both undergraduate and postgraduate level (1996: 45), and as with the BAWE corpus (Figure 2.6, Appendix 2) Exercise genres, 'were more common in the physical / mathematical science and engineering group than the social sciences and humanities group' (1996: 45).

## … *more diagrams*

In the corpus as a whole (see Table 1.5), assignment length in words, sentences and paragraphs tends to increase proportionally with number of figures. In Table 3.1, however, Explanations and Exercises are not only shorter than average, and include fewer block quotes, but they also include more figures than average. While figures or diagrams are not exclusive to Explanations or Exercises, they are a significant feature in demonstrating knowledge and understanding. In Computer Science, students may use a diagram to explain a coding (Computer Science lecturer). In Economics:

*A typical 'essay' would contain diagrams and formulae, as the spine of the essay. For example, in an essay of 5 or 6 pages you'd normally find 2 or 3 pages with 1 or 2 diagrams on each of them. Good students would surround the diagrams with lots of writing explaining what is going on. Weaker students would have the diagrams but little prose, or else prose paragraphs that don't really relate to the diagrams. On the other hand, words alone, without figures, are not enough. Quite a challenge to marry the diagrams with the text.*

(Economics lecturer)

In such assignments, diagrams and words are employed together (as in Figure 3.4, the anatomy of the eye) to demonstrate knowledge and understanding. This partly explains why assignments in the Exercise and Explanation genre families are shorter in terms of words and sentences than average.

In addition to figures, Exercises contain more paragraphs, formulae, tables and lists than average, as illustrated in Figure 3.1, the answer to Question 1 in a Level 3 telecommunications module assignment from Engineering.

This extensive use of formulae suggests that preparation for writing such an Exercise would be quite different from preparation for writing a diagram-driven assignment as described by the Economics lecturer, or for writing a conventional words-only essay.

## 3.3 Explanations across disciplines

Explanations occur across all disciplinary groups in the corpus (see Section 2.4). They occur as simple assignments or as parts of compound assignments where they may occur with other genres or more usually with other Explanations. For example, one magazine publishing portfolio from Publishing is a compound assignment that includes four explanations, each on a different type of magazine (men's, food and drink, teens', music) each with its own title, word count (around 500 words each) and bibliography. Similarly, an 18-page assignment from Mathematics includes two main parts, one an explanation of coding theory, the other an explanation of cryptography, each with its own introduction and concluding summary sections. As shown in

---

### Question 1

Normalised colour signals are given as $R = 0.5$, $G = 0.4$, $B = 0.1$. The system gamma value is given as $\gamma_s = 3$ and display gamma value as $\gamma_d = 2$. Luminosity coefficients are taken as $l_1 = 0.299$, $l_2 = 0.587$ and $l_3 = 0.114$. This allows corrected luminance values for each colour to be calculated as follows:

$$R' = R^{\frac{1}{\gamma_s}} = 0.5^{\frac{1}{3}} = 0.794$$

$$G' = G^{\frac{1}{\gamma_s}} = 0.4^{\frac{1}{3}} = 0.737$$

$$B' = B^{\frac{1}{\gamma_s}} = 0.1^{\frac{1}{3}} = 0.464.$$

Transmitted luminance can then be calculated:

$$Y' = l_1 R' + l_2 G' + l_3 B' = 0.299 \times 0.794 + 0.587 \times 0.737 + 0.114 \times 0.464.$$
$$= 0.723$$

Colour difference signals are then:

$$R' - Y' = 0.794 - 0.723 = 0.071$$

$$B' - Y' = 0.464 - 0.723 = -0.259.$$

The displayed luminance can also be calculated:

$$Y \propto (Y')^{\gamma_d} = 0.723^2 = 0.522.$$

---

Figure 3.1    An entry from an Engineering exercise

Table 3.2, the 214 Explanation texts occur in 185 assignments, across all four disciplinary groups.

Explanation texts are typically found in Life Sciences (LS) such as Biology, Agriculture and Health, and in Physical Sciences (PS) such as Engineering, Physics and Chemistry. They also occur across the Arts and Humanities (AH) and the Social Sciences (SS).

### Explanations in the first two years

We have seen that Explanation genres occur in the BAWE corpus more frequently at the first two levels of study (see Section 2.4) than at upper levels, and that they are on average shorter than most assignments (see Section 3.2). It therefore makes sense, and was clear from interviews, course materials and assignments set, that assignments

Table 3.2    Number of Explanation texts and assignments in the corpus

|  | Explanation texts (assignments) |
| --- | --- |
| LS (Biology, Agriculture, Health, Food Science, Psychology, Medicine) | 117 (113) |
| PS (Engineering, Physics, Chemistry, Meteorology, Computer Science, Mathematics) | 65 (50) |
| AH (Linguistics, Archaeology, Publishing) | 19 (10) |
| SS (Business, HLTM, Anthropology) | 13 (12) |
| Total | 214 (185) |

which require students to demonstrate knowledge and understanding are often, but not always, a basis for further development.

*In year 1 a student can gain a first-class grade without really being clever or any good at psychology: lecturers are looking for the ability to describe theories or experiments clearly and evaluate them in a reasonable manner. The crucial requirement is that the writing be 'accurate, concise, explicit and unambiguous'. It isn't about novel thinking.*

(Psychology lecturer)

Explanations are therefore more common at Levels 1 and 2:

*The first essay that we ever had to do was to explain a cell and the bits in it. You were starting from the beginning and literally detailing the bits in it. It's quite a dull essay really.*

(Level 2 Chemistry student)

With the exception of Level 4 in Arts and Humanities, Explanations occur at all levels in each disciplinary group, but as Figure 2.7 shows, the proportion of Explanations is larger in Levels 1 and 2, and smaller in Levels 3 and 4. More marked are disciplinary differences with the highest proportions in Life Sciences (25% compared to 9%), and in Physical Sciences (13% to 7%), in comparison with Arts and Social Sciences where numbers and differences between levels are smaller (3% or 4% to 0–1%).

## Explanations in Life and Physical Sciences

Explanations are widespread in the Sciences where students may be asked to explain the nature of stem cells, human molecular disease, tsunamis or epiphytes. The Explanation genre family for university student writing therefore encompasses classifications and descriptive reports which have a similar function to Report genres in the schools literature in that they tell us 'what an entire class of things is like' (Martin, 1989: 15). In research on writing from secondary schools, Report genres are distinct from Explanations (Christie and Derewianka, 2008; Veel, 1997), but for university student writing it seems that explanation is an important feature of descriptions of classes of things, needed if students are to demonstrate their understanding, and we have therefore prioritised explanation as the overarching function. Students may also be asked to explain techniques such as Positon Emission Tomography (Physics) or processes such as the making of a vertebrate limb (Biology), or evaporation in yogurt (Food Sciences). That an explanation is required is often clear from the title or rubric:

*HTTP is the "stateless" protocol used by Internet browsers for most communications on the Internet. Using the seven OSI layers as reference model describe in detail how data (TCP segments) travels from a home user's browser to a website during a typical ecommerce transaction. You are required to elaborate on any encapsulations and de-capsulations that occur during this process.*

(Computer Science task)

The macrostructure of an Explanation may be given by the lecturer, or may be developed by the student as part of the explanation process. It generally contains a definition of whatever is being explained, descriptions of its properties, functions, uses or how it works, and a conclusion which sums up the significance of the facts concerning what has been explained. This example of a short (700-word) Explanation uses bullet point lists extensively to present a clear, informative and concise explanation of hydroponics for a postgraduate course in horticulture (see Figure 3.2).

The emphasis on facts is clearly shown in this Explanation about hydroponics, where all verbs are in the present tense, and most pieces of information are presented as bullet point lists, some with no grammatical subject, and most with no lexico-grammatical links connecting them.

As is typical of scientific writing, the Explanation is general, and does not refer to a specific instance of hydroponics even though this particular assignment was inspired by a specific farm visit; the clauses are predominantly relational processes with the main verbs *be* and *have*; and the grammatical subjects and complements include technical nominalisations as in: '*Hydroponic cultivation* is characterised by *high cost*'. This is typical of Explanations – they are impersonal (no human

---

# Hydroponics

**Definition:** [2 sentences]
**History of hydroponics:** [2 sentences]
**Crops that can be grown in hydroponic systems:** [2 sentences]
**Advantages of hydroponic systems:**
- Water as well as nutrients is always available so the plants are never stressed.
- [6 further advantages]

**Disadvantages of hydroponic systems:**
- Hydroponic cultivation is characterised by high cost.
- [3 further disadvantages]

**Growing media used in hydroponics:**
There is a great variety of growing media. Several media that can be used in hydroponics include:
- **Sand:** this medium exists in abundance and is of low cost. It has the disadvantages that it has to be sterilised after use as well as poor drainage.
- [7 further bullet points of growing materials]

**The role of growing media:**
- Provide support for the roots of the plants.
- [2 further bullet points]

A good growing medium … must also … be sterile, of neutral pH and finally it must not break down.
**Nutrient solution – a key factor in hydroponics:**
The most important factor in terms of hydroponics is the nutrient solution. [2 sentences describing the solution]
**General conclusion:**
[2 sentences omitted] Apart from advantages these systems also have disadvantages but the fact is that the benefits deriving from hydroponic systems outnumber the disadvantages.

---

Figure 3.2    Hydroponics Explanation

participants), describe states, qualities and properties rather than actions, and are concisely and precisely written. As with Reports and Explanations in school Science, information is typically construed as 'general, well-established and timeless facts' with 'no scope for questioning or challenging the information presented' (Veel, 1997: 166).

Explanations in student writing, however, cannot be verbatim replications of textbook knowledge either in wording or in information content and structure. Students have to decide what to include, how to link sections and how to frame the assignment. Thus some Explanations include specific motivation for detailed understanding and knowledge. For example, a detailed explanation of the optic nerve system can be motivated by possible future developments. As one student states at the end of her abstract and again at the end of her conclusion:

> ... *artificial impulse creation ... could enable completely blind and partially sighted individuals to have some sight stimulation. This ... will improve the qualities of lives of countless individuals, and so it is important to further understanding of the optic nerve system, and conversion of these signals to produce an image, within the occipital lobe of the brain.*
>
> (Biomedical Engineering student)

This rationale allows the student to demonstrate an understanding of the significance of what she is explaining. From the subheadings below we can see that the space devoted to these future possibilities is small, and indeed the 175-word discussion and conclusion section mainly summarises the explanations in the bulk of the assignment (pp 3–15).

This assignment is fewer than 3,000 words, but 18 pages long, because of the extensive use of diagrams, as illustrated on page 3 in Figure 3.4.

In addition to the prominent position of diagrams, which complement the written text in the Explanation in that both should be read for full understanding, it is noticeable that the paragraphs are short, each one describing a feature of the eye on the diagram.

| | |
|---|---:|
| 1.0 Abstract and Keywords | 1 |
| 2.0 Introduction | 2 |
| 3.0 The Eye | 3 |
| 3.1 The Eyelids and Lacrimal Apparatus | 4 |
| 3.2 The Iris and Genetics of Eye Colour | 5 |
| 3.3 Extrinsic Eye Muscles | 7 |
| 3.4 The Cornea (Penetrating keratoplasty) | 9 |
| 3.5 The Lens | 10 |
| 3.6 The Retina | 13 |
| 3.7 The Sensory Connections | 15 |
| 4.0 The Future for Eye Surgery | 16 |
| 5.0 Discussion and Conclusion | 17 |
| 6.0 References | 18 |

Figure 3.3   Subheadings of an Explanation with diagrams

I will begin my discussion with a basic anatomy of the eye. Fig. 1. indicates the main areas that are of importance when regarding the eye systems[i].

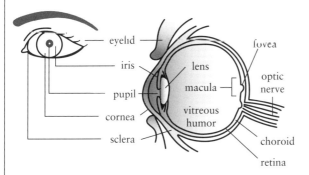

Fig. 1.   The Anatomy of the Eye.

Each has a specific function that helps to maintain the eye. A brief indication of these would be:[ii]
The Lens bends the light entering the eye so that it forms an image on the retina at the back of the eye. The lens can change shape because it is held in position by the ciliary body.
The Cornea is a transparent membrane that covers the iris and pupil. It helps to focus the light.
The pupil is the dark hole in the ...

i.  http://www.mvrf.org/images/eye_anatomy.gif
ii. http://www.college-optometrists.org/index.aspx/pcms/site.Public_Related_
    Links.Parts_of_the_Eye.Parts_of_the_Eye_home/

Figure 3.4   The anatomy of the eye

If we check the reference for the text, we see the first feature in the source text on the Internet is given as:

The lens is a transparent body behind the iris, the coloured part of the eye. The lens bends light rays so that they form a clear image at the back of the eye – on the retina. As the lens is elastic, it can change shape, getting fatter to focus close objects and thinner for distant objects.
www.college-optometrists.org/index.aspx/pcms/site.Public_Related_Links.
Parts_of_the_Eye.Parts_of_the_Eye_home/

It is clear that the student has not copied this, but has used her own wording to explain the functions of the components of the eye. As appropriate for writing scientific explanations, she has used technical language (*lens, bends, retina, ciliary*), general participants (*the lens, the light, the eye*), specific circumstantial details (*on the retina, at the back of the eye, by the ciliary body*) and causal conjunctions (*so that, because*).

Moreover, the diagram and layout of text in this example illustrate well how layout in Explanations is a crucial feature of planning and producing high-quality assignments.

The next example illustrates how upper level student writing is generally expected to draw on several expert sources. The explanation of the digestion system in horses is ascribed significance through the claim that colic is one of the most frequent causes of veterinarian visits to horses in the UK. At 2,900 words, with two figures and twenty-one references, this assignment is also more essay-like in appearance than those in the previous two examples.

This Level 3 assignment was written by a student who is a native speaker of English and was fully educated in the UK. It earned a 'distinction' (top) mark, despite grammatical slips (e.g., *i.e.* for *e.g.*; *There is ... studies* for *There are*; *the risks of death ... remains* rather than *remain*). The marker's leniency in this respect suggests that including relevant, comprehensible information in a conventional Explanation format is more important than using standard grammar throughout. It should be noted, however, that some lecturers we interviewed were more concerned with grammatical accuracy than others.

---

ENTERAL PROBLEMS OF THE HORSE – COLIC

Colic, which refers to a 'severe pain in the abdomen caused by wind or obstruction in the intestines' (Soanes, 2005), is a term used for a wide range of causes and symptoms that all affect the gastrointestinal system. There seems to be no gender that is more prone to colic, although types of colic may be gender specific, i.e. uterine torsion in mares. There is conflicting studies regarding breed and age risks. For example, Tinker *et al.* (1997) identify Arab horses to be at a reduced risk of developing colic, whereas Cohen *et al.* (1999) describe the opposite, where Arab horses are actually more prone to colic. However, in all horses that develop colic, the risks of death still remains high, despite improved medical and surgical techniques (Greet, 1993).

---

Figure 3.5    Negotiating multiple citations in an Explanation

Explaining colic at Level 3 involves not only collating the generally agreed 'facts' about digestion in horses, but also pointing to gaps in knowledge (*there seems to be no gender that is more prone*) or to conflicting findings (*Cohen et al. describe the opposite*). Nevertheless, this is not a discussion genre – the aim of the assignment is not to consider the conflicting evidence in detail, but to demonstrate 'acquisition of coherent and detailed knowledge, at least some of which is at or informed by, the forefront of defined aspects of a discipline' (QAA, 2001).

## Initial Explanations in Arts and Social Science Explanations

While some Social Sciences include Explanations that are very similar to scientific Explanations (e.g., a general account of the white-throated capuchin monkey in Anthropology), Explanations in Arts and Humanities and in Social Sciences are often implied in the first part of a two-part assignment question. For example, in Economics, students may be asked to (1) explain a theorem, and (2) apply it to the real world. In Anthropology, students may be asked to explain a concept and develop an argument about its prevalence: 'What is meant by the term "human–wildlife conflict"?' Is this a phenomenon that only occurs within tropical regions of world? In Linguistics, students may be asked to explain a theoretical concept and then develop an argument about related empirical research.

*What is meant by code-switching? Discuss the main types and functions of code switching that have been identified.*

(Linguistics assignment)

*Explain what is meant by 'Quick Incidental Learning' and 'Fast Mapping' in relation to lexical acquisition. What do investigations in this area tell us about vocabulary learning?*

(Linguistics assignment)

In Law this may not be as explicit in the title of an assignment, but students figure out this dual requirement from the assessment criteria and the emphasis in the teaching:

*The lecturers emphasise the need for people to understand the basics of their modules. After that they would value the extra research and after that they think that the writing style is most important. Of course, you need this writing style for a good essay but the knowledge comes first.*

(Level 1 Law student)

It is important to note that although the responses to these two-part questions could be written as a compound assignment of two texts, they are often written as one integrated text, a fact which underscores the importance of Explanation in many genres beyond those whose primary purpose is to explain. As in the Linguistics assignments above, the wording of the title set by the lecturer to include '[explain] what is meant by' makes explicit one common assumption underlying assignments which include an element of explanation, and those which belong to the Explanation genre family: that there tends to be a widely agreed rationale or detailed definition for the phenomenon or concept students are asked to explain. Explanations are therefore frequent in 'hard' disciplines where knowledge acquisition is emphasised over interpretation and skill in argument (Neuman, Parry and Becher, 2002: 408).

One corollary of how knowledge and understanding are presented as factual, or at least as shared current state of knowledge in the field, is that when students were asked about the extent to which they had to write for individual lecturers, or whether all lecturers would mark using the same criteria, it was clear that in some disciplines students believed that the assessment criteria were objective and objectively applied, whereas in others it was necessary to figure out what individual lecturers wanted and to write accordingly.

*Basically, [the lecturers] all think the same. We need a good understanding. Then a good amount of extra research. And also a good writing style. It is like a check box effect. There are other criteria too.*

(Level 1 Law student)

Explanations seem to have the added benefit that they can be marked relatively objectively. In these ways writing Explanations is a convergent translation task that requires students to demonstrate shared knowledge and understanding in their own words.

## 3.4 Exercises across disciplines

Although the number of Exercises in the corpus is about half that of Explanations (only 114, or 4 per cent), Exercises, unlike Explanations, are found across all four disciplinary groups and all four levels. They represent 6–10 per cent of texts in the Physical Sciences and Engineering disciplinary group, which includes Mathematics, Engineering and Computer Science, but are spread across other disciplines including Food Science, Business and English, as shown in Table 3.3.

In Business, Exercises occur in modules such as accounting and finance or statistics for business, which is consistent with their frequency in Mathematics and Computer Science where the Exercises

Table 3.3   Number of Exercise texts and assignments in the corpus

|  | Exercise texts (assignments) |
| --- | --- |
| PS (Mathematics, Engineering, Computer Science, Chemistry, Meteorology, Cybernetics, Architecture, Physics) | 49 (49) |
| LS (Food Science, Agriculture, Biology, Psychology) | 33 (21) |
| SS (Business, Economics) | 17 (17) |
| AH (English, Linguistics, Archaeology, Publishing, History) | 15 (15) |
| Total | 114 (102) |

require students to perform calculations using the MatLab software or statistical programs (as in the Archaeology assignment in Figure 3.7). Exercises may expect calculations using techniques such as spectophotometry in Food Sciences, or they may ask for terms to be defined, or graphs to be interpreted. Exercises can thus provide good evidence of student progress, as in the example in Figure 3.6 which asks for a short explanation.

This is one of a series of answers to six questions, and is less than 150 words in length, with no introduction, no elaboration and no conclusion; no motivation or justification; simply a direct, informative, concise reply to the question asked.

## Repeated headings in Exercises

Exercises are easily recognisable from their macrostructure, which in 80 per cent of Exercises is indicated by the headings used (Gardner

---

(i) Why is a mixture of 80% $O_2$: 20% $CO_2$ frequently used to package fresh beef? Why would such a system not be useful for white fish? (5 marks)

The high oxygen level, relative to air serves to increase the depth of the oxymyoglobin layer at the meat surface. ... 80% $O_2$ extends the colour shelf life of the beef because it delays the oxidation of oxymyoglobin to the brown pigment metmyoglobin, which gives the meat an unattractive brown colour. The high $CO_2$ level improves the microbial stability of the meat, because it provides unfavourable conditions for microbial growth. ...

Figure 3.6   An Exercise question and answer in Food Science

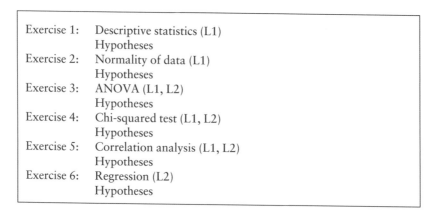

Figure 3.7    Archaeology Exercise headings in student text

and Holmes, 2009). They tend to have a series of headings such as Question 1, Question 2 and Question 3, which Gardner and Holmes (2010) have called 'interpersonal' headings because they are labelled as responses to questions set by the lecturer. They may also have headings which highlight the topic of the section, or headings which suggest how the section is organised, as in the extract from an Archaeology student text shown in Figure 3.7.

Thus the 'Exercise 1-n' part of the headings responds interpersonally to the lecturer's questions and tells us this is an Exercise, while the second parts, such as 'Descriptive statistics, Normality of data, etc.', provide ideational content about the topic of each exercise, and the addition of 'Hypotheses' indicates the organisation of the reply.

## Use of formulae and diagrams

Many Exercises focus on demonstrating knowledge and understanding using technical language and equations (Figure 3.8) or calculations (Figure 3.9).

In Figure 3.8, Question 2 relates specifically to Question 1, as is often but not necessarily the case.

Where the questions in an Exercise lead students through a series of steps, the final question tends to involve pulling together information from earlier questions and explaining the overall significance of the findings. Figure 3.9 makes this cumulative relationship explicit in its references to Questions 4, 5 and 6. This highlights the important role of Exercises in shaping how learners build understanding and demonstrate knowledge.

## Question 1

The system equations, given that the initial conditions are zero, are
$x_1 = k_{12}x_2 - k_{01}x_1$ and $x_1 = -k_{12}x_2 + b_2u_2(t)$ with $x_1(0) = 0$ and $x_2(0) = 0$
and observation $y = c_1x_1$.

## Question 2

These system equations may be written in matrix form as follows:

$$\begin{pmatrix} x_1 \\ x_2 \end{pmatrix} = \begin{pmatrix} -k_{01} & k_{12} \\ 0 & -k_{12} \end{pmatrix}\begin{pmatrix} x_1 \\ x_2 \end{pmatrix} + \begin{pmatrix} 0 \\ b_2 \end{pmatrix}u_2(t) \text{ and } Y = \begin{pmatrix} c_1 & 0 \end{pmatrix}\begin{pmatrix} x_1 \\ x_2 \end{pmatrix}$$

Note that $u_2(t) = D_2\delta(t)$, i.e. an impulsive input, therefore:

$$\begin{pmatrix} x_1 \\ x_2 \end{pmatrix} = \begin{pmatrix} -k_{01} & k_{12} \\ 0 & -k_{12} \end{pmatrix}\begin{pmatrix} x_1 \\ x_2 \end{pmatrix} + \begin{pmatrix} 0 \\ b_2 \end{pmatrix}D_2\delta(t) \text{ and } Y = \begin{pmatrix} c_1 & 0 \end{pmatrix}\begin{pmatrix} x_1 \\ x_2 \end{pmatrix}$$

Figure 3.8    Equations in an Exercise text

The relationship between equations and words is quite differ-ent from that between figures and words, as we see in Figure 3.9. Equations and other formulae are included in the grammar of the sentences. The writing demand is therefore not to explain diagrams in words, but to make sense using these highly specialised and highly technical semiotic entities. As we heard from the Economics lecturer in Section 3.2, Extract 2.8 (page 63), formulae can be the backbone of the answer to the question. In contrast, when diagrams are included, they tend to duplicate the written information. The written text may fully explain the information presented in the diagram making the 'reading' of both diagram and writing com-plementary (or redundant), or the writing may be secondary to the diagram and function simply to label or highlight features of the diagram. In such cases the diagram conveys a more essential part of the message of the text. This is not to say that diagrams or writing can be omitted, as both are expected in many student Exercises and Explanations.

### Exercises as portfolios of unrelated parts

In addition to answers to a set of cumulatively related questions, Exercises can also form a portfolio of work. For example, there may be different Exercises given from seminars each week. In Figure 3.10,

# Question 7

The two sum of exponential curves obtained in questions 4 and 5 are as follows:

- $y = \dfrac{1.520 \times 10^{-8} c_1 k_{12}}{k_{12} - k_{01}} \left( e^{-k_{01}t} - e^{-k_{12}t} \right) = 1.337 \times 10^{-8} \left( e^{-5.00 \times 10^{-6}t} - e^{-1.80 \times 10^{-3}t} \right)$

Obtained by substituting values of $k_{01} = 5.00 \times 10^{-6}$ and $k_{01} = 1.80 \times 10^{-3}$ (as given on the question paper) and $c_1 = 0.877$ (as calculated in question 6) into equation from question 4:

- $y = \dfrac{1.520 \times 10^{-8} c_1 k_{12}}{k_{12} - k_{01}} \left( e^{-k_{01}t} - e^{-k_{12}t} \right)$

  $y(t) = 1.3347 \times 10^{-8} e^{-6.7598 \times 10^{-6}t} - 1.3347 \times 10^{-8} e^{-8.6085 \times 10^{-3}t}$.

These equations were plotted in MatLab using the following code:

```
t = 0:1000:75000;
y1 = 1.3368e-008*(exp(-5.00e-006*t)-exp(-1.80e-003*t));
y2 = 1.3347e-008*exp(-6.7598e-006*t)-1.3347e-008*
    exp(-8.6085e-003*t);
data = [y1; y2];
plot (t, data)
plot (t, abs(y1-y2))
```

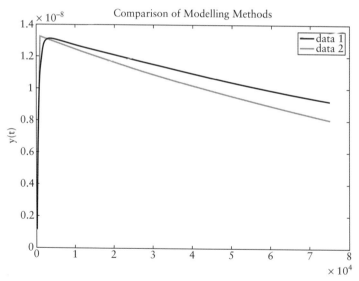

Figure 1    Comparison of Modelling Methods

data1 is the plot of the model generated theoretically in question 4; data2 is the plot of the model generated using the Nelder-Meade simplex algorithm in question 5. Both models provide a reasonable match to most of the data, however the difference between the two methods can be seen below:

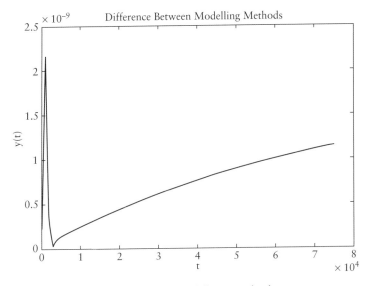

Figure 2    Difference Between Modelling Methods

The magnitude of the difference spikes initially very early on, however it rapidly drops and then increases more gradually over time. This suggests that the models diverge over time; assuming the trend continues, this means that eventually one model is likely to provide a far better fit to the data than the other. In this case, it appears that, while data1 gives a smoother fit, data2 takes account of the detailed experimental data and therefore initially fits the data very well. However, as data2 takes account only of the provided experimental values whereas data1 uses the average values over time, it is likely that data1 would provide a much better fit after a significant period of time.

Figure 3.9    The cumulative nature of the final question in an Exercise text

the work submitted for Seminar 2 involves demonstrating understanding of how 'synetics' can assist in the design process. This shows how a table is used to present a succinct response to the short task or Exercise.

---

## Seminar 2 – Extracting mechanical work from compressed gas

The best way to go about creating initial designs of solutions to a problem is to look at 'synetics'. This strips the problem down into different analogies that we can work with. For extracting work from a compressed noncombustible gas, we can split synetics into the following categories and create words that work with these analogies:

| ANALYTICAL LOGIC | ORGANISATIONAL LOGIC |
|---|---|
| Pressure, momentum, rotation, displacement, explosion, motion, pump, jack | External pressure |
| **INTERPERSONAL LOGIC** | **FANTASY** |
| Breaking wind, blow, suck, squashed, crushed, leak, breathing, inflates, spray, tube, nozzle, efficiency | Smell, rockets, hurricane, weather, space travel, heat exchange |

With these keywords in mind, I can now take one of them to create an initial sketch for an idea and use other words from the list also to develop the idea.

---

Figure 3.10   Demonstrating understanding of a technical concept

This highlights another advantage of the multimodal nature of Explanations and Exercises – they are often amenable to quick marking.

To sum up, Exercises occur across disciplines and levels and are widely used for demonstrating mathematical-type calculations, not only in the hard physical and mathematical sciences but also across applied and social sciences. They are recognisable by their headings which are typically numbered 'Question 1, 2, 3', and by the responses to these questions which may be short (50–150 words), and which often require calculations or demonstrations of proficiency in the use of a technique or the interpretation of data. Thus Exercises serve an important function of monitoring progress, similar to formative assessment. They require students to demonstrate knowledge and understanding of discrete pieces of information or discrete skills, and the expectation is that these pieces will be used later in more elaborate assignments.

## 3.5  Demonstrating knowledge and understanding across genre families

As demonstrating knowledge and understanding is such a central function in university assessment, it is evident across genre families. In this section we explore the similarities among Explanations, Exercises and other genres. Our decisions along the borders of genre families are guided by our focus on academic writing and our interpretation of educational purpose based on interviews and other disciplinary evidence as described in Chapter 2.

### From Exercises to sets of Explanations

Just as there are Exercises that include Explanation in answer to individual questions, there are also compound assignments that consist of a set or portfolio of Explanations which in some respects resemble a large Exercise. In theory there could be a continuum between an Exercise which required a series of Explanations and a compound assignment which consisted of a series of Explanation genres. In practice, however, Exercises tend to contain shorter, numbered parts and to mix Explanations with other types of question such as calculations. These differences in length reflect their different purposes and mean that the language in a short answer exercise is also more constrained than in a full-length Explanation genre.

### Demonstrating understanding in Empathy Writing

Assignments which demonstrate knowledge and understanding for a non-academic audience in a non-academic setting belong to the Empathy Writing family. For example, in an Engineering assignment students are required to prepare a poster for a transport museum explaining to the general museum-going public how a particular engine works. As with Explanations, one of the aims of such Empathy Writing genres is to demonstrate knowledge and understanding, however not all empathy writing includes this focus on explanation, so Empathy Writing remains a distinct, though fairly small, genre family.

Assignments which we have classified as Explanations, but which are close to Empathy Writing in that their content is not typically associated with assessed academic writing, include an Explanation of the role of a nature conservation officer. This assignment begins, 'A nature conservation officer is responsible for protecting, managing and enhancing natural habitats', and continues to explain in general the responsibilities of such a position.

## *Demonstrating knowledge in Essays*

As we shall see in Chapter 4, the principal function of Essays is to demonstrate the ability to develop and sustain an argument, supported by reasoning and evidence. Explaining the evidence used in argumentation typically involves demonstrating knowledge and understanding. From this perspective, argumentation as a cognitive process in higher education builds on Explanation.

> On the one hand, argumentative assignments provide students with an opportunity to develop and eventually display for evaluation, their knowledge and understanding of a given subject area, its canonical works and its key debates. At the same time, however, the defining characteristic of the argumentative essay is precisely that it requires students *to argue*; this is to make "their own" claims, to make a contribution to the current debates by adding their voices to the ongoing academic conversation, and in so doing to claim membership of the discourse communities into which they are being apprenticed.
>
> (Groom, 2000: 66)

This relationship is made explicit in the QAA criteria which expect students to demonstrate 'conceptual understanding that enables the student to devise and sustain arguments ...' (QAA, 2008: 18). This means that explanation would extend into persuasion in Essays. Given this relationship, it is not surprising that there are student assignments which lie close to the boundaries of Explanation and Essay genres.

It does not necessarily follow however that students will progress from Explanations to argumentation, as most Life and Physical Sciences Explanations lead to experimental research rather than essay-like argument. The final section of this chapter looks in greater detail at the lexico-grammar of Explanations and Exercises.

## 3.6  The language of Explanations and Exercises

An examination of the five Biber dimensions (see Section 1.6) for Exercises and Explanations (see Section 2.3) shows that these genre families are positioned fairly centrally and close together along most dimensions, which suggests their language displays many features typical of academic writing in general. The exception is along Dimension 1 (involved versus informational) where Explanations (at −15) are more informational than Exercises (at −12). This suggests they may have longer words, as well as longer sentences and paragraphs than Exercises.

To uncover more of the specific lexico-grammar associated with demonstrating knowledge and understanding, we search first for key-words and clusters in Explanation genres, then follow this with an exploration of the use of EXPLAIN and UNDERSTAND across the corpus as a whole.

## Clusters and keywords in Explanations

A keyword search[3] of the language of Explanation genres compared it to the language of the BAWE corpus as a whole. The lexis of Explanations was not found to differ markedly from the lexis of the whole corpus. Two words which frequently form a collocational framework for nominal groups, THE and OF, are the most positively key (18.895 and 10.109 respectively), indicating that Explanations are written in a dense, nominalised 'literate' style. ALTHOUGH, HOWEVER, THAN, DIFFERENT and THEREFORE, indicating a concern with comparison, contrast and causality, are all positively key at lower levels. Similarly and predictably from the data in Table 3.1 FIGURE is significantly more frequent in Explanations than in the BAWE corpus as a whole.

The list in Table 3.4 shows four-word clusters (or 4-grams) occurring at least fifteen times in at least ten different assignments in Explanations. The clusters indicate a concern with structure (*in the form of, is made up of, the surface of the*), with causality (*is due to the, as a result of, this is due to, an important role in, this means that*

Table 3.4   Frequent clusters in Explanation genres

| as well as the | 34 | as a result of | 19 |
|---|---|---|---|
| in the form of | 32 | in the case of | 19 |
| the end of the | 28 | the surface of the | 18 |
| can be seen in | 25 | a wide range of | 17 |
| in the absence of | 24 | on the other hand | 17 |
| one of the most | 23 | that there is a | 17 |
| the development of the | 23 | this is due to | 17 |
| is believed to be | 22 | an important role in | 16 |
| is due to the | 22 | on the surface of | 16 |
| is made up of | 22 | the rest of the | 16 |
| at the end of | 20 | to be able to | 16 |
| at the same time | 20 | is considered to be | 15 |
| in the development of | 20 | this means that the | 15 |
| is thought to be | 20 | | |

*the*) and with the representation of received knowledge (*is believed to be, is thought to be, is considered to be*).

Clusters such as *is due to the* and *as a result of* point to the extent of nominalisation (Halliday, 1998; Martin, 1993) in the language of Explanations, as indicated in these examples from Biology, Food Science, Computer Science, Meteorology, Anthropology, Physics, Engineering and Business respectively:

> is the process by which ATP is formed. As a result of the transfer of electrons from NADH or
> Diabetes Study Group, 1991). As a result of persistently raised blood glucose worsening
> Protection Act must show that, as a result of the defect in the product, it was reasonably
> warmed up more rapidly, presumably as a result of an increase in greenhouse gas emissions
> via a process of parallel evolution as a result of exposure to similar environmental and
> Graph showing mesogen tilt angle as a result of the voltage applied
> Drag occurs as a result of the interruption of a flow by a body.
> consequential (not pure) economic loss as a result of a negligent misstatement was

This is typical of the lexically dense language where processes are packaged as nouns such as *transfer* or *worsening* in what can be quite complicated nominal groups, such as *persistently raised blood glucose worsening*. This might be unpacked in two clauses: *the amount of glucose in the blood rose persistently* and *this condition worsened*.

### The lemmas EXPLAIN *and* UNDERSTAND *in the corpus*

We have argued that demonstrating knowledge and understanding is fundamental to university student writing, and that explanation is in many respects the foundation upon which other genres are built. It therefore perhaps makes sense that when we look at lemmas, such as EXPLAIN and UNDERSTAND, we find they are both widespread across genre families, as can be seen from Table 3.5. Tables 3.5 and 3.6 are presented according to the relative frequency of EXPLAIN, which closely parallels that of UNDERSTAND. The main differences are that Research Reports and Methodology Recounts are more likely to involve EXPLAIN, where Narrative Recounts are more likely to involve UNDERSTAND. Otherwise, they have a similar distribution across genre families, levels of study and disciplinary groupings, occurring most frequently in Narrative Recounts, Research Reports and Essays, in Arts and Humanities and Social Sciences in Levels 3 and 4 of study (Table 3.6).

What is paradoxical, and rather surprising perhaps, is that EXPLAIN and UNDERSTAND are used relatively infrequently not only in Explanations, but also in the Life Sciences, and in Level 2, which

Table 3.5   Lemmas EXPLAIN and UNDERSTAND across genre families

| | EXPLAIN | | UNDERSTAND | |
|---|---|---|---|---|
| Genre family | Frequency | Relative % | Frequency | Relative % |
| Research Report | 112 | 183.7 | 58 | 100.8 |
| Essay | 1481 | 122.6 | 1420 | 124.5 |
| Narrative Recount | 71 | 116.5 | 127 | 220.7 |
| Critique | 337 | 109.1 | 278 | 95.4 |
| Literature Survey | 33 | 103.2 | 31 | 102.7 |
| Case Study | 142 | 75.6 | 174 | 98.1 |
| Methodology Recount | 219 | 67.9 | 114 | 37.4 |
| Problem Question | 25 | 67.6 | 18 | 51.6 |
| Proposal | 45 | 63.4 | 62 | 92.6 |
| Exercise | 64 | 62.8 | 50 | 52 |
| Design Specification | 53 | 59.6 | 50 | 59.6 |
| Explanation | 92 | 49.8 | 96 | 55 |
| Empathy Writing | 10 | 35.7 | 6 | 22.7 |
| Compounds | 62 | -- | 92 | --- |
| Total | 2746 | | 2484 | |

Table 3.6   EXPLAIN and UNDERSTAND across disciplinary groups and levels

| | EXPLAIN | | | UNDERSTAND | |
|---|---|---|---|---|---|
| Discipline | Frequency | Relative % | Discipline | Frequency | Relative % |
| SS | 992 | 128 | AH | 872 | 133 |
| AH | 789 | 113 | SS | 830 | 115 |
| PS | 457 | 77 | LS | 534 | 84 |
| LS | 508 | 75 | PS | 340 | 61 |
| Total | 2746 | | | 2576 | |
| Level | Frequency | Relative % | Level | Frequency | Relative % |
| 3 | 730 | 124 | 4 | 654 | 119 |
| 4 | 627 | 107 | 3 | 583 | 106 |
| 2 | 707 | 93 | 2 | 705 | 99 |
| 1 | 670 | 84 | 1 | 629 | 84 |
| unknown | 12 | | | 5 | |
| Total | 2746 | | | 2576 | |

is exactly where Explanations are most frequent (Figure 2.7). Thus Explanations do not need framing moves such as *I shall first explain…*; they simply explain, as in the horse colic example (Figure 3.5). The most frequent uses of the lemmas involve non-human subjects in expressions such as *this explains why / how* and implicit human subjects in *is not fully understood*.

In order to make these numbers more concrete, we conclude this chapter with concordance lines from Explanations in the BAWE corpus organised according to moves in the discourse. This helps us appreciate the language of explaining how, why and that, and finishes with a reminder that Explanations in student writing may be more or less successful and more or less complete.

(1) *Explain* is used as a reporting verb in direct and indirect citations with authors as subjects. This use is not specific to Explanation genres, and since Arts and Humanities and Social Science writing generally cites more widely, we would expect this move to occur more frequently in those disciplinary groups.

Campbell and Reece (2005) **explain how** antimicrobial proteins attack microbes
suggested by Dudley et al in 2002 to **explain** the phenotype **that** results from AER removal
In their 1999 review, Stock et al. **explain that** the number of c subunits in the ring
as a three-cylinder engine." Hence they **explain that** two sites are not enough and that

Secondly, EXPLAIN can be used as a framing device with the writer as subject, but this type of framing is not widespread in Explanations.

, I will briefly outline each scale and **explain how** it relates to the relationship between
now I will attempt to **explain why** RSA has proved so successful at
tells us about the family. I also hope to **explain what** genetic assessment and counselling

A more important use of EXPLAIN in Explanations is where abstract concepts such as theories, concepts, distributions, mechanisms and (2) factors explain. Of course there are people involved in these theories, but scientific language tends to avoid the use of *I* (see Section 4.3), and in Explanation writing in particular there is little expectation of personal involvement or individualised argument.

and some theories that might **explain** aspects of these. Averil appears to be
of contrast. Quick incidental learning **explains how** children are able fast map words in
this he created three models that could **explain** the possible fates of the universe. To

Interestingly in explaining *why*, we find mostly examples with modality (*would, can, may*) or negative polarity (*doesn't, failed*). This points to the difficulty of stating reasons baldly and without the hedging found in much scientific writing. In addition to the face-threatening aspects of stating individualised claims directly, Basturkmen points out that in some areas (language teaching in her 2009 study), it is usual for writers to consider several alternative explanations for findings. From this perspective, not explaining can be baldly stated (*this doesn't explain how or why...*), but explaining why *may* require a little more hedging:

function without the other, which would **explain**   **why** neither mitochondria nor chloroplasts
  (adjectives and adverbs). This can be **explained** by the fact **that** these various parts of
    more complicated". This may **explain**   **why** people view the 'H' variety as more
      This interpretation doesn't **explain**   **how** the wavefunction collapses, or why
    higher than the usual sea level. This **explains**   **why** the Japanese fishermen failed to notice

If we turn to UNDERSTANDING in Explanations, we see more assertive language where specific features are signalled as 'important' or 'essential'.

sheep meat year round, it *is* essential to **understand** the production system(s) in place on the
  on energy transfer. It *is* important to **understand** some basic transfers of heat energy to
    its contagiousness, it *is* important to **understand** the pathogenesis of SARS and its affect

But it is worth remembering that they may also be partial:

    The germ line lineage is fully **understood** unlike the mechanism which differentiates
establishment of the a-p axis is not fully **understood** , however, the cues seem to reside in
  the formation of rain are not yet fully **understood** , however, there are two important processes
      up for debate and a lot is still to be **understood** , as many other diseases express the same
and cancer formation is beginning to be **understood** biologists can start to produce more

This reminds us that while Explanation genres do serve a basic function of developing knowledge and understanding in students, the quest for more knowledge and deeper understanding is at the heart of the academic and scientific enterprise, and students are expected to recognise the need for further research.

## 3.7 Conclusion

In this chapter we see that demonstrating knowledge and understanding are fundamental concerns of all student writing genres, but they shape the central purposes of genres in the Explanation and Exercise genre families. Explanations aim to demonstrate and develop student understanding of an object of study and its significance, while Exercises provide practice in key skills and an opportunity for students to briefly explain technical terms or concepts. Both Explanations and Exercises provide a foundation for students to build on in subsequent assignments. This is evidenced by the relative frequency of Explanations at Levels 1 and 2.

Explanations differ from Exercises in being longer, using longer paragraphs, sentences and words, and thus generally being more elaborate in their demonstration of understanding. Exercises are organised into a series of answers to questions which are usually related in content, but not connected into one piece of cohesive, continuous prose. While both Explanations and Exercises use more figures than average, Exercises use many more figures, formulae and lists than Explanations. As Exercises consist of a series of short answers or calculations, the language of each short answer is considerably shorter and more constrained than that of an Explanation genre.

The challenges for writing Explanations and Exercises lie in the expectation that students will have understood the received knowledge – if they merely write their own opinion on the topic this will not normally receive a pass grade. They also have to be able to present this knowledge in their own words, to write in ways that incorporate figures and diagrams and to write with an appropriate degree of sophistication for an educated audience.

The cluster analysis of the language of Explanations suggests that students will need to be able to represent received knowledge in their explanations of structures and causality. This is achieved through attribution to others (*Wang et al. explain that...*) and more often through nominalisations (*Drag occurs as a result of the flow by a body*) and lexically dense language (*persistently raised blood glucose worsening*). The language is generally clear, concise, technical and with fewer of the evaluative features of Critiques or the persuasive features of argumentative Essays that we shall see in Chapter 4.

## Notes

1. Students in England typically follow three Advanced (A) level courses in the sixth form, or last two years of secondary school. They are therefore relatively specialised when compared with the International Baccalaureate or qualifications from most other secondary school systems.
2. These statistics were calculated for the 185 Explanations and 102 Exercises in non-compound assignments (i.e., those assignments realised by one genre only, see Section 2.1). Results are rounded to whole numbers.
3. Keywords were identified using WordSmith Tools Version 5 (see Section 1.6).

# References

Basturkmen, H. (2009). Commenting on results in published research articles and masters dissertations in Language Teaching. *Journal of English for Academic Purposes*, 8, 241–51.

Bloor, M. (1999). Variation in the methods sections of research articles across disciplines: The case of fast and slow text. In P. Thompson (Ed.), *Issues in EAP writing research and instruction*. CALS: The University of Reading, 84–106.

Christie, F., & Derewianka, B. (2008). *School discourse*. London: Continuum.

Drury, H. (2001). Short answers in first-year undergraduate science writing. What kind of genres are they? In M. Hewings (Ed.), *Academic writing in context, papers in honour of Tony Dudley-Evans*. Birmingham: University of Birmingham Press, 104–21.

Gardner, S., & Holmes, J. (2009). *Can I use headings in my essay?* Section headings, macrostructures and genre families in the BAWE corpus of student writing. In M. Charles, S. Hunston & D. Pecorari (Eds.), *Academic writing: At the interface of corpus and discourse*. London: Continuum, 251–71.

Gardner, S., & Holmes, J. (2010). From section headings to assignment macrostructure in undergraduate student writing. In E. Swain (Ed.), *Thresholds and potentialities of Systemic Functional Linguistics*. Trieste: Edizioni Universitarie Trieste, 254–76.

Groom, N. (2000). A workable balance: self and sources in argumentative writing. In S. Mitchell & R. Andrews (Eds.), *Learning to argue in higher education*. Portsmouth, NH: Boynton/Cook, 65–73.

Hale, G., Taylor, C., Bridgeman, B., Carson, J., Kroll, B., & Kantor, R. (1996). *A study of writing tasks assigned in academic degree programs*. Research Report 54. Princeton, NJ: ETS.

Halliday, M.A.K. (1998). Things and relations: Regrammaticising experience as technical knowledge. In J. Martin & R. Veel (Eds.), *Reading science: Critical and functional perspectives on discourses of science*. London: Routledge, 236–65.

Martin, J.R. (1985/1989). *Factual writing: Exploring and challenging social reality*. Oxford: Oxford University Press.

Martin, J.R. (1993). Life as a noun: Arresting the universe in Science and Humanities. In M.A.K. Halliday & J.R. Martin, *Writing science: Literacy and discursive power*. London: The Falmer Press, 221–67.

Neuman, R., Parry, S., & Becher, T. (2002). Teaching and learning in their disciplinary contexts: A conceptual analysis. *Studies in Higher Education*, 27, 405–13.

QAA (2001) Quality Assurance Agency Framework for Higher Education Qualifications in England, Wales and Northern Ireland – January 2001 (www.qaa.ac.uk/academicinfrastructure/FHEQ/EWNI/default.asp accessed 03/06/2008).

QAA (2008) Quality Assurance Agency Framework for Higher Education Qualifications in England, Wales and Northern Ireland – Draft for consultation April 2008 (www.qaa.ac.uk/academicinfrastructure/FHEQ/EWNI08/default.asp accessed 03/06/2008).

Veel, R. (1997). Learning how to mean – scientifically speaking: Apprenticeship into scientific discourse in the secondary school. In F. Christie & J. R. Martin (Eds.), *Genre and institutions: Social processes in the workplace and school.* London: Continuum, 161–95.

# 4  Developing powers of informed and independent reasoning

> [A]ssumptions of rationality ... underpin the processes of higher education. .... Graduates ... are expected to be able to 'think' creatively and imaginatively about their discipline but also ...to be able to apply that creativity to different contexts. Learning to argue, then, could be seen to be a central purpose and activity of attendance at the university.
>
> (Andrews, 2000: 5)

In Chapter 3 we examined the importance of developing disciplinary knowledge, and how arguments at university build on such under-standings (Section 3.5). We start this chapter with an exploration of expectations of evaluation and argumentation from different per-spectives. In Section 4.2 we introduce the six genres in the Critique genre family and the six genres in the Essay genre family. We then focus on shared and contrasting genre features found in introduc-tions, headings and hyperNews. These give us a sense of the organi-sation and stages of Critiques and Essays. In Section 4.3 we explore disciplinary variation through moves involving the use of first person *I* and IF–THEN reasoning. In the final section (4.4), we review the basic statistics and multidimensional analysis of Critiques and Essays, then explore keywords in the two genre families, and conclude with a focus on disciplinary variation in the language of Essays, the most populated genre family in the BAWE corpus.

## 4.1  Critical evaluation and argumentation

Independent reasoning is developed through critical evaluation and the devising of sustained arguments, which we suggest are semioti-cally rather distinct processes. They involve the construal of knowl-edge and understanding in support of a critical appraisal or of a position on an issue. Such links between understanding, argumen-tation and evaluation are echoed in the Quality Assurance Agency (QAA) frameworks for England, Wales and Northern Ireland:

89

Bachelor's degrees with honours are awarded to students who have demonstrated

- conceptual understanding that enables the student **to devise and sustain arguments,** ... and **comment upon particular aspects** of current research, or equivalent advanced scholarship, in the discipline

  ...

Typically [BA Hons] holders will be able to: ... **critically evaluate** arguments, assumptions, abstract concepts and data ...

(QAA, 2001/2008: 18–19, emphasis added by authors)

*in extricable (adj) (formal)*
*too closely linked to be*
*separated*

As we explained in Section 3.5, there is an assumption that conceptual understanding (such as that displayed in Explanation genres) is inextricably linked to 'devising and sustaining arguments' as well as 'evaluating current research, concepts and data'. This is what typically distinguishes assessed student writing for credit from pre-university writing for academic purposes. It is the work of the student writer to become expert at being able to 'comment on' – which we interpret here as to critically evaluate – current theory and research as well as to construct arguments and develop a coherent position or thesis throughout an assignment. This evaluation and argumentation requires individual creativity and initiative, which by graduate level has become an aspiration of originality, though as we shall see such originality is bounded by disciplinary practices and understandings.

*To get beyond a 2.1, [to get a first class degree] individuality is the key. 'This is what I want to say, and that's how I will say it.' If we curb subjectivity, how would we deserve the marks?*

(Level 2 Philosophy student)

This creativity and initiative is explained in Creme and Lea's advice to students on how to develop argumentation around the idea or thesis that 'famine was caused by factors other than lack of food':

The important point to remember is that, unlike the central idea, an argument is not a tangible thing that you can identify somewhere else and import into your assignment. The argument is developed through your writing, and you as the writer make the decision about what weight to give to the different topics and themes that you will be drawing on to build your argument and to express your central idea...

(Creme and Lea, 1997: 96)

Thus in contrast to Explanation genres, one important dimension of argumentation is the involvement of a degree of personal commitment to, or at least original development of, a sustained argument;

in this way students increasingly participate in the debates of their disciplines. In critical evaluation and argumentation, therefore, students are expected to develop independence of thought, the power of reason and the capacity to build a convincing case based on knowledge and understanding, all qualities expected of the university graduate.

## The three-part cognitive structure of arguments

Traditionally students in England are expected to acquire an understanding of what counts as evaluation and argumentation through reading and discussion (e.g., Andrews, 2010: 197); lecturers will declare themselves able to recognise a good argument when they see one, but may have difficulty explaining to struggling students how to improve. So can argumentation be taught? One approach that persists is the study of logical argumentation, where students develop an explicit understanding of deductive and inductive reasoning, and related fallacies or errors in reasoning, such as straw man, false dilemma or circular reasoning[1]. While this may provide a useful foundation in certain modules in Law or Philosophy, in other disciplines argumentation may rest on the acceptance of widely held theories (e.g., in the Sciences) or on conventional, discipline-based strategies of persuasion (e.g., in the Humanities).

In Mitchell's five-year study of learning to argue in higher education, case studies conducted across disciplines and genres suggested that while academics were in agreement that argument is highly valued, researchers found it difficult to pin down a general understanding, or to see where the development of argumentation would fit explicitly in the curriculum. 'From the disciplines' point of view argument is about writing; from the writing specialists' it's about content' (Mitchell, 2000: 149). In order to develop 'a common basic understanding about argument among mainstream disciplinary staff' the project team adapted Toulmin's (1958) influential theory that argument consists of three basic parts: grounds, claim and warrant, where the claim (or argument) is based on certain grounds (or evidence) and supported by a warrant (or generally held theory). In other words, SINCE x (grounds), THEN y (claim), BECAUSE z (warrant), where the grounds provides support for the claim, and the warrant justifies the argument from grounds to claim (Riddle, 2000: 57). Thus at the heart of academic argumentation claims have to be supported by evidence and related to theories of the disciplines. This means that students need to develop a discipline-based understanding of

*arguments*

3 part

2 part

1 part

what counts as evidence, and which warrants can be used to build an argument.

Interestingly, the three-part argument is not necessarily fully realised in writing. Riddle found that the two-part argument (SINCE–THEN) is 'very much the norm in student writing' since 'students assume their assessors will know the theories [warrants] underpinning relevant academic positions' (Riddle, 2000: 59). He also suggests that a one-part THEN argument structure that presents a commonly held position without evidence or warrant may effectively evoke the straw man logical fallacy, and yet still be a useful strategy for student writers to create a rhetorical space within which to insert their own arguments (Riddle, 2000). This one-part argument was found in the introduction and literature review stages of assignments, rather than in the argument steps themselves.

The three-part argument structure, whether made explicit or not, can apply to individual steps in an argument across a few sentences as well as to the larger macroargument as it accumulates across longer stretches of text (Mitchell, 2000: 151). From what we know of differences in writing across disciplinary groups, where scientific disciplines are characterised by shared theories, Social Sciences by contested theories, and Humanities by greater appeal to individual appraisal (Neuman, Parry and Becher, 2002), we might expect to see three-part arguments more regularly in the Social Sciences and disciplines concerned with explicit argumentation such as Philosophy and Law, while two-part arguments may be more usual in the Sciences. Alternatively, with the foundation of *demonstrating* knowledge and understanding, it may be that student writing in Sciences leans more towards the three-part argument structure. Such disciplinary differences are explored further in Section 4.3.

## Developing arguments: Participant perspectives

Argument in this two or three-part sense has been seen in Explanations (Chapter 3) where students learn to replicate conventional arguments, and it is relevant in subsequent chapters. The distinctive aspect of argumentation for this chapter is the ability to build a sustained argument, and the expectation that, unlike in Explanations, different students drawing on the same evidence and literature base are expected to develop arguments that are individualised, and yet also constrained by the evidence, reasoning, literature and conventions of the field. Before we examine how arguments are shaped, individualised and sustained, we shall review student and staff perspectives.

In our research we found that some students were very aware of how they develop arguments *as a student*. This history student describes accumulating data (here the views of different historians) and making claims within the constraints of her position as a novice, the generally held wisdom of the field, and the approach of the individual professor for whom the assignment was written:

*I try to use different opinions. I say someone's opinion, then counter it with someone else's. I weave my own perception in but I'd never say "this is what I think" directly. I use some arguing and counter but I always go back to my introduction stance.*

*… I put across my argument always and (a) you have to consider the popular argument at the time. You don't want to go against the flow completely as you don't have the skill to do that. But (b) I consider what the professor will think.*

(Level 2 History student)

While some students had faith in the objective application of assessment criteria, more experienced students realise the importance of considering who might be assessing their work. Compare the following perspectives:

*No it doesn't vary from marker to marker; they have to follow a very specific set of marking guidelines, you see.*

(Level 1 Philosophy student)

*I cater my essays to the first marker.*

(Level 3 English Literature student)

*It's easier to know what they want, and write to them, when you've read their papers and interests.*

(Level 4 Chemistry student)

Underpinning the advice from the Level 3 and 4 students is the importance of recognising which areas are open to discussion, debate and argumentation, what counts as support and where justification is, or is not, expected.

Notions of building a sustained, individual argument were also emphasised by lecturers: an essay would be not just a summary of understanding but 'an integrated piece of work' where students have the '*freedom* to shape their understanding into a particular form' (Biology lecturer). 'That's the good thing about the openness of essays – it lets you pursue the subjects you're really interested in' (Level 2 Psychology student). Yet students should not simply 'pile up example after example', they have to integrate them into an argument

(Business lecturer), and through critical reading and writing the ability to structure an argument improves over the years of study (Agriculture lecturer).

Thus argumentation involves the ability to report and critically evaluate the work of others in ways that support a macroargument or thesis.

*An essay is 'well structured, it's well organised, it engages with the texts, the main texts, it has an argument, a critical argument, critique is crucial'.*

(Sociology lecturer)

One of the most frustrating feedback comments for students, however, is that work is 'not critical enough'. As argumentation is so desirable, it is perhaps not surprising that a common assignment task involves the critique of other people's work. This develops general critiquing strategies such as evaluating 'how far the author does what the author says he / she's going to do' (Agriculture lecturer), as well as discipline-specific understanding of the nature of conventional arguments (grounds, claims and warrants) and how these are constructed in different disciplines. Although arguments in student writing may differ in writer positioning from expert arguments in published sources, one of the main rationales for assigning review and evaluation tasks is to immerse students in the critical thinking and writing practices of a discipline.

## 4.2  Evaluation and argument genres: Critiques and Essays

While evaluation and argumentation can be found across all genre families, we focus in this chapter on the Critique and Essay genre families. Critiques and Essays build on developing understanding or explanation to include a critical evaluation or the development of an argument. Specifically, the central purpose of Critiques is to demonstrate and develop understanding of the object of study and the ability to evaluate and / or assess its significance; the central purpose of Essays is to demonstrate / develop the ability to reason independently and construct a coherent argument.

Critiques and Essays were found across all departments (see Table 2.10) and comprise the majority of Level 1 and 2 Arts and Social Sciences assignments (see Figure 2.6). As Table 4.1 indicates, Essays are considerably more numerous than Critiques, particularly in Arts and Humanities and the Social Sciences, while Critiques slightly outnumber Essays in the Physical Sciences.

Most Essays involve discussion of an issue or developing arguments to support a thesis (exposition). In departments such as History,

Table 4.1   Distribution by disciplinary group

|  | Arts and Humanities | Life Sciences | Physical Sciences | Social Sciences | Total |
|---|---|---|---|---|---|
| Critique | 48 | 84 | 76 | 114 | 322 |
| Essay | 601 | 127 | 65 | 444 | 1237 |
| Total | 649 | 211 | 141 | 558 | 1559 |

English and Philosophy, undergraduate students may be assessed predominantly by Essays with an occasional Critique. Critiques span the assignment range from reviews of books, articles and websites, to evaluations of products and procedures, to appraisal of theories and concepts, to assessments of research approaches and methods.

## The Critique genre family

The stages of Critique genres tend to correspond to the main two purposes: to describe or summarise, and then to review, evaluate or critique. Tutors are well aware of the importance of these two stages, grounded in the concerns of the discipline:

*A book review should say what is in the book and how well its contents hang together. It should relate this to the real world and academic disputes and then reach an evaluative conclusion.*

(Psychology lecturer)

These stages may be realised recursively, rather than as just two discrete stages; students may summarise one aspect of the entity being evaluated, evaluate it, then move on to another feature, or another perspective. Indeed, a study of article critiques in Sociology (Mathison, 1996) found that students who interwove topics and comments tended to produce better Critiques.

Across disciplines we see Critique genres given different names, but the functions are similar whether they be reviews of semiotic entities such as books, films or plays, or analyses of social entities such as businesses or organisations, or evaluations of physical entities such as tools, machines and equipment. In the Humanities the book review is a typical Critique genre, whereas in the Social Sciences typical Critiques are evaluations of research articles, theories and techniques, and in the Physical and Life Sciences typical Critiques are evaluations of equipment and systems (Gardner, 2009).

The following assignment titles indicate the range of Critique genres:

**1 Academic paper review**
Article Critique (Archaeology, Computer Science)
Journal Refereeing (Chemistry)
An analysis of Dirichlet's paper of 1829 (Mathematics)

**2 Theory / approach / method / tool evaluation**
Evaluate Esping-Anderson's classification of welfare states (Politics)
Outline and evaluate the doctrine of transcendental idealism (Philosophy)
A Critical Analysis of Extension Approaches by CATI in Brazil (Agriculture)
Evaluation of COSMOS use in designing Microneedle Arrays (Engineering)
Critical analysis of a diagnostic tool used within clinical practice (Health)

**3 Interpretation of results**
Palaeopathology lab reports (Archaeology)
Dietary survey questionnaire results interpretation (Food Science)

**4 Business / system / proposal evaluation**
Marketing Assignment: Lastminute.com (Business)
Compare and contrast the various systems of local government revenue collection (Planning)
CFS Insurance Restructuring Proposal Review (Computer Science)

**5 Case / curriculum / product evaluation**
Analysis of Pepper vs Hart (Law)
Evaluation of FCE Reading paper (Linguistics)
Bread-Maker Critical Review (Engineering)

**6 Review of a book / film / play / website**
Write a review of Blackmore (1999) *The Meme Machine* (Psychology)
Book review: M. I. Finley *The World of Odysseus*. (Classics)
Analysis of Jules Verne's *Journey to the Centre of the Earth* (pp. 24–27) (Meteorology)
Book Review essay – *Geisha*, by Liza Dalby (Anthropology)

The first three categories of Critiques (1–3) are designed to prepare students for developing their own research projects, while the next two categories (4–5) are more closely linked to Case Study genres. They differ from Case Studies in their focus on evaluation per se, rather than on developing recommendations for future action. In all Critiques it is important to demonstrate awareness of disciplinary values. As Mathison found, 'Critiquing required students to go beyond the personal to make their positions relevant to the content about which they had been learning' (1996: 344). Thus a book review (6) in Meteorology or Anthropology is expected to draw on knowledge and understanding of the discipline concerned in its evaluation.

Of course, titles alone are not sufficient to predict genres, and indeed some of the above were described as Case Studies or Essays *title* by the participants. In our classification, however, titles of Critiques tend to follow a pattern exemplified by 'Critique article x', 'Evaluate product y' or 'Review entity z'. They thus have one main object of evaluation (or one participant in transitivity terms as described by Halliday, 2004). In contrast, titles of Essays, as we shall see in the next section, tend to relate two participants in a pattern of 'How does x relate to y'.

## The Essay genre family

The structure of essays is three parts: ①Introduction: introducing topic, defining key terms, explaining structure, a logical sequence of arguments, a conclusion.

(Health Studies lecturer)

Many Essays in our corpus correspond to this three-part structure of introduction followed by a sequence of arguments and a conclusion, and as a result the type of Essay can be determined from the introduction where students state the issue or thesis and the slant they plan to take in developing their individual arguments, and from the conclusion, where students review what they have done and how they reached their final position or thesis. There does seem to be a shared cultural awareness of these three stages from school essays, and the expectation of multiple steps building an argument:

*Intro – general info about the essay topic, clearly lay out what the essay will cover. Body – usually split into 4/5 different paragraphs covering the main areas of the question. Each paragraph perhaps a different argument or view point. Conclusion – a summary of all the points made in the essay and perhaps my own opinion on the topic at hand.*

(Level 1 Psychology student)

This is reminiscent of the 'five-part essay structure' (Warschauer, 2002) with an introduction, three distinct arguments, and a conclusion, taught in some university preparatory courses.

The main Essay genres are introduced here through their titles (which typically correspond to a question posed by the tutor), introductions and conclusions. The next section highlights the focus move which reveals one strategy for developing an individualised argument, and we then move on to illustrate the importance of the hyperTheme and hyperNew (Martin, 1992), or the initial and final moves in constructing each step of the argument in the body of the Essay.

Essay introductions and conclusions differ in the amount of background or contextual information they include, whether key terms are defined, whether an issue or a thesis is introduced, and in the extent to which the structure of the Essay is made explicit. For instance a comparison of ten Sociology and ten English Essays from the BAWE corpus found that

> ... the sociology essays had a more developed move structure in their introductions and generally contained more metadiscoursal mapping of the essay at the outset and through the essay. ... English essays appeared to assume greater reader responsibility, and used less metadiscourse to explain the shape of the essay and less overt direction of the reader towards the arguments or points being made by the writer.
>
> (Bruce, 2010: 162)

While Essays share the general aim of developing an argument, they also differ in how the argument unfolds. Table 4.2 shows the stages of the Essay genres in the order in which they are subsequently discussed. Identification of these genres draws heavily on the work of Coffin (2004, 2006) and Martin (1992).

The introduction stage of an exposition is distinctive in its statement of the thesis. The series of arguments in an exposition provide evidence to support the thesis, and the conclusion summarises by restating the thesis in the context of the supporting arguments. Thus the three stages of an exposition are thesis, evidence and restate thesis. Consecutive stages of a genre are conventionally joined by the carat sign '^' (see p. 99):

Table 4.2   Six Essay genres with stages

| Genres | exposition | discussion | challenge | factorial | consequential | commentary |
|---|---|---|---|---|---|---|
| **genre stages** | thesis, evidence, restate thesis | issue, alternative arguments, final position | challenge, evidence, thesis | state, contributory factors, summary thesis | state, ensuing factors, summary thesis | text(s) introduction, comments, summary |

EXPOSITION ESSAY
(Thesis^Evidence^Restate thesis)

An expository Essay sets out the claim or thesis it argues for in the introduction, as in this example:

*Does Functionalism Offer a more Plausible Theory of Intentional States than it does of Sensations and other States of Consciousness?*
*Yes, functionalism offers a more plausible theory of intentional states than it does of sensations and other states of consciousness.* [Thesis] *I intend to argue my thesis by initially providing an account of the functionalist theory. I will then outline the criticisms that have been raised in response to functionalism concerning the theories' ability to account for sensations and phenomenal consciousness and evaluate whether they are successful in disproving functionalism. Finally I will illustrate how I arrived at my thesis* [preview].

(Philosophy)

Each stage of a genre can be characterised in terms of moves. Thus in addition to stating the thesis, this introduction in Philosophy, like introductions in Sociology (Bruce, 2010), contains a preview move which allows the reader to anticipate the structure of the essay and how the argument will develop. In this example and throughout this chapter, key moves are indicated in square brackets after the move they describe.

Here are further examples of question titles that invite an Exposition:

*Did Neolithic People really hate fish?*

(Archaeology)

*Grazing – good or bad for Britain's landscape?*

(Biology)

*Can the economic history of Britain in the late 18th and early 19th centuries be described as an industrial revolution?*

(Economics)

*Do male and female poets use the dramatic monologue form to different effect?*

(English)

*In what ways has feminism challenged conventional thinking about politics?*

(Politics)

An alternative approach to answering the Philosophy question would be to treat it as a more open discussion and respond using a discussion genre, which presents an issue, then considers, perhaps more objectively, the arguments that can be developed to support different positions on the issue. A discussion genre thus involves more weighing up or evaluation of evidence to ascertain how strong it is in relation to a position on an issue, rather than presenting evidence in ways that argue for a stated position from the outset.

DISCUSSION ESSAY
(Issue^Alternative Arguments^Final Position)

Discussions involve entertaining alternative positions on an issue before reaching a position or thesis that reconciles them in line with the evidence discussed. These alternative positions might be pros and cons, or alternative claims, as in this example:

*This essay will look at continuity and departure through these two periods thematically, and **attempt to form a conclusion as to whether the 'Age of Braudel' conserved or contradicted original Annales historiography.***

(History)

Discussion questions may be worded as comparisons:

*How does Kant's Theory of Freedom differ from Hume's?*

(Philosophy)

Here students are expected to realise that both Kant and Hume are addressing issues of determinism and free will, to consider their two perspectives, and to come to their own position on the issue. The following is taken from an introduction to the Essay prompted by this question:

*We all feel as though we are truly interacting in the world. Every day we face a variety of options from which we can freely choose. We buy into the idea that we have a complex process of reasoning and deliberating that can override our natural instinct or change the effect that external influences have upon us. [context] The popular belief is that our action is free, but how can we account for the spontaneity of human freedom in a world follows natural laws of causality? ... The idea behind determinism is ... The prima facie implication ... if determinism exists, free will is not possible. [issue] This essay will discuss two fundamental philosophers who both argue that despite the reality of determinism we can have freedom. Hume ... the Compatibilist position. Kant ... complex metaphysical theory. [preview]*

(Philosophy)

The assignment rubric or question may indicate a preference for Exposition or Discussion, though this is not always followed. Gardner (2008a) found an even balance of Discussion and Exposition in History Essays from the BAWE corpus, and to some extent it can be a matter of personal preference. For example, the History student cited in Section 4.1 claimed she would 'always go back to [her] introduction stance,' while this Law student in contrast tends towards discussions:

*I just argue for and against the title to provide as balanced a view as possible and to cover the subject matter in enough depth.*

(Level 1 Law student)

Essays that challenge established positions and theories are unusual for the reasons suggested earlier. Students are very aware of the views of their tutors when they write, and may also feel they are not 'expert enough' to develop challenges to received wisdom. Although challenges to existing theories are essential for the development of science and knowledge in general, they are relatively rare in student essays. In a comparative study of assignments in History and Engineering, Gardner (2008a) found four Challenges in fifty-nine History Essays.

CHALLENGE ESSAY
(Challenge^Evidence^Thesis)
The question, 'Are you convinced by the view of the Levellers on franchise reform as expressed by McPherson in his *Political Origins of Possessive Individualism?*', could have been answered as an Exposition, but as this introduction shows, the response in this instance was a Challenge. The purpose of the Essay is stated in the introduction:

*An attempt will be made, therefore, not only* **to dispute much of Macpherson's argument, but to propose a different hypothesis of how the** *Levellers interpreted franchise reform, based around notions of compromise and heterogenity.* [Challenge]

Following a series of arguments, the challenge is then reinforced or stated in the conclusion or thesis stage where the alternative theory is restated:

*The aim of this essay has been not only to highlight many of the problems of MacPherson's thesis, but also* **to propose an alternative interpretation** *of Leveller franchise reform proposals. … Not only does this highlight the main problem with MacPherson's thesis, but illustrates one of two factors that this* **essay has stressed as vital** *in understanding …. **What also needs to be stressed is …*** *They proposed an incredibly radical and 'modern' set of ideals that …*

A second example of a challenge is provided here, from the introduction to a Philosophy Essay. We can see how a challenge involves disagreeing with a given theory and proposing an alternative.

*Why does Anscombe think we ought to abandon the concepts of moral obligation and duty?*
*I do not agree with Anscombe's idea that we should abandon moral obligation and duty. Anscombe does point out some problems with two major*

*and conflicting ethical views of consequentialism and deontology, but her alternatives are unsound and there is contradiction in her argument. I shall argue that though her principal thesis and ideas seem sound, when Anscombe tries to explain differences between what is intrinsically 'just' and what can be 'just' depending on circumstances, she misses the point. I also think that her link between the 'just' and the 'right' is flawed (or as she says that we as yet do not have a link). I shall argue that moral obligation will occur with any theory and that by waiting for her "adequate philosophy of psychology", she is postponing what is inevitable. I do not think that moral obligation is a "survival", but something that is a necessity for any ethical theory.*

The question does not seem to call for a challenge genre; it seems to call for an Explanation genre, though in the context of Philosophy, an Evaluation or an Essay genre would be expected. From this perspective we can see how a challenge builds on explanation (of the theory to be challenged), evaluation (of the evidence and arguments that support the theory), and exposition (of an alternative thesis).

FACTORIAL ESSAY (State^Contributory Factors^Summary Thesis) and
CONSEQUENTIAL ESSAY (State^Ensuing Factors^Summary Thesis)

Factorial and Consequential Essays are similar in that both are organised around factors that either lead to and / or result from a state of affairs. They are found across disciplines, as can be seen in these assignments:

*Outline the social and political factors that led to the development of feminism in Japan*

(Sociology)

*What factors caused a gladiator to be viewed as a hero in ancient Rome?*

(Classics)

*Factors Affecting Degree of L2 Foreign Accent*

(Linguistics)

*Was the Collapse of the Bretton Woods System Inevitable? And what were its long-run Consequences?*

(Economics)

*Why are some children more popular than others and what consequences does this have for psychological development?*

(Psychology)

The aim is firstly to construe factors, but also to come to a conclusion which summarises the factors identified and makes sense of them in a thesis. Sometimes the thesis is previewed in the introduction, as in this Level 3 History Essay:

*This essay will account for and analyse these separate reasons and come to the conclusion that the vast difference in belief systems was undoubtedly the primary cause for the failure of the mission.*

(History)

In her study of secondary school texts Coffin describes similar texts with factors and consequences as 'Explanations', whose purpose is 'the explanation of past events through the examination of causes and consequence' (2006: 67). Although our classification has been greatly influenced by Coffin's, we have distinguished Explanations, where an individual interpretation is not expected, from Essays, where independent reasoning and the ability to construct a persuasive argument are valued. At university, Factorials go beyond explanation to offering an individualised argument, as in this conclusion, taken from the same Essay as the previous example:

*Therefore, in conclusion, there were a huge variety of factors which explain the failure of the Church Missionary Society's Wellington Valley Mission. Some of these were specific to this particular mission, namely a lack of funding …. However, it is important to recognise that the most important reasons for its failure were those which affected almost every mission in Australia: …. However, one factor stands above all others in explaining the failure of the mission: the vast differences in the highly incompatible belief systems of the Aborigines and the missionaries meant that the Wellington Valley Mission was doomed to failure from the start.*

(History)

As we can see in this Factorial Essay example, the factors are grouped, evaluated and marshalled as arguments in support of a summary thesis. This thesis will not necessarily be the same as that of another student responding to the same question, and is not expected to be found in a textbook. The individualised nature of the argument differentiates Factorial Essays and Consequential Essays from Explanations, though among Essays, these two genres are most similar to Explanations. In contrast, Commentary Essays are most similar to Critiques.

COMMENTARY ESSAYS
(Text(s) Introduction^Comments^Summary)
Unlike most Essays which focus on an issue, Commentaries focus on one or more texts. The introduction therefore introduces the texts, and the series of comments or claims tend to follow the sequence of

the texts. These Essays conclude with a summary of comments, as in this commentary on Plutarch, *Life of Pericles*:

*This extract of Plutarch's Life of Pericles contains a number of features that appear in the life as a whole. It shows Pericles' virtues of calmness, self-control and lack of superstition, whilst also defending him from the charge of being a demagogue. It shows common methods that appear both in ancient biographical writing, such as comparison between the protagonist and other figures in order to elevate the former, and in Plutarch's own writing, such as using criticisms and taunts, or ignoring some aspects of his subject's career in order to show virtue.*

(Classics)

Where this extract focuses on a single text, others involve comparison:

*Contrastive Analysis of Two Short Texts; Linda France and John Agard*

(English)

*Source Criticism – The Lyon Tablet and the Claudius Speech on the Gallic senators Annals 11.23–5*

(Classics)

*Compare the two poems: 'upon his leaving his mistress' by John Wilmot, and 'I am very bothered when I think' by Simon Armitage.*

(English)

*Comparative Discourse Analysis of a Political Speech and an Academic Journal Article*

(Linguistics)

Although the questions do not suggest that theses are required, the summary in commentary essays can be similar to a thesis. The greater attention paid to the analysis (*the analysis will show*) rather than the argument (*I will argue that*) is typical of commentaries.

This completes our overview of six genres in the Essay family, the largest and most widespread of all genre families in the BAWE corpus. Before we turn to disciplinary variation, we highlight features worthy of attention in identifying Critique and Essay genres.

## *Headings and assignment macrostructure*

Critiques and Essays require student writers to develop claims and shape them into a coherent evaluation or argument. The resulting structure can be signalled through headings in the macrostructure of the assignment discussed here, through preview and review moves in introductions as examined next, and through hyperThemes and hyperNews which are found at the beginning and end of paragraphs respectively, as will be illustrated at the end of this section.

Two-thirds of Critiques have headings which, together with the title, contribute to the assignment macrostructure (Gardner and Holmes, 2009). This suggests how the argument develops. In our first example, the organisation of the assignment follows the stages of the research article being evaluated initially, then comments on style and concludes with a discussion of its contribution to the debate.

ARCHAEOLOGY CRITIQUE: *Article review*

---

*ARTICLE CRITIQUE*

Svenning, J.-C. (2002). A review of natural vegetation openness in north-western Europe, *Biological Conservation* 104: 133–148
Background
Research methodology
Results and interpretation
Style and presentation
Impact on the debate
References

---

The headings of the Engineering Critique also indicate the organisation of the assignment. This review of a bread-maker includes the results of tests conducted on the machine, and is organised according to the qualities being evaluated.

ENGINEERING CRITIQUE: *Product Evaluation*

---

*- Bread-Maker Critical Review -*

Introduction
Specification: market & performance
Performance & reliability
Value
Ergonomics
Aesthetics
Safety
Noise & vibration
Type of motor
Use of materials
Clever features
Conclusion
References

---

In contrast to Critiques, only one-third of Essays use headings. In the 363 Essays where they do occur, they also usefully indicate the macrostructure. The typical format of Essay macrostructures involves (Introduction)^Ideational Heading 1-n^(Conclusion) (Bibliography/References), where an ideational heading points to the field or subject rather than the function or genre (Gardner and Holmes, 2010) as in the following examples.

LAW ESSAY: *Discussion*

> *"The development of international criminal law in the latter half of the twentieth century demonstrates that governments can no longer behave with impunity". – Discuss –*
>
> 1. Introduction
> 2. Historical development of international criminal law; the emergence of individual accountability
> 3. The International Criminal Tribunals for the former Yugoslavia (ICTY) and Rwanda (ICTR)
> 4. The International Criminal Court
> 5. Conclusion – an end to impunity?

POLITICS ESSAY: *Exposition*

> What, if anything, has membership of a political community in common with membership of a family? Can this tell us anything about our obligations?
>
> 0. Introduction
> 1. The analogy
> 2. Simmons' Objection
> 3. Hardimon's Role Obligations
> 4. Reflective Acceptability
> 5. Conclusion
> Bibliography

ENGLISH ESSAY: *Commentary*

> Close Textual Analysis of the Ball Scene (0:32:48) in Dragonwyck
>
> Brief synopsis
> Narrative structure
> Visual style
> Mise-en-scène
> Conclusion

The macrostructures of assignments indicated in these extracts provide the skeletons for the different Essay and Critique genres. Further details and examples can be found in Gardner and Holmes (2009).

## Angle on topic and narrowing scope in introductions

The argument developed in the body of an assignment often begins in the first few words of the first sentence, where a particular focus or slant on the topic is introduced. The angle on the topic or field can be given in the subject of the first sentence of the introduction, or Initial Sentence Subject (ISS), as in these assignment beginnings from Gardner (2008b).

---

1 **The Dutch Republic** was something of an anomaly in seventeenth century Europe.

2 Until the last few decades, **the accepted view amongst historians of Mexico** was that the seventeenth century was indeed one of crisis.

3 **Memory** is a topic of study with which psychologists have grappled experimentally for over a century.

4 **The work of Jean Piaget (1896–1980)** has informed the developmental psychology paradigm for many years.

5 **The pursuit of an acceptable definition of schizophrenia** has tested researchers and clinicians since the classifications proposed by K.

6 **Escherichia coli O157:H7** is a particularly high-profile bacterium in modern times, not least as a result of its ability to inflict …

7 **Examination of the subcellular distribution of molecules** is an important tool in cell biology.

---

A comparison of the initial sentence subjects in (1), (3) and (6) clearly indicates the different objects of enquiry across disciplines – *the Dutch Republic, Memory, Escherichia coli O157:H7*. Moreover a comparison of (1) and (2), or of (3) and (4), reveals differences between the phenomena under scrutiny and the related academic literature. An Essay about the Dutch Republic engages directly with the phenomena, whereas an essay about 'the accepted view amongst historians' enters the academic debate and intends to focus on what Halliday (2004) refers to as metaphenomena. A comparison of (3), (4) and (5) suggests an intermediate step of focusing on the work of a particular academic, *the work of Jean Piaget*, while a comparison of (6) and (7) suggests that the sciences are less concerned with the 'who' and more likely to write about either a particular entity (*E coli*) or a broader tool or field of enquiry (*Examination of the subcellular distribution of molecules*). In this way the Initial Sentence

Subject (ISS) indicates the intended angle the writer will take on the topic. This highlights where the topic at lower levels of study is more concrete and specific (Gardner, 2008b; Hewings, 2004) in comparison with more theoretical and abstract topics at higher levels. Once the angle on the field has been established, this is often followed by a narrowing of focus.

Critiques and Essays differ from Explanations specifically in that there is an expectation that students will develop different arguments and that each Essay will be individual. The selection of a particular angle on the topic or a specific definition of a key term allows students to declare from the outset how they narrow the scope of their paper and to develop an argument in more specific detail than if a wider scope had been chosen:

*There are several different theories about what truth actually is, however,* **truth in this essay is being taken as** *agreement with reality.*

(Philosophy Essay)

*In particular* **I would like to focus on** *Britain ...*

(Economics Essay)

*While I will incorporate other theories* **my focus will be on** *the ethical principle of respecting patient autonomy* **as I feel this is central to the dilemma described and integral to** *the nursing role.*

(Health Essay)

*However,* **the general focus of the essay will be on** *the early years of the Revolution* **because it could be argued that** *it lasted until 1815 with the fall of Napoleon and* **covering this whole period would be both unfeasible and lacking in depth for such a short essay.**

(History Essay)

*This debate* **is too large to be explored in this essay** *and an agent centred theory of justice* **will be assumed** *to be valid.*

(Philosophy Essay)

**I will focus mainly on** *the issues of attraction, mate selection methods and criteria and rape,* **because** *these are areas causing controversy amongst academics.*

(Psychology Essay)

*In order to answer this question I have chosen to evaluate Amnesty International's Stop Violence Against Women campaign. This campaign aims to tackle violence against women in the family and in conflict / post conflict situations across the globe. However,* **for reasons of time and space I will focus on violence against women in the family in the British context.**

(Sociology Critique)

As can be seen here, the focus can be developed through defining terms or narrowing the focus of attention. A range of reasons can be given, from personal preference, through the relatively weak 'lack of space' to stronger claims of academic centrality. Too broad a scope can make the Essay or Critique unwieldy, too narrow a scope can be perceived as exactly that, too narrow. Generally a clear, well-justified focus leads to a more comprehensive and in-depth analysis and a more effective evaluation or argument is developed. Once the focus has been established, the body of the assignment can be developed accordingly. This development may be reflected in headings, and is typically also reflected in hyperThemes and hyperNews.

## Cumulative evidence and claims: HyperThemes and hyperNews

The structure of assignments can be revealed by examining how writers abstract from, organise and shape evidence. This can often be read from the initial and final sentences of each paragraph, as this is where the hyperThemes and hyperNews are likely to be (Martin and Rose, 2003). In the following example, the hyperThemes themselves are not given in full, but we can see how they are connected by phrases such as *x too meant...*, *furthermore*, and *another reason why* which occur in many but not all first sentences of paragraphs:

*The traditions of the artisan, **too, meant that** they already ...*
***Furthermore**, the Revolution ...*
***Another reason why** artisans were more likely to ...*
*However despite the above reasons as evidence for 'radical artisan' discourse, it is **not** so simple to ...*
***There is also criticism** of ...*
***As well as seeing why** artisans ... it is important to look at why ...*

(History Essay)

If we read down the first sentence in each paragraph, we could extract hyperThemes (which are very similar to topic sentences) and see how they link the argument steps through markers such as *furthermore, another reason* and *as well as* into an argument structure. For Factorial Essays and Critiques this cumulative building of features signalled in the initial sentences of paragraphs may be the main organisational feature.

Each step may begin with a claim (hyperTheme), proceed to add and evaluate details, and conclude at the end of one or more paragraphs by summing up how this new evidence contributes to the developing argument, expressed as a hyperNew (Martin and Rose, 2003):

Table 4.3   From hyperThemes to hyperNews

| hyperTheme | Evidence | hyperNews |
|---|---|---|
| **A prime characteristic** of modern environmentalism **was** an endeavour to conserve exhaustible sources of energy by conducting searches for safe, renewable sources. | ...... | **This clearly represents how** modern environmentalism adapted qualities from the path set down by Romantic Movement as both encouraged the return of man to nature. |
| When Germany attacked Moscow in 1941, it appeared that ... | ...... | **This illustrates that** left to their own devices the Russian people could not defend the capital. |

Topics are introduced in the hyperTheme, and grounds (evidence) are in the middle of paragraphs, but it is important to notice the end of paragraphs, as this is where the hyperNew or claims tends to be most explicit.

HyperNews are made explicit through lexical bundles such as *This clearly shows that, It can be seen that, This illustrates that,* and *We can see that,* which are spread across Critiques and Essays in all four disciplinary groups. Here are some examples of '*this shows that*' from the BAWE corpus. As the left hand columns indicate, most of these extracts occur in the final sentence of a paragraph, and they occur in paragraphs throughout the assignments (e.g., s8.8 p4.10 means Sentence 8 of 8 in Paragraph 4 of 10). This hyperNew position at the end of paragraphs is where the claims are made that will build up to a concluding thesis for the assignment.

In this section we have described the Critique and Essay genre families by subclassifying each into six genres, by showing how students structure the assignments through headings, how they begin to individualise their arguments in the introductory focus moves which narrow the scope, and how they link steps in the overall argument or evaluation through explicit metadiscourse in the hyperThemes and through the use of hyperNews which build on evidence presented to make claims worded as *This (clearly) shows (that)* ... and other similar phrases. We now turn to disciplinary differences in Critiques and Essays.

Occurences of *This shows that*

| | | | |
|---|---|---|---|
| s8.8 | p4.10 | each piece had a specific place.' | *This* shows *that* in Alba's eyes, Esteban's place |
| s10.10 | p6.10 | which govern that society." | *This* shows *that* society ( or control of the |
| s15.27 | p3.6 | limitations and conditions. | *This* clearly shows *that* being an EU citizen |
| s2.6 | p6.9 | with arising ethical issues. | *This* clearly shows *that* there is a considerable |
| s13.13 | p6.45 | (Gordon et al, 1997). | *This* shows *that* internet is still used as a source |
| s3.4 | p8.41 | within the peer report. | *This* shows *that* out of this group Renold Plc |
| s10.10 | p4.13 | than the medical profession. | *This* shows *that* lay people may never be lay |
| s9.9 | p9.14 | was no static element present. | *This* shows *that* elements in the objects |
| s6.6 | p12.14 | thought this to be unlikely. | *This* shows *that* knowledge of what consists of |
| s5.5 | p13.30 | the insider does not trade". | *This* shows *that* investors' confidence should |
| s4.4 | p13.23 | cited in Barnard, 2003, p69). | *This* quote shows *that* Malinowski's theory |
| s4.5 | p7.7 | but also inter-cultural level. | *This* ethnography thus clearly **shows** *that* |
| s9.11 | p2.7 | " (l.7 ) and "people" (l.5). | *This* shows *that* everybody, even children, |

## 4.3 Disciplinary variation in Critiques and Essays

> [in Medicine] it's proof, proof, proof, a fixed journey on a
> regimented path... [but in Philosophy] the more unique, the
> higher the mark; they don't agree with set structures.
> (Philosophy, then Medicine student)

Many students in the British education system remain within one or
two related disciplines and so do not develop a contrastive sense of
disciplinary norms. For those who do, however, such as this student
who studied Philosophy as an undergraduate and then moved into
Medicine, the different expectations become clear.

We assume that disciplinary differences in the nature of evaluation and argument are reflected in the linguistic features of the
student texts. Preliminary evidence can be found in the use of section
headings in Critiques and Essays: while Essays account for only 65
(11 per cent) of all Physical Science texts, 58 per cent of these have
headings. In contrast, Essays account for 554 (82 per cent) of all Arts
and Humanities texts, of which only 14 per cent have headings. In discipline terms, more than 65 per cent of Essays in Physics, Agriculture,
Law, Planning and Business have headings while less than 15 per cent
of Essays in History, English, Psychology, Philosophy and Classics
have headings (Gardner and Holmes, 2009). This suggests that in the
Sciences, where students are used to writing assignments with headings, such as Reports and Case Studies, this may carry over into their
Critique and Essay writing.

While headings can show how students organise their writing, the
heart of the differences lies in the arguments they make: what counts
as evidence, the claims they can make, and the warrants they invoke,
if any. As the Philosophy turned Medicine student suggests, evidence
in the Sciences is more to do with proof, while argumentation in the
Humanities is more individualistic. In this section we will search for
disciplinary differences, first with the aim of uncovering variation in
individualisation, and then in reasoning across disciplines.

### *Disciplinary variation in use of first person I*

If argumentation in the Humanities and Social Sciences is more concerned with the expression of individualised arguments, we will be
able to find evidence of this in the lexico-grammar. As studies on
published research have shown (e.g., Hyland, 2002; Samraj, 2008),
an investigation of the lemma *I* should throw some light on such disciplinary differences. Moreover, the question of whether to avoid the
use of *I* in assignments is one that vexes many students, and on which

some staff have rather fixed views. It may be that in an effort to move away from expressing personal unsubstantiated views as arguments (*I think...*), and knowing that some scientific writing omits reference to the author, they have become uncertain whether it is appropriate to use *I* in introductions and conclusions to declare their essay plan or thesis. Whatever the reasons, the advice given to students tends to be contradictory. There is 'current confusion in teaching materials and style guides ... [and the materials seem] uncertain whether to encourage or prohibit [first person] use' (Hyland, 2004: 131).

Our data shows that the lemma *I* is used widely and, surprisingly perhaps, in the corpus as whole lemma *I* is a top keyword (see Appendix 1.4). It is approximately nine times more frequent in the BAWE corpus (925.1 ARF per million words) than in the British National Corpus of general English (108.8 ARF per million words), with roughly equal frequency in both Critiques and Essays (Table 4.4). Subsequent analysis therefore combines these genre families.

This search for the lemma *I* in assignments found *I* to be eight times more frequent than *me* – *me* occurs 105 times in Critiques, as in *this leads me to believe / question,* and 589 times in Essays, as in *it seems to me that.*

Studies of other types of academic writing have found disciplinary differences. Hyland's study of dissertations in Hong Kong ranked self-mention in six disciplines from Applied Linguistics at the high end through Business Studies, Computer Science, Public Administration and Electronic Engineering to Biology at the low end (Hyland, 2004: 144). In a similar pattern, we see four Arts and Humanities disciplines at the high end (22–35 words per 10,000 words); we see Social Sciences in the middle (6–13), with Engineering (6) and Biology (3) at the lower end. In fact *I* only occurs in 4 of the 31 Essay and Critique texts in Biology.

Why is *I* so much more frequent in Philosophy? *I* typically is followed by *have*, and when we compare examples in a concordance, we can see how important framing moves are in guiding the reader through the decisions made (*I have chosen his work for two reasons...*) and

Table 4.4   Use of first person in Critiques and Essays

|  | frequency of *I/me* | total number of words | frequency of *I/me* per 10,000 words |
|---|---|---|---|
| Critiques | 1023 | 853,956 | 12.0 |
| Essays | 5092 | 4,010,103 | 12.7 |
| Critiques and Essays[2] | 6115 | 4,864,059 | 12.6 |

Table 4.5    Lemma *I* across disciplines in Critiques and Essays

| discipline | frequency of *I/me* (N) | words (N) | *I/me* per 10,000 words |
|---|---|---|---|
| Philosophy | 1025 | 294,769 | 34.8 |
| English | 833 | 283,280 | 29.4 |
| Linguistics | 603 | 242,111 | 24.9 |
| Classics | 519 | 230,881 | 22.5 |
| Economics | 244 | 197,658 | 12.3 |
| Sociology | 424 | 348,298 | 12.2 |
| Law | 335 | 436,434 | 7.7 |
| Business | 158 | 232,132 | 6.8 |
| History | 221 | 358,079 | 6.2 |
| Engineering | 77 | 130,290 | 5.9 |
| Biological Sciences | 24 | 93,045 | 2.6 |

keeping track of the steps in the argument throughout the assignment: '*on the account that I have given, the problem then arises: how...*'. *I* is also used to make claims (*I have come to the conclusion that...*).

## *I* IN PHILOSOPHY

*I* in framing moves

interpretation of Husserl as a metaphysical idealist, I have chosen his work for two reasons. first

this makes the tripartite theory sound. I have also tried to address the point that

ground the subject. On the account that I have given, the problem then arises: how

Conclusion: In order to evaluate the theory I have considered several objections to the

any reason to abandon moral obligation. I have discussed Anscombe's use of different

*I* in claims

perhaps not be attributed to the same mind, I have argued that they can still be attributed

properties originally assigned to the mind, I have come to the conclusion that it does

*I* in evidence: generic *I*

I have a body and I can understand that I have a hand. this does not mean that my

that it is right to uphold my promises, I have a normative reason to uphold them.

qualities directly. On this account, when I have a perceptual experience of a square

if I see a tomato, R would require that I have a round and red idea. this account

*I* in evidence: *I* as an example

through the senses. But from time to time I have found that the senses deceive, and

Physically functional human adult male. Thus far I have gained the ability to walk, talk and

I have been born and for over 21 years I have gradually grown from being a small

This strong authorial presence guiding the reader through the argument in Philosophy is consistent with earlier studies of Masters dissertations (Samraj, 2008) and research articles (Chang and Swales, 1999; Hyland, 2002).

The concordances show that the evidence used to support claims in Philosophy can also be worded as personal experience, as in '*I have a body and can understand that I have a hand*'. *I* in Evidence is used as a rhetorical device both when it is used generically to mean 'anyone' and when it is personalised slightly to give an example, as in '*I have been born, and for over 21 years ...*'. As such it can be repeated many times in a sentence: '*I know I exist because I think I exist, as long as I'm thinking I'm certain that I exist*'. In both cases it is unlike the *I* in framing moves which refers uniquely to the writer's signalling of the discourse, or metadiscourse (Hyland, 2005). This need to keep track of a developing argument combined with the use of *I* in evidence explain the frequency of *I* in Philosophy and give us a good sense of the language of Philosophy, and what can count as evidence in Philosophy argument.

What about English? Many students of English believe that they should not use *I* in their writing, and yet it is relatively frequent. A closer study of the use of *I* in English is equally revealing. *I* is used in framing moves (*I have argued, I have chosen to*) in ways similar to Philosophy. It is also used to make claims (*I believe .., I know…*).

## *I* in English

| *I* in framing moves | |
|---|---|
| 2002) esp. pp.21–34 In conclusion, | I have argued that Heart of Darkness represents |
| The Complete Essays p353 | I have argued within this essay that the |
| selection of the texts studied. For this essay | I have chosen to examine the representation |
| language is created and represented. | I have chosen to examine how gender, discourse |
| response could have been given in many ways and | I have chosen to make a simple list. As for |
| In the hope of illustrating these points, | I have chosen to look at Part II of Coleridge |
| 108. In the Box Hill scene, which | I have chosen, Emma's imagination again leads |
| understanding to occur. The particular sections | I have chosen from each piece of literature |
| *I* in claims | |
| different occasions, helping advocate why | I believe it to be too limited in its division |
| Psychological and emotional complexity, | I believe it to be a pioneering example of |
| one solution to the problems presented. | I believe Murphy encapsulates Eliot's intention |
| poem that deliberately rejects coherency. | I believe Structuralism to be the most effective |
| nature repair[ing] her ravages." Ultimately, | I believe Tom's death is more significant |

of his meetings with O'Brien and Julia. I think this demonstrates even on a small

words appear to be spoken to suit them. I think this is the essence of what John

freedom, expression and perhaps hope. Yet, I think ultimately it is powerless because

*I* in quotations as evidence

envious Cannot be damn'd; Alas; why should I bee? (Sonnet IX, 1–4) John Donne, The

particularly female gendered activities, " I began with cooking." Freud proposed that

Brabantio he says, " My services, which I have done the signog, shall out-tongue

he is telling. 'This is the saddest story I have ever heard' (p.13) is how Dowell begins

died, saying 'It suddenly occurs to me that I have forgotten to say how Edward met his

see that thou art angry with me; I know I have given thee just cause of anger; and

love, we ave all the dregs you do to. Me? I know my ends, it knows me. I love my blads

that she thanked men for gifts 'somehow - I know not how' (32), but unintentionally

complaints. 'Tis yet to know – which, when I know that boasting is an honour, I shall

And grandmother who "were such good cooks I left everything to them", and "Jody, my

separate from it; when she has sex she says " I let them do anything to me and tried to

The writers could have chosen a similar degree of certainty using other features (e.g., *Murphy convincingly demonstrates; this seems to be the essence*). Instead, here, they choose *I believe* and *I think* as projecting clauses, as in *I believe Murphy demonstrates...* and *I think this is the essence...* In this way they emphasise the individual aspect of the claim, as expected in Essays. These claims have to be supported, however, and in English *I* is used frequently in quotations which are interpreted to develop arguments about the literary texts. This feature of Essays in English is also noted by Bruce who compares ten Essays in English with ten Essays in Sociology and finds that 'The English essays ... made greater use of direct quotation to convey the arguments of the essay with an average use of 37 evidentials[3] per essay compared with an average of 20 for the sociology essays.' (2010: 162)

This brief examination of lemma *I* in Philosophy and English has provided useful insights into the nature of evidence and argument in these disciplines, and illustrates the type of analysis that could be done for the 6,000 instances of *I* and its collocates across the disciplines. We would find that the Linguistics and Classics assignments do include a high proportion of framing and arguing moves, but also use *I* in examples such as '*I wanna be ...*' when analysing spoken interaction in Linguistics, or in extracts from ancient texts in Classics such as '*this mania has not left me, Though I am forced to suffer adverse gods*', from the Latin poet Propertius.

The analysis in this section has shown that the frequency of *I* varies little across Critiques and Essays. It occurs more in the Humanities than Sciences, which reflects not only the extent to which first person framing and claiming moves are used extensively, or hardly at all (e.g., in Biology), but also the fields of evidence drawn upon in those Humanities disciplines where *I* occurs frequently. Where *I* is used in *I think* or *I believe* to make claims, it may be redundant in one sense – *I believe Murphy encapsulates...* could have been written *Murphy encapsulates...* Its inclusion may underscore the writer's commitment to a developing personal thesis, or paradoxically may weaken that thesis where it is interpreted as similar in meaning to *Murphy probably encapsulates...* (see Halliday, 2004: 626–630).

Ultimately, some differences can be partially attributed simply to disciplinary culture. In disciplines where lab reports are frequent, Essays and Critiques are more likely to have headings, and less likely to use *I*, suggesting a possible trade-off between headings and framing moves with *I*. In disciplines assessed largely through Essays, headings tend not to be used. Here *I* is readily available and widely used with the disciplinary differences suggested in Table 4.4 being largely explained by differences in the nature and sources of evidence.

## Reasoning across disciplines

We have seen differences in the nature of evidence used in arguments across disciplines. We now turn to the 'if–then–because' logic that supports a grounds–claim–warrant type argument to explore whether there are differences in how evidence is used to make claims. Giltrow (2000) describes the difficulties of generalising about 'argumentation' across disciplines from the perspective of readers' reactions to student writing. She points out the disciplinary variation in, for example, the acceptability of 'making broad statements about human nature'. Students in History and Sociology were cautioned against this, while assessors of English Literature arguments had no similar objections. (Giltrow, 2000: 134). In her analysis of reasoning (CAUSE: reason) in Education assignments with a focus on the *why* of explanations, Woodward-Kron (2009) found that students constructed reasoning congruently (e.g., using *therefore* or *because*) more often than incongruently (e.g., using *reason* or *means*), and that such reasoning and explaining took on an increasingly significant role, the further students advanced in their studies. The salience of *therefore* in the BAWE corpus as a top keyword (Appendix 1.4) suggests reason is similarly expressed in student writing in general, as in these examples from Essays in Law, Sociology and Classics:

*Without consideration, a contract is declared legally void. It is **therefore** commonplace for the courts to have to deal with cases in which parties...*

(Law)

*There is much agreement among feminist researchers that many of society's rules are made by men wanting to retain power over women's behaviour ([references]) and when it comes to the justice system, women are **therefore** judged by men's ideas about how women should behave ([references]).*

(Sociology)

*Even if this was not the case, it seems to be what the elite feared ([references]). **Therefore** we can see how the cult of Bacchus could be viewed as a political threat to the Roman elites, since in their view it collected people who wished for an alternative religious system.*

(Classics)

These examples indicate the nature of claims being made in different disciplines and the grounds on which they are made. More direct access to the grounds–claim–warrant structure of argument in student writing can be seen by comparing the use of the congruent IF–THEN across disciplines:

### Reasoning in Philosophy: Logical deduction
- If humans live in a deterministic universe, *then* our actions may also be fixed by determinate causes.
- If Descartes' argument is guilty of circularity *then* it can be entirely dismissed because, being self-contained, it is impossible to prove one way or another.

### Reasoning in Law: Legal consequence
- Therefore the courts have made the presumption that if agreements are made in a social / domestic context *then* there will be no intention, and the reverse will be true in commercial contexts.
- If the problem is still not resolved *then* the Commission issues a reasoned opinion which lays down the grounds for dispute.

### Reasoning in English: Persuasive interpretation
- If Mrs Alving represents modernism, *then* Pastor Manders is the voice of Victorian values.
- If female is multiplicity *then* man is unity according to much feminist criticism.

### Reasoning in Archaeology: Hypothetical inferencing
- If this was why they were hunting them *then* you would expect to see occupation during summer and autumn.
- If this is the case *then* status is defined by a series of cultural practices which ...

Although IF–THEN constructions are used in each discipline, the nature of the argument from evidence to claim is, we suggest, different in each case. Though the warrant is not always stated, we can infer the basis for the claims. In Philosophy, where IF–THEN is frequent (215 instances, or 44 per cent, of the 487 in all undergraduate native speaker[4] Essays[5]), the argument rests on the force of logical deduction; in Law it rests on an understanding of legal consequences: the logic of inferring from one legal case to another with reference to real world legal cases. In English the basis seems to be more persuasive interpretation, and in Archaeology the argument is based on hypothetical inferencing to try and make sense of the past. Such insights are important because as Carter-Thomas and Rowley-Jolivet have shown,

The comparison ... of *if-* conditionals between the general theory and rather prescriptive rules found in learner manuals on the one hand, and specialised [medical] discourse practice on the other, has highlighted many important discrepancies between the two, both formally and functionally.

(Carter-Thomas and Rowley-Jolivet, 2008: 203)

For instance, fewer than six per cent of the *if*-conditionals in the research articles they analysed were of the three *if*-clause types taught in general English classes. In other words, not all argument is founded on an abstract, universal principle of causality; and the way IF–THEN constructions are taught in English classes is unlikely to capture the way they are used across disciplines.

We have begun to see how arguments in the body of Essays and Critiques are developed through different types of evidence or grounds, and different reasoning from grounds to claims using *therefore* and constructions such as IF–THEN in discipline-specific ways rather than as they are taught in general English lessons. Disciplinary differences based on individual search terms here are clear. In order to try and uncover differences in the discourse in general, we now examine basic statistics, then keywords in the genre families across disciplines.

## 4.4  The language of Critiques and Essays

In this final section we explore how the different functions of Critiques and Essays are reflected in their language. As a preliminary, we consider the basic statistics for Critiques, Essays and the BAWE corpus average. Table 4.6 shows that Critiques are more likely than Essays to have an abstract, lists, tables and figures, which reflects their more analytical nature. In contrast, Essays have more block quotes than average, and more than twice as many as Critiques, which supports

Table 4.6    Length of Critiques and Essays[6]

| | words | s-unit | p-unit | w/s | s/p | block quotes | figures | tables | formulae | lists etc. | abstracts |
|---|---|---|---|---|---|---|---|---|---|---|---|
| Critiques | 2155 | 88 | 25 | 25 | 4.3 | 0.5 | 1.6 | 0.5 | 3.2 | 0.4 | 0.1 |
| Essays | 2455 | 92 | 20 | 28 | 5.6 | 1.3 | 0.3 | 0.1 | 2.7 | 0.1 | 0.0 |
| average | 2357 | 98 | 30 | 25 | 4 | 1 | 1 | 1 | 4 | 3 | 0.1 |

the expectation that the arguments developed in Essays draw on long quotes from published literature, which may be objects of study or may provide direct evidence from sources to support arguments being developed.

Essays with a median length of 2,201 and average of 2,455 words tend to be longer than Critiques with a median of 1,961 and average 2,155 words. Essays also have longer sentences (average 28 words) and longer paragraphs (average 5.6 sentences), with most Essays having an average sentence length of between 25 and 40 words. Very long sentences tend to include quotations, as in these examples, where the first sentence has 52 words and the second 66:

*There existed, to some extent, interdependency between women and the state, though Yosano Akiko, a prominent feminist at the time, argued that 'it is slave morality for women to be dependent on men because of their procreational role [and therefore women] must refuse dependency on the state for the very same reason'.*

(Sociology Essay)

*In his concluding remarks to The Anarchical Society, Bull says that 'it has been contended that order in world politics conflicts with goals of justice – international, human and cosmopolitan – and that while there is a sense in which order is prior to justice, it does not follow from this that goals of order are to be given priority over goals of justice in any particular case'.*

(Politics Essay)

In terms of the language features identified in the multidimensional analysis, the language of Critiques and Essays is very similar, and represents the mid-point of student academic writing on the informational (first), persuasive (fourth) and impersonal (fifth) dimensions. Critiques and Essays are placed towards the elaborated end of the student writing continuum on the third dimension suggesting high use of nominalisations (such as *interdependency* and *remarks*) in both genre families, while the language of Essays is relatively more narrative than Critiques on the second dimension, reflecting the sizeable number of History, Classics and other Essays which report past events as evidence to support claims in argumentation.

These basic statistics and multidimensional analyses suggest Critiques use more figures than average, while Essays are longer than average, with longer sentences, longer paragraphs, more block quotes and more narrative language features. The language of both genre families is towards the elaborated end of student writing. We now turn to the qualitative nature of these wordings.

## Keywords in Critiques

Table 4.7 provides the verbs, nouns, adjectives, and adverbs with the highest keyness scores[7] for undergraduate Critiques written by native speakers[8] of English compared with the BAWE corpus as a whole.

Most of these keywords suggest a general vocabulary of critique and evaluation where precision (*accurate[ly], correct, exactly*) and extent (*fully, extra, sufficient*) are among the properties critiqued. These and others such as (*currently, unlikely, assumption*) if explored further would help us see how student writers express evaluation through 'both a statement of personal judgement and an appeal to shared norms and values' (Hunston, 1994: 191).

Keyword searches can be a useful starting point for a concordance collocation study across disciplines. We shall illustrate this here with a focus on the most key verb and adverb – *account* and *accurately* in Critiques–, and later for *assert* and *perhaps* in Essays, but each of the key items merits further investigation.

Table 4.7   Top keywords in undergraduate Critiques

| Verbs | Adverbs | Adjectives | Nouns |
| --- | --- | --- | --- |
| account | accurately | extra | critique |
| analyse | really | beneficial | collection |
| aid | fully | reliable | interview |
| collect | enough | fair | insight |
| answer | necessarily | accurate | sequence |
| combine | currently | correct | assumption |
| employ | etc | scientific | acid |
| predict | exactly | useful | animal |
| review | later | sufficient | application |
| complete | relatively | unlikely | bibliography |

*Account* in Critiques is used across disciplines, with positive and negative polarity. Thus one line of critical evaluation is to explore which features are *not* accounted for by the entity concerned, be it a theory, system, model, instrument, approach, outcome or other entity:

| | | | |
|---|---|---|---|
| Agriculture | The appendix. This, therefore, does *not* account | *for* this trend. The trend may be accounted |
| Biology | of DNA in the mitochondria can not be accounted | *for* in most autogenous theories. |
| Computer Sci. | The system is known well, it is hard to account | *for* every instance in which something |
| Economics | unhappiness 4 and this model does *not* account | *for* any psychological effects of unemployment |
| Engineering | with digital callipers. The error bounds account | *for* instrumental inaccuracies |
| Law | Legal advisor examined. This does *not* account | *for* the multitude of reasons an innocent |
| Linguistics | perception theory as a whole can *not* account | *for,* but I shall return to this point |
| Philosophy | what Jackson was suggesting was not accounted | *for* by physical facts. This new perspective |
| Physics | is accepted. Bohmian mechanics does *not* account | *for* phenomena such as the pair creation |
| Politics | decommodification binary is *not* sufficient in accounting | *for* the bewilderingly complex relationship |
| Psychology | further research it may be beneficial to account | *for* these individual factors |

The specific features reflect disciplinary differences, while the common evaluative strategy is to identify gaps in explanatory power. The concordance lines suggest, for example, that Economics is concerned with explaining the effects of unemployment; Engineering with instrumental (in)accuracies, Law with reasons and Psychology with individual factors. Not all evaluation is negative, of course, but pointing to omissions and shortcomings is one of the perceived aims of Critique genres.

In contrast to *perhaps* for Essays, in Critiques, the most key adverb *accurately* indicates certainty, particularly in the sciences, where typical collocates are *predict, represent* and *describe*:

*Therefore, coronary angiography* **can accurately predict** *IRA patency, leading to a prognosis for failed / successful reperfusion.*

(Health)

*The simple graphical interface allows the user to create kinematic vector diagrams that* **accurately represent the** *mechanism characteristics and display it in a simple and easy to comprehend graphical layout.*

(Engineering)

*The model* **fails to describe the** *spectrum of larger atoms* **accurately**, *merely being able to make weak* **predictions** *of* **certain** *emission spectrum of atoms only with a single outer shell electron (namely the Alkali metals).*

(Physics)

In the Social Sciences '*accurately*' is used more persuasively to indicate possibility:

*The coverage and scope of this pressure group's website* **can be labeled accurately** *as extensive enough for its agenda and whether you are a* *researcher, journalist, student, teacher or activist, there is **definitely** a piece of information **relevant** and **useful** to a certain extent.*

(Politics)

*However, **when it** is **accurately** calibrated it **can often** provide the archaeologist with an **efficient** way of dating sites over a wide area, unlike tree ring dating.*

(Archaeology)

While accuracy is a desirable quality, *really*, the second most key adverb in Critiques, is similar to *perhaps* in its use to hedge, negatively, as illustrated here with *only*:

*The **only** thing we can **really** say about general iteration is exactly what it says itself, that it is a repeated application of a simple procedure until a rather trivial condition is satisfied and is inaccurate just because it takes so long to arrive at a solution.*

(Meteorology)

*It is **really** applicable **only** to ensembles of particles; ...*

(Physics)

*Really* is seldom used as a booster, as it might be in conversation, but it does occur positively:

*The fact that mathematicians and physicist are forever finding new applications for Green's techniques is evidence of just **how** flexible and powerful they **really** are.*

(Mathematics)

*From these graphs it is very clear **how** close the model **really** is to the experimental data.*

(Engineering)

It is also used in rhetorical questions to engage the reader:

*But if we take a closer look, have **they really** proved this?*

(Philosophy)

The complexities of evaluation illustrated here for *really* are similar to other adverbs identified as keywords for Critiques: *fully, enough, necessarily, exactly* and *relatively*. Their polarity is established through prosodic relationships across clauses and sentences.

The full list of 64 key adjectives is given in Appendix 4.1, and it is tempting to sort them into categories of evaluation such as status (*likely, stable, potential*), value (*interesting, useful, beneficial*) and relevance (*essential, extra*) (Hunston, 1994) or of appraisal such as appreciation (*complex*), affect (*interesting*), judgement (*obvious, serious, easy*) (Martin and White, 2005), but this cannot really be done for words in isolation as the words acquire different evaluative meanings in context. For instance, they can be used to evaluate claims, and they can be used to evaluate entities. Moreover, each of these would be interpreted in different senses from a disciplinary perspective, as these examples of *fair* suggest:

*Evaluation of claims*

| | | |
|---|---|---|
| inelastic for the same reasons therefore it is | **fair** | to assume that the impact of the tax is (**Agriculture**) |
| described as courtesans, I think it is | **fair** | to say that they are courtesans of a much (**Anthropology**) |
| it in such a form. Additionally, it is | **fair** | to suspect, that Crumlin-Peredsen and Olsen (**Archaeology**) |
| would cause for the company. It is | **fair** | to say however that even if the system (**Computer Science**) |
| For most of these machines its | **fair** | then to say that for the price of the product (**Engineering**) |
| Emerson's sample, however so it would not be | **fair** | to say that his theory is irrelevant in (**Psychology**) |

*Evaluation of entities*

| | | |
|---|---|---|
| management should ensure that queues are | **fair** | (e.g. no pushing in, stealing waiting (**Business**) |
| they receive a wage that is considered | **fair** | and equal. The adherence to group norms (**Economics**) |
| Reporting Standards indicates that a true and | **fair** | view of the company is being given, (**Engineering**) |
| with the outcome of the case. It was only | **fair** | that the creditors did not lose out their (**Law**) |

The evaluation of an argument or claim as *fair* suggests it is reasonable or rational within the conventions of the discipline; the evaluation of an entity as *fair* tends to have more to do with morality or justice in the world of the entity being described.

It is helpful here also to look at frequency. Biber et al. (2002: 200) found that *good, best, right, important, simple* and *special* were frequent attributive adjectives in academic prose; Thetala (1997: 114) identifies *significant, important, interesting, remarkable* as frequent in research articles. In a similar study of the BAWE Critiques, Gardner (2009) found that particularly frequent collocates of *very* were *different* and *important* in Arts and Humanities; *important, similar, small, little* and *useful* in Life Sciences; *difficult, important, limited, little, good* and *different* in Social Sciences; and *useful, accurate, important* and *simple* in Physical Sciences. Interestingly Social Sciences is the only disciplinary group here with frequent negative evaluation (*difficult, limited*).

Moreover, *important, significant* and *useful* are frequent across all four disciplinary groups in the BAWE corpus. Their use with the following collocates in Critiques[9] suggests the nature of entities being explicitly evaluated:

- *important*: aspect, factor, element, consideration, implication
- *significant*: impact, reduction, difference, growth, effect
- *useful*: tool, information, model, source, site

*Important* is the most frequent, and widespread, occurring in over 200 Critiques across 28 disciplines. Its collocation with *aspect, factor, element* and others (see Appendix 4.2 for the full list) suggests a pervasive analytical perspective to evaluation. In contrast, significance is associated with impact and change in size, where usefulness is associated with tools and information. The terms *important* and *significant* are relatively more frequent in the Social Sciences, whereas *useful* is relatively more frequent in the Physical Sciences (see Figure 4.1 in Appendix 4.2).

Explicit evaluation involving these three adjectives is most evident in the Social Sciences, and least evident in Arts and Humanities, but of course this does not mean that Critiques in Arts and Humanities do not use evaluative language as there are many alternative ways of expressing evaluation. Indeed, much evaluation is cumulative and not construed through adjectives (e.g., see Hunston and Thompson, 2000; Martin, 2000) as in the examples of *not account for* and *assert that*.

Our analysis of keywords and frequent adjectives in Critiques has provided useful perspectives from which evaluation can proceed. It has highlighted the need for claims and entities evaluated to account for a range of factors, and the suggested perspectives from which evaluation stems within disciplinary groups and across the academy. In general, the language of Essays is less analytical and more persuasive.

## Keywords in Essays

In contrast to the keywords in Critiques, Table 4.8 shows the keywords in Essays clustering around specific fields of the Humanities and Social Sciences, verbs of argumentation (*assert, portray, criticise, deny*) and adverbs used for hedging and boosting arguments (*perhaps, certainly*).

*Assert* occurs across disciplines in Essays and, unlike *account* in Critiques, it is typically used with positive polarity, collocating strongly with *that*:

*Plude and Hoyer (1985)* **assert that** *"… measuring attention consists of evaluating the selectivity of information processing" (p.52).*

(Life Sciences)

*Davis is unique in* **asserting that** *because there were no concrete evidences of the 'Ranter's' practical antinomianism, therefore they do not exist.*

(Arts and Humanities)

Table 4.8    Keywords in undergraduate Essays

| Verbs | Adverbs | Adjectives | Nouns |
|---|---|---|---|
| assert | perhaps | moral | man |
| die | merely | religious | century |
| fight | ultimately | ancient | religion |
| portray | ever | modern | belief |
| criticise | certainly | sexual | death |
| deny | entirely | civil | god |
| fear | essentially | contemporary | society |
| kill | seemingly | historical | truth |
| refuse | socially | liberal | war |
| born | surely | male | character |

*Evolutionary ecologists attribute behavioural patterns to the influence of natural selection over time, **asserting that** choices are made within a pre-developed framework.*

(Social Sciences)

These keywords play an important role in positioning students' voices in the context of debates in the disciplines (Groom, 2000), which are accessed through published academic writing. By reporting that a published author *asserts* something, the student writer is endorsing the idea. It is noteworthy that *claim* is not a top key verb in student Essays. This suggests that students are more likely to endorse published ideas through the use of *assert* than to challenge the validity of the published ideas through the use of *claim* or other more negative reporting verbs.

*Perhaps* is the most frequent keyword in Essays occurring more than 1,000 times in almost 300,000 words (35.4 per 10,000 words), collocating with *the* and many other items, including modal verbs (*could*, *would*) and suasive verbs (*suggest*). As we see in these examples, it is not *perhaps* itself that indicates an argument, but its combination with other persuasive features, as illustrated in bold here:

*Perhaps it **can be suggested** that, the above **arguments** regarding economic and cultural aspects were **merely** the manifestation of the broader concept of European rivalry.*

(History)

*However, perhaps, almost equally, their charismatic **claim** falls **just** short.*

(Comparative American Studies)

*In contrast to other communities who **are believed** to have worshipped the ancestors, the inhabitants of Knap of Howar **may** have separated themselves* *from the dead; **alternatively**, there **may** be a correlation to the rising sun in the east, **perhaps** a belief in rebirth.*

(Archaeology)

In one sense the use of *perhaps* in these examples is redundant – it adds nothing to the propositional meaning of the first example, for instance. Instead, its function is to contribute to an evaluation that builds up over a longer stretch of text. This can be described as the prosodic nature of evaluative language (Halliday, 2004; Martin, 1992). Thus *perhaps* indicates the persuasive function of Essays, and the rather tentative nature of some arguments particularly in the Humanities.

As the Essay genre family is large, it was decided to conduct a further keyword search across Essays in disciplines where they are frequent: Law, Philosophy, Sociology, English and Classics. The aim was to search for disciplinary variation in persuasive language. Table 4.9 shows the twenty most key adverbs and verbs[10].

From this table it seems that argumentation in Law is distinct in its focus on what is *consequently, legally right*; in Philosophy on what is *absolutely, morally* or *logically accepted*; and in Sociology on what is *arguably, fundamentally, increasingly, importantly, socially* and *predominantly challenged*.

*To conclude, State A cannot **legally impose** a new tax on imported furniture, whether or not it is being dumped.*

(Law)

*Action against their respective State to **enforce** the directive they are **relying** upon. Usually the Commission takes action against ...*

(Law)

The key verbs suggest that laws, which can be *binding, enforced* and *justified*, enable states to *impose, deter, prohibit* and *protect*. In Philosophy, student writers are concerned with concession (*accept, admit, concede*), critique *(criticise, imagine, question)*, entertainment *(claim, imagine, postulate)*, justification *(entail, justify)* and renunciation *(deny, doubt, refute)* in their search for truth, while the distinctive features of argumentation in Sociology focus on how theories and ideas '*embrace, reproduce, shape, transcend, reinforce, redefine, legitimise, question, portray* and *challenge*' our understanding of Society.

*The depiction of the street child as a social menace **could arguably** be **construed as** a conscious effort to maintain the flourishing child labour market.*

(Sociology)

Table 4.9    Key adverbs and verbs in Essays across disciplines

| Law | Philosophy | Sociology | English | Classics |
|---|---|---|---|---|
| **Adverbs** | | | | |
| alone | absolutely | arguably | away | actually |
| arguably | actually | critically | certainly | all |
| better | causally | ever | constantly | alone |
| consequently | certainly | fundamentally | entirely | away |
| course | else | historically | essentially | BC |
| entirely | entirely | importantly | ever | certainly |
| essentially | essentially | increasingly | immediately | completely |
| ever | ever | instead | indeed | eventually |
| increasingly | exactly | is | instead | ever |
| legally | independently | largely | merely | instead |
| merely | infinitely | longer | never | later |
| necessarily | logically | merely | perhaps | never |
| neither | merely | naturally | similarly | once |
| nevertheless | morally | no | specifically | particular |
| no | necessarily | predominantly | | probably |
| potentially | really | socially | | rather |
| right | somewhat | today | | really |
| surely | surely | totally | | there |
| ultimately | truly | truly | | today |
| | ultimately | whereby | | yet |
| **Verbs** | | | | |
| acknowledge | accept | challenge | capture | attack |
| afford | admit | cite | convey | born |
| assert | appeal | constitute | depict | defeat |
| bind | claim | criticise | desire | defend |
| commit | commit | dominate | die | depict |
| deem | conceive | embed | emphasise | desire |
| deter | concede | embody | escape | die |
| enforce | criticise | embrace | evoke | fight |
| impose | deny | emerge | explore | kill |
| intervene | distinguish | legitimise | force | let |
| justify | doubt | oppress | hear | love |
| prohibit | entail | police | imagine | marry |
| protect | imagine | portray | imply | portray |
| refuse | justify | question | love | remind |
| rely | perceive | redefine | portray | rule |
| | possess | reinforce | read | send |
| | postulate | reproduce | refuse | tell |
| | reason | retain | speak | translate |
| | refute | shape | witness | win |
| | shall | transcend | write | worship |

*Giddens outlines four **key** principles that shape the Third Way (2001, p.50–56). Firstly and most **fundamentally**, the Third Way rests on the belief that both globalisation and Thatcherism have brought **profound** change.*

(Sociology)

Similarly, we can infer that in English writers are concerned with verbal processes in communication (*read, speak, write*) and how authors *capture, convey, depict, emphasise, evoke, explore, imagine, imply, portray* and *witness*; whereas in Classics, the debate is worded more in material processes of life (*born, die*), love (*love, desire, marry, worship*) and battle (*attack, defeat, fight, kill*).

*Eliot 'others' Hetty by **portraying** her as **never** fully human; she is **consistently referred to as** a 'cat' or 'kitten'.*

(English)

*is an 'animated image of death carved out of ivory.' The image of white bones **evokes** notions of fossils, thus **implying** that humanity faces moral extinction if ethical ...*

(English)

These examples show how arguments work in English; how a claim is made, supported by an interpretation of the data, where the interpretation is realised by processes such as *portray* or *evoke*. These processes are a matter of personal interpretation (the writer thinks Eliot portrays Hetty as never fully human), supported by evidence cited from the text (that Hetty is referred to as 'cat' or 'kitten').

In Classics, Essays focus on the battles and marriages of ancient civilisations as told in ancient texts read in translation and depicted on pottery and other artefacts.

*Another source of evidence that can **tell** historians about the way of **life** in fifth century Athens is archaeological evidence, mainly the discovery of decorated pottery that **shows** scenes of Athenian everyday **life**.*

(Classics)

*In W. K. Lacey's 'The Family in Classical Greece', we are **told** of two stories that **present** these types of situations.*

(Classics)

This keyword analysis in Essays across disciplines complements our findings from IF–THEN across disciplines. Together they provide evidence of the disciplinary nature of argumentation, with its claims, grounds and warrants. They also suggest where argumentation is explicit and logical, and where it is more nuanced and persuasive.

## 4.5 Conclusion

This chapter has considered the nature and language of Critique and Essay genres. The development of independent reasoning, in the context of disciplinary knowledge and understanding, is central to higher education and evidenced across genre families. The main functions of Critiques and Essays are to display informed rationality in terms of critical evaluation and the development of sustained arguments. Six Critique genres and six Essay genres were identified in Section 4.2 and explored through their titles, introductions and conclusions. Examination of headings, macrostructure, and angle on field revealed variation across assignments, though ways of narrowing the focus and building hyperNews suggest common strategies for individualisation and making claims across disciplines. Disciplinary differences were identified in Section 4.3 in terms of author presence in framing moves, and in the nature of evidence cited. Further disciplinary differences were inferred in terms of reasoning, claims and warrants from an examination of IF–THEN structures. Basic statistics and exploration of keywords provided clear evidence of the distinctive language of each genre family. They point to further disciplinary differences in the prosodic nature of the language of evaluation and argumentation. Critiques may involve *accounting for beneficial factors*, while Essays *perhaps merely assert*.

## Notes

1. In a straw man argument, a weak position is introduced so that it can be countered; in a false dilemma, alternatives are proposed as if they were alternatives, or the only options, when they are not; and in a circular argument, claims are interdependent and not open to testing with independent evidence.
2. Calculations for Critiques and Essays are for all non-compound assignments, using SketchEngine.
3. Evidentials, such as 'according to x', '(Y 1990)' or 'Z states', refer to information in other textual sources, as do quotations in English Essays.
4. A subcorpus of native speaker Essays is possible due to the large number of Essays in the corpus. It was intended to reduce the influence of taught uses of IF–THEN from English language classes, which may or may not reflect specific disciplinary norms (see Carter-Thomas and Rowley-Jolivet).
5. T-score=14.652, MI=10.408; range -1 to +20
6. These statistics were calculated for the 1,222 Essay texts and 315 Critique texts from assignments realised by one or more text of the same genre family.
7. Calculated by SketchEngine where F=15, simple math parameter =50, and scores >1.4 are listed.
8. A native speaker subcorpus was created with the aim of focusing on the departmental disciplinary influences and reducing influences from generic English preparatory sessions.

9. SketchEngine F>5, MI>4
10. SketchEngine amp=100, undergraduate Essays by native speakers

# References

Andrews, R. (2000). Introduction: Learning to argue in higher education. In S. Mitchell & R. Andrews (Eds.), *Learning to argue in higher education*. Portsmouth, NH: Boynton/Cook, 1–14.

Andrews, R. (2010). *Argumentation in higher education: Improving practice through theory and research*. New York: Routledge.

Biber, D., Conrad, S., & Leech, G. (2002). *Longman student grammar of spoken and written English*.

Bruce, I. (2010). Textual and discoursal resources used in the essay genre in sociology and English. *Journal of English for Academic Purposes*, 9(3), 153–66.

Carter-Thomas, S., & Rowley-Jolivet, E. (2008). *If*- conditionals in medical discourse: From theory to disciplinary practice. *Journal of English for Academic Purposes*, 7, 191–205.

Chang, Y-Y., & Swales, J. (1999). Informal elements in English academic writing: Threats or opportunities for advanced non-native speakers? In C. N. Candlin & K. Hyland (Eds.), *Writing, texts, processes and practices*. Harlow: Longman, 145–63.

Coffin, C. (2004). Learning to write history: The role of causality. *Written Communication*, 21, 261–89.

Coffin, C. (2006). *Historical discourse*. London: Continuum.

Creme, P., & Lea, M. (1997). *Writing at university: A guide for students*. Maidenhead: Open University Press.

Gardner, S. (2008a). Integrating ethnographic, multidimensional, corpus linguistic and systemic functional approaches to genre description: An illustration through university history and engineering assignments. In E. Steiner & S. Neumann (Eds.), *ESFLCW 2007: Data and interpretation in linguistic analysis*. Saarbrücken: Universität des Saarlandes. http://scidok.sulb.uni-saarland.de/sulb/portal/esflcw/.

Gardner, S. (2008b). Mapping ideational meaning in a corpus of student writing. In C. Jones & E. Ventola (Eds.), *New developments in the study of ideational meaning: From language to multimodality. Functional Linguistics series*, edited by R. Fawcett. London: Equinox Publishing, 169–88.

Gardner, S. (2009). Evaluation across disciplinary groups in university student writing: The critique genre family as texts and text. In M. Edwardes (Ed.), Proceedings of the BAAL annual conference 2008. *Taking the measure of applied linguistics. Swansea University*. London: BAAL/Scitsiugnil Press, 47–50.

Gardner, S., & Holmes, J. (2009). Can I use headings in my essay? Section headings, macrostructures and genre families in the BAWE corpus of student writing. In M. Charles, S. Hunston, & D. Pecorari (Eds.), *Academic writing: At the interface of corpus and discourse*. London: Continuum, 251–71.

Gardner, S., & Holmes, J. (2010). From section headings to assignment macrostructure in undergraduate student writing. In E. Swain (Ed.), *Thresholds and potentialities of Systemic Functional Linguistics.* Trieste: Edizioni Universitarie Trieste, 254–76.

Giltrow, J. (2000). 'Argument' as a term in talk about student writing. In S. Mitchell and R. Andrews (Eds.), *Learning to argue in higher education.* Portsmouth, NH: Boynton/Cook, 129–145.

Groom, N. (2000). A workable balance: Self and sources in argumentative writing. In S. Mitchell & R. Andrews (Eds.), *Learning to argue in higher education.* Portsmouth, NH: Boynton/Cook, 65–73.

Halliday, M.A.K. (2004). *Introduction to functional grammar* (3rd edition). CMIM Matthiesson. London: Arnold.

Hewings, A. (2004). Developing discipline-specific writing: an analysis of under-graduate geography essays. In L. Ravelli & R. Ellis (Eds.), *Analysing academic writing: Contextualized frameworks.* London: Continuum, 131–52.

Hunston, S. (1994). Evaluation and organisation in a sample of academic written discourse. In M. Coulthard (Ed.), *Advances in written text analysis.* London: Routledge.

Hunston, S., & Thompson, G. (Eds.) (2000). *Evaluation in text.* Oxford: Oxford University Press.

Hyland, K. (2002). Authority and invisibility: Authorial identity in academic writing. *Journal of Pragmatics,* 34(8), 1091–112.

Hyland, K. (2004). Disciplinary interactions: Metadiscourse in L2 postgraduate writing. *Journal of Second Language Writing,* 13, 133–51.

Hyland, K. (2005). *Metadiscourse.* London: Continuum.

Martin, J.R. (1992). *English text: System and structure.* Amsterdam: Benjamins.

Martin, J.R. (2000). Beyond exchange: Appraisal systems in English. In S. Hunston & G. Thompson (Eds.), *Evaluation in text: Authorial stance and the construction of discourse.* Oxford: Oxford University Press, 142–75.

Martin, J.R., & Rose, D. (2003). *Working with discourse.* London: Equinox.

Martin, J.R., & White, P.R. (2005). *The language of evaluation: Appraisal in English.* Basingstoke: Palgrave Macmillan.

Mathison, M. (1996). Writing the critique, a text about a text. *Written Communication,* 13, 314–54.

Mitchell, S. (2000). Putting argument into the mainstream. In S. Mitchell & R. Andrews (Eds.), *Learning to argue in higher education.* Portsmouth, NH: Heinemann/Boynton-Cook, 146–54.

Neuman, R., Parry, S., & Becher, T. (2002). Teaching and learning in their dis-ciplinary contexts: a conceptual analysis. *Studies in Higher Education,* 27, 405–13.

QAA (The Quality Assurance Agency for Higher Education) (2001, 2008) *The framework for higher education qualifications in England, Wales and Northern Ireland.* August 2008. Mansfield: QAA.

Riddle, M. (2000). Improving argument by parts. In S. Mitchell & R. Andrews (Eds.), *Learning to argue in higher education.* Portsmouth, NH: Heinemann/Boynton-Cook, 53–64.

Samraj, B. (2008). A discourse analysis of masters theses across disciplines with a focus on introductions. *Journal of English for Academic Purposes,* 7, 55–67.

Thetala, P. (1997). Evaluated entities and parameters of value in academic research articles. *English for Specific Purposes*, 16(2), 101–18.

Toulmin, S. (1958). *The uses of argument*. Cambridge: Cambridge University Press.

Warschauer, M. (2002). Networking into academic discourse. *Journal of English for Academic Purposes*, 1, 45–58.

Woodward-Kron, R. (2009). "This means that ...": A linguistic perspective of writing and learning in a discipline. *Journal of English for Academic Purposes*, 8, 165–79.

# 5  Developing research skills

> Typically holders of an honours degree will be able to apply the
> methods and techniques that they have learned to review,
> consolidate, extend and apply their knowledge and
> understanding, and to initiate and carry out projects.
>
> (QAA, 2008: 19)

For some students the aim of demonstrating 'an ability to deploy
accurately established techniques of analysis and enquiry within
a discipline' (QAA, 2008: 18) involves developing arguments as
in Essay genres, whereas for others greater emphasis is placed on
conducting empirical studies, on solving practical problems, and
on the ability to 'apply the methods and techniques that they have
learned to review, consolidate, extend and apply their knowledge
and understanding, and to initiate and carry out projects' (QAA,
2008: 19). This chapter focuses on ways in which students prepare
for and demonstrate their abilities to initiate and carry out projects
in their respective disciplines, with specific reference to the genre
families of Research Reports, Literature Surveys and Methodology
Recounts.

## 5.1  Developing research skills

Perhaps because there is an abundance of professional research
writing available to students, less attention has been paid to training students to write research reports than to write essays. Published
literary essays by Hazlitt, Montaigne, Will Self or other essayists
bear little resemblance to student essays in purpose or nature. This,
together with the quantities of essays written, the fact that students
seldom see other people's essays, and the wide distribution of essays
across the academy, helps to explain why textbooks for developing
student writing focus on essays (Tribble, 2009). In contrast, examples
of research articles are readily available in academic journals, and
there has been a productive line of inquiry in Applied Linguistics that

analyses reported research that broadly follows the Introduction–Methodology–Results–Discussion (IMRD) framework (e.g., Swales, 1990; Lewin, Fine and Young, 2001). Students across the Sciences in particular are expected to read such professional research reports published in academic journals. In some cases journal articles are presented as models for student writing, and assignments from disciplines, such as Biology and Hospitality, Tourism and Leisure Management, appear in the guise of journal articles with volume and page numbers, acknowledgements, keywords and formatting such as double columns and fonts associated with published work in their disciplines.

As a Physics lecturer explained, 'We're trying to get them to write like a scientific paper, as would be published in a scientific journal, but for an audience of their peers'. In a similar way, a Psychology lecturer reported that their aim is to 'cultivate a scientific formal writing style' where the 'gold standard' is the research article. Although he acknowledges that all assignments may be called 'essays', students also produce practical reports and project reports which are meant to be written in essentially the style of a research article.

Thus, in Psychology, students are introduced to the published journal article format in their first year, and are expected to produce assignments which report a small experimental study, including sections such as abstract, introduction, methods, results and discussion (IMRD). This format is repeated over the years leading to a longer final year project written up as a Research Report.

This practice is in contrast to that of some Humanities disciplines where students may engage initially with 'real-world' literature or historical events, answer a pre-set question, and only later in their studies situate their writing explicitly in the context of theories and approaches to their disciplines (Gardner, 2008).

In many Sciences disciplines the full empirical research report does not appear until the final year project, with assignments targeting specific sections of the report over the years. Thus, in Engineering, students may write product evaluations, lab reports and design specifications over Levels 1 and 2, and then produce a complete Level 3 project on an original topic which contains elements of all these genres together with a literature review.

This progression may be reflected in what students are expected to read:

*In year 1 they are reading textbooks and websites almost exclusively; by the second year they should be reading key review articles (syntheses of research on a given topic); by the third year, they should be going to the primary literature. They change in being able to draw in a wider range of information and being able to deal with more sophisticated sources. Weaker students find certainly that last step quite difficult.*

(Biology lecturer)

From these introductory comments we can anticipate significant differences across disciplines in the nature and progression of genre families that focus on the development of research skills.

## 5.2 Genre families for demonstrating research skills: Research Reports, Literature Surveys, Methodology Recounts

In our interviews with students and tutors, one key difference that emerged between Research Reports and assignments such as lab reports and Essays concerned the origin of the assignment or research question. Thus although a research project and a lab report assignment may have a very similar IMRD generic structure, there are important differences in their educational purpose. In a given Level 1 or 2 module all the students might be introduced to the same concepts and theories, conduct the same experiment and produce very similar lab reports, so that they might acquire an understanding of the techniques, methods and knowledge of the discipline. In contrast, in Level 3 and 4 research projects, there is an expectation that each piece of research will be different, and that students will identify their own perspective and methodology, informed by a review of the literature, and thus develop the ability to 'initiate and carry out projects' (QAA, 2008: 19). Because many experimental Research Reports include stages which are very similar to those of lab reports, and therefore the language of the central stages is substantially the same, we consider both together in this chapter. And because a central feature of Research Reports, such as Level 3 projects or dissertations, is the literature review, we also examine Literature Surveys in this chapter.

The difference between the two genres resides in whether the student has developed the design him- or herself in the context of the literature, and has presented it in a format similar to published research (a Research Report), or whether the student has been told what to do and the assignment is basically a write-up of an experiment (a lab report, one type of Methodology Recount). The section headings in both cases may be the same, as suggested in the following quotes from lecturers:

*Lab reports have a distinctive formal structure. Final-year project reports have a similar structure, though are longer.*

(Biology)

*They do lab reports in all 3 or 4 years, culminating in a final year project report which has the same structure but is larger (6000–7000 words).*

(Physics)

*[in the first year] students have to learn to explain: what happened; why it is interesting; how it relates to psychological theory. [at upper levels] the main difference is that students set themselves the problem.*

(Psychology)

In a similar way, in disciplines which favour Essays, Level 1 and 2 assignments tend to answer questions set by tutors. In contrast, a Level 3 assignment, such as a dissertation, develops a particular focus in the context of a review of the relevant literature. The gap between tutor-set Essays and a dissertation can be filled by a Literature Survey, a popular developmental assignment which may be followed by a literature-based Research Report where the relevance or value of the investigation is demonstrated in the context of the literature. Experimental and literature-based Research Reports can serve to bring to the attention of tutors those students who would be well suited to continue to doctoral research.

In this chapter we examine the genre families of Research Reports, Literature Surveys and Methodology Recounts. Table 5.1 shows their distribution across disciplinary groups in the BAWE corpus, and the predominance of Methodology Recounts in the Life and Physical Sciences.

## Research Reports

Research Reports may be written throughout a student's years at university, or may represent the culmination of undergraduate study. Their function is to report on research conducted independently by students, individually or in teams, and to demonstrate familiarity with and expertise in the research methods of the discipline. They

Table 5.1   Distribution by disciplinary group

|  | Arts and Humanities | Life Sciences | Physical Sciences | Social Sciences | Total |
|---|---|---|---|---|---|
| Research Report | 9 | 22 | 16 | 14 | 61 |
| Literature Survey | 7 | 14 | 4 | 10 | 35 |
| Methodology Recount | 18 | 157 | 170 | 16 | 361 |
| Total | 34 | 193 | 190 | 40 | 457 |

may be similar in structure to other assignments in the discipline, either in full or in part, but they include specific attention to developing, justifying and embedding the research question in the literature of the field, and therefore generally include more references to 'theory' sources (Bizup, 2008).

In the BAWE corpus we aimed to include a limited number of Level 3 projects to explore the boundaries of undergraduate writing. The numbers are small, partly because comparative research across disciplines already exists in this area, for example with reference to Hyland's corpus of 240 Masters and Doctoral dissertations across six disciplines (Hyland, 2005: 55ff), partly for corpus design reasons, because dissertations are disproportionately longer than other assignments, and partly for practical reasons, because we did not want to collect assignments before their grades were published (Alsop and Nesi, 2009) and it was hard to persuade students to submit projects after they had left the university at the end of their final year. We excluded Level 4 (postgraduate) dissertations for similar reasons.

Those Research Reports that are included in the corpus are dissertations, long essays, project reports and experiment reports. The Research Reports fall into two distinct types, within which there are disciplinary differences. The first distinct type has a complex, topic-based macrostructure (Gardner and Holmes, 2009), with chapter or section headings that carry primarily ideational meaning (such as *magic* or *revolution*), which point to the field rather than the genre. The second distinct type has a complex, genre-based macrostructure (ibid.) with headings that carry primarily textual meaning (such as *methods, results*), which point to the genre rather than the content or field.

### COMPLEX TOPIC-BASED MACROSTRUCTURE: *Dissertations and long essays*

Research Reports with complex topic-based macrostructures are found primarily in Arts and Humanities where semiotic entities are interpreted, and in Sciences where research draws on secondary sources. Research Reports of this kind may be presented as dissertations, research articles or long essays. The table of contents in Figure 5.1 is from a level 3 Classics dissertation.

The basic structure of the assignment is similar to a five-part essay format (Warschauer, 2002): it starts with an introduction chapter, which is followed by three equally weighted argument chapters on state magic, funerary magic and popular magic, and ends with a concluding chapter. The development of the focus of the study

# Contents

Figure 5.1   Table of contents from a Classics dissertation

towards the end of the first chapter and the evaluation of its contribution to the field in the final chapter, the overall length (9,000 words), and the extensive bibliography (over 100 entries) mark this as a dissertation. A similar macrostructure is seen in the Sociology dissertation (Figure 5.2), which is of similar length although it contains only fourteen references.

This dissertation explains realist ontology and then takes a particular framework (morphogenesis) and applies it to debates in the field. Following this analysis, the student positions his views in the literature, and in the final chapter uses the arguments developed throughout to critique a position adopted in a recent journal article.

Some Humanities disciplines require a 'long essay' rather than a dissertation in the final year of study. Figure 5.3 is an example from Philosophy.

This assignment is very similar to an Exposition in its development of a thesis, but the 'question' was not set by a tutor, and the length (over 9,000 words) forces not only the development of an extended argument, but also division into chapters, which has an inevitable effect on how the language unfolds.

## Contents

Figure 5.2    Table of contents from Sociology dissertation

## Table of Contents

**Introduction (P. 3)**
This includes a brief discussion of the relation between different forms of pacifism and just war theory, settling on anti-war pacifism as the type to defend.
**Chapter 1: War and the Rule of Law (P. 6)**
The just war theorist proposes an analogy between war and punishment, which is discussed and refuted in this section.
**Chapter 2: Self-Defence (P. 9)**
The issues surrounding both individual and large-scale violent self-defence are explored, with the conclusion that it is legitimate in the case of the former but there are problems in arguing for the latter.
**Chapter 3: Humanitarian interventions (P. 17)**
Is there a moral obligation to use military force in cases of gross human rights violations? A discussion of possible anti-war pacifist approaches to this issue.
**Chapter 4: Alternatives to Violence (P. 25)**
After discussing some of the criticisms levelled against anti-war pacifism, the argument turns to positive alternatives to violence and the need for new international institutions.
**Conclusion (P. 29)**
The main points made in the essay are revisited, and it is argued that ...

Figure 5.3    Contents of a Philosophy long essay

COMPLEX GENRE-BASED MACROSTRUCTURE: *Project reports versus experiment reports*

Just as topic-based assignment headings are found in dissertations and essays, so too are genre-based IMRD headings found in research project reports and experiment reports. There is broad agreement across systemic functional linguistic (e.g., Lewin, Fine and Young, 2001) and Swalesian (e.g., Kanoksilapatham, 2005) approaches to genre analysis about the linguistic distinctiveness of the different sections of published experimental research articles. Because of this distinctiveness the different stages can be readily examined in relative isolation, as in recent papers on the abstract (Lores, 2004), introduction (Loi, 2010; Samraj, 2008), methods (Lim, 2006; Bruce, 2008), results (Williams, 1999; Basturkmen, 2009), discussion (Peacock, 2002) and conclusion (Bunton, 2005). Our approach here is rather different. We aim to demonstrate the distinctiveness of two IMRD experiment report genres through examples of paired texts from three different disciplines where experimental studies are common: Psychology, Engineering and Biology.

The two assignments selected from Psychology are similar in many ways: both report studies which involved administering questionnaires to fellow students to test psychological theories. In the project report the aim is to find out about links between avoidance coping and alcohol consumption, and in the experiment report the focus is on links between experiences and the emotions of guilt, shame and embarrassment. The macrostructure of the two assignments is very similar, but the proportion of the assignment allocated to each section is different, as Table 5.2 illustrates.

Table 5.2    Psychology project and experiment section weightings

| Psychology project headings | N words | %* | Psychology experiment headings | N words | %* |
|---|---|---|---|---|---|
| abstract | 116 | 2 | abstract | 98 | 6 |
| introduction | 1913 | 30 | introduction | 179 | 11 |
| method | 641 | 11 | method | 330 | 20 |
| participants | 36 | | design | 40 | |
| materials | 357 | | participants | 79 | |
| design & procedure | 248 | | materials | 86 | |
| – | | | procedure | 125 | |
| results | 1281 | 20 | results | 611 | 38 |
| discussion | 2343 | 37 | discussion | 403 | 25 |
| | 6294 | 100 | | 1621 | 100 |
| references (51) | | | references (1) | | |
| appendices (4) | 1761 | | – | | |

*of assignment

While the introduction to the project report is almost 2,000 words long (30%) and contains over 40 citations, the introduction to the experiment report is only 180 words (11%), with one citation. This means that the research project assignment resembles a published journal article where the aims of the study are contextualised in the literature, while the experiment is written up primarily for the module tutor who appreciates why this is an appropriate topic to investigate and is more interested in what the student does (methodology), what she finds (results) and whether she can write appropriately using the IMRD framework. Thus most of the experiment assignment (58%) is concerned with a recount of the study. Only six sentences are devoted to other sources in the introduction and only one in the discussion, as we can see in the following extract.

---

**Introduction**

Guilt, shame and embarrassment are emotions of similar origin and type, in that they are moments of unpleasant self-consciousness that we all experience. It is sometimes believed that they are basically the same. However Tangney et al., (1996) described these emotions as distinctly separate experiences. A study was conducted amongst undergraduates to determine what sort of experiences lead to feelings of guilt, shame and embarrassment, and how different the three emotions were considered to be. It seemed that shame and guilt were similar emotions, with shame a more public experience, and that embarrassment was the most public of all, and milder than shame or guilt, (Tangney et al., 1996)....

**Discussion**

...This was generally as expected and followed the pattern of results given by Tangney (1996)...

---

This distribution of information suggests that the aim of the study was not to generate new knowledge, but to demonstrate an understanding of disciplinary procedures. Thus, as Table 5.3 shows, where the bulk of the research project is devoted to the literature review and

Table 5.3   The contrasting 60:40 splits in Psychology report and experiment

| Psychology | Research Report % | Methodology Recount % |
|---|---|---|
| Introduction + Discussion | 67 | 36 |
| Methods + Results | 31 | 58 |

the discussion (67%), the bulk of the small empirical study is devoted to an account of the methods and the results (58%).

Thus, we generally find that final year project reports are members of the Research Report genre family, while small experimental studies and practicals are members of the Methodology Recount genre family (see Section 5.2 for further discussion of this genre family).

The differences are similar across the disciplines. For example, in Engineering we can compare headings in a Level 3 project and a Level 2 Fluid Mechanics lab report (Table 5.4). Both are reports of experiments conducted by a team rather than individuals. The project includes a literature review with 29 citations and 19 references, while

Table 5.4   Engineering project and practical section headings

| Engineering Level 3 project (main headings only) | Engineering Level 2 practical (all headings) |
| --- | --- |
| Author's Assessment of the Project | |
| 1.0 Summary | Summary |
| 2.0 Contents | |
| 3.0 Introduction | |
| 4.0 Literature Review (29 citations) | |
| 5.0 Theory | 1. Apparatus and Method |
| 6.0 Research Methodology | 2. Theory |
| 7.0 Experimental Equipment (11 figs) | |
| 8.0 Set Up and Experimental Procedure | |
| 9.0 Flat Plate | |
| 9.1 Introduction | |
| 9.2 Results | 3. Results |
| 9.3 Observations and Interpretation | 3.1 Laminar flow |
| 9.4 Additional Observations and Interpretation | 3.2 Turbulent flow |
| 9.5 Additional Notes and Evaluation of Methods | |
| 10.0 120mm Tube | 4. Discussion |
| 10.1 Introduction | |
| 10.2 Observation and Interpretation | |
| 10.3 Evaluation of Methods | |
| 11.0 Conclusions | 5. Conclusion |
| 11.1 Costing | |
| 11.2 Flat Plate | |
| 11.3 120mm Tube | |
| 11.4 In Reference to Specification | |
| 12.0 Acknowledgements | |
| Appendices (4) | 6. Bibliography (3) |
| References (19) | 7. Appendix (Graphs) |

there is no literature review section in the lab report, and only three references, all of which are course materials (lecture notes, a textbook and a data book).

The comparison in Table 5.5 of the weighting of the main sections shows the importance of the Literature Review (16% > 0%) in the research project in comparison to the 'Theory' (18% > 2%) in the practical project.

The practical assignment emphasises results (15% > 7%) over interpretation and discussion of the project (42% > 28%), though the headings and sections do not match exactly across the two assignments.

Our third example comes from a similar pair of assignments in Biology: a Level 3 aquaponics project and a Masters level practical report on vegetation after burning. Again the project contains detailed headings, as can be seen in Table 5.6.

The main differences between the two assignments are shown in Table 5.7 – the project includes a literature review of over 2,000 words, 43 citations and 50 references; while the results and analysis sections in the practical report amount to almost half the assignment wordcount (49% > 29%).

The comparison of projects and practical experiments across these pairs of similar assignments in three disciplines supports what the tutors told us: that although both could be considered experiment reports, they differ in function. This functional difference is evident

Table 5.5    Engineering project and practical section weightings

| Research Report | | Engineering | Methodology Recount | |
| --- | --- | --- | --- | --- |
| Project N words | %* | Main sections | Practical N words | %* |
| 250 | 3 | Summary | 214 | 10 |
| 216 | 2 | Introduction | 0 | 0 |
| 1523 | 16 | Literature Review | 0 | 0 |
| 230 | 2 | Theory | 397 | 18 |
| 1517 | 16 | Equipment & Methods | 323 | 15 |
| 694 | 7 | Results | 326 | 15 |
| 4065 | 42 | Observations and Interpretation / Discussion | 612 | 28 |
| 1114 | 12 | Conclusion | 300 | 14 |
| 9609 | 100 | | 2172 | 100 |

*of assignment

Table 5.6    Biology project and practical section headings

| Project main headings | Practical headings |
|---|---|
| Abstract | Introduction |
| Introduction | |
| Principles of an aquaponic system | |
| Literature review (43 citations) | |
| Objectives | Methods & Materials |
| Materials and Method (11 sections) | |
| Results (7 sections) | Results & Analysis (2 tables, 2 figures) |
| Discussion | Discussion |
| Conclusion | |
| Future Work | |
| References (50)Appendices (4) | |

Table 5.7    Biology project and practical section weightings

| Research Report | | Biology | Methodology Recount | |
|---|---|---|---|---|
| N words | %* | Main sections | N words | %* |
| 427 | 4 | Abstract + Intro + Principles | 118 | 13 |
| 2146 | 20 | Literature Review | 0 | 0 |
| 2456 | 24 | Objectives, Methods, Materials | 116 | 12 |
| 3033 | 29 | Results [Analysis] | 460 | 49 |
| 2408 | 23 | Discussion [Conclusion, Future Work] | 241 | 26 |
| 10470 | 100% | Total % | 935 | 100% |

*of assignment

from the inclusion of a significant literature review in the research project reports, and the proportionally greater attention given to methods and results sections in the practicals.

The Research Report genre family includes dissertations with topic-based macrostructure and research projects with genre-based macrostructure; in both cases students have developed the research question themselves, in the context of a literature review, and the conclusions of the research are discussed as contributions to the field of study. For most the Research Report is a final year undergraduate dissertation or project that provides an opportunity for students to participate in their disciplines as researchers. As most undergraduate students write only one such Research Report, which may count double the credits of other assignments, the transition from Essays or Methodology Recounts to Research Reports is a critical step. A useful bridge for students and tutors can be a Literature Survey assignment.

## Literature Surveys

In our interviews one of the key qualities lecturers looked for in their students, alongside 'the ability to manage their own learning', was the ability to 'make use of scholarly reviews and primary sources'. By setting an assignment with the express purpose of surveying the literature, tutors aim to develop such skills. In format Literature Surveys range from library searches where students have to find a number of sources on the topic they wish to research, to something more akin to an essay. A Psychology lecturer informant cited the following prompt, for example: 'Review research on subliminal perception and comment on how it has changed over the past 20 years'.

We identified seven main Literature Survey genres in the BAWE corpus, and will discuss them in this order: annotated bibliography, analytical bibliography, research methods review, literature review, review article, literature overview and anthology.

### ANNOTATED BIBLIOGRAPHY

The annotated bibliographies in the corpus all have a similar format, namely a series of paragraphs each of which starts with the full reference to a text (article, book chapter, website, etc.) and is followed by a summary of that text. Some contain longer summaries of as few as five texts, others contain shorter summaries of as many as fifty texts. The assignments demonstrate and develop the students' abilities to conduct a library search and find appropriate sources around a topic, often in preparation for a subsequent essay or project. They also allow the tutor to see how well the student has been able to extract or summarise key information. The summary should extract relevant information and evaluate its significance, as in this entry from an annotated bibliography:

*4. Paterson, H.E.H. (1985). The recognition concept of species. In* Species and speciation, *Transvaal Museum monograph; no. 4 (Ed, Vrba, E. S.) Transvaal Museum, Pretoria, pp. 21–29.*
*The author, researcher at the University of the Witwatersrand, provides his view of theoretical species concepts. The Biological Species Concept (=Isolation Concept) is criticized for its inconsistency in function and logic in contrast to the Recognition Concept of Species (= Specific-Mate Recognition System or SMRS). SMRS is the prevalent species concept that*

*is used by researchers of galagos and indirect responsible for the recent upsurge in new found species. This seminal paper is a good source for the theoretical framework encompassing SMRS and contains vital information for any biologist and especially taxonomist.*

(Anthropology)

An annotated bibliography, like a dictionary or encyclopaedia, is what Hoey (1991) calls a 'colony' text in that although each entry is complete in itself, a set or colony of such entries is required to form the superordinate assignment. Although 'annotated bibliography' is the term typically used for this type of Literature Survey, other terms such as 'Dissertation field' (English 3012c) or 'Reading portfolio' (Publishing 3037a) are also found. The title 'Dissertation field' concentrates attention on the preparation for the dissertation, whereas 'portfolio' suggests a demonstration of the range and breadth of reading.

ANALYTICAL BIBLIOGRAPHY

A very similar genre is the analytical bibliography. The entries here, as the name suggests, are more than a summary; they involve explicit analysis of each text, as the headings in Figure 5.4 demonstrate:

---

Notes
• Examines the effects on the Djabugay people of the presentation of their culture at the Tjapukai Aboriginal Cultural Park. Advantages and disadvantages of their involvement in tourism.
• …

Comment & Analysis
• …
• Highlights the importance of including local people in the management of the Park. At the time of the study, the Djabugay had no representative on the Park's board.
• …

Evidence to support argument
• Own research at Tjapukai Aboriginal Cultural Park, with cooperation of staff at all levels and the Djabugay people.
• …

Key Links
[3 references]

---

Figure 5.4    An example of analytical bibliography headings

Each of the four entries in this assignment has the same five-part structure, with bullet points under the three middle parts that summarise the article. It is thus similar to an annotated bibliography, but provides more scaffolding to help students identify the information expected from each text.

## RESEARCH METHODS REVIEW

As with the analytical bibliography, the research methods review focuses on identifying and summarising the research methods used to investigate a specific topic. It is presented discursively rather than in bullet point form.

*Research Review: Tackling Truancy*
*This literature review will examine the different approaches used to tackle truancy within schools. It will in look in detail at the methodology used to research the effectiveness of such interventions.*

(Health introduction)

This assignment continues with a summary of seven articles with sub-headings for methodology and results. In the following example the writer shows awareness of the dual aims of the assignment: to review methods used and to review research in a specific area.

*In choosing articles to examine in more depth, I was interested in pursuing the debate regarding integrated programmes, however I also wished to reflect a range of research methodology. I have therefore selected, the only randomised control trial of ...*

(Health)

## LITERATURE REVIEW

In the literature review genre, the main focus shifts from methodology to topic area, though both are relevant. The specific topic may vary according to the level of study, as in this example from History:

*For literature reviews undergraduate students choose a controversial topic and must include foreign language material. Postgraduate students review relevant theoretical literature.*

(History lecturer)

These assignments are essentially the literature review chapters of planned dissertations or research projects. They are written as chapters, and their aim is to review (usually through analytical summary and evaluation) the literature on a specific topic and identify a niche or gap which the student's research will occupy.

In the example in Figure 5.5 the final paragraph or sentence of the review points to the aims of the intended study. The study indicated may or may not actually take place, but the pedagogical aim of setting a Literature Survey as an assignment can be to check that the student is on the right track before a dissertation or project develops further.

REVIEW ARTICLE

Similar to a literature review chapter is the review article which is written as a state-of-the-art article for an audience of peers. It is formatted as a journal article, and concludes with general areas where further research is needed, rather than specifying a student dissertation project. This shift in audience is noted in the surface features of the assignment, and may also be present in the more highly academic register of the language used. Nevertheless the central aim and content is the same: to review earlier studies on a specific topic.

The extent to which the assignments represent published articles varies. At the extreme end they include all the features found in published research articles, including publication date, copyright, author affiliation and acknowledgements, and are presented in columns with the page format of a specific journal. In the example in Figure 5.6, the

---

2.1 Introduction
The purpose of this chapter is to provide a review of the literature on the Polish agriculture and in particular the fruit production. Moreover, the effects of foreign direct investment (FDI) in the Polish agri-food chain on Polish farms are investigated
2.2 Agriculture in Poland: An overview
2.3 The fruit sector
2.4 Relations to upstream agents
2.5 FDI, vertical integration and grower restructuring
2.6 Spill-over effects
2.7 Conclusion
Poland is a leading European …The objective of this study will be to find out whether and to what extent Polish fruit growers actually benefit from this cooperation.
References
[18 references]

(Agriculture)

---

Figure 5.5    Example literature review headings

Annu. Rev. Eco. Syst. 2005. 43: 1–7
Copyright © 2005 by Annual Reviews inc.
All rights reserved

# A REVIEW OF THE GENETIC CONTROL OF PLANT MORPHOLOGY

{anonymised: student name}
*Department of Plant Sciences, {anonymised: university}, England*

KEY WORDS:*Aribidopsis thaliana*, Homeobox, *KN 1*. ROTUNDIFOLIA 3, Photoreceptors, MADS box, *KNOX*, S-gene, AMOVA, QTL

**Abstract**
A number of individual genes have been identified within species of plants that are responsible for particular characteristics. Some papers given in this report involve the identification of a single gene with respect to one characteristic. The need to study genes within many species and in conjunction with other acting genes has also been found to be relevant and is likely to prove useful in the understanding of the evolution of plant morphology and in turn the applications of this understanding. It is hoped that the applications of the understanding of the genetics of plant morphology will enable the improvement of crop yields and have massive economic advantages.

**INTRODUCTION**
Genetic control of plant morphology has been investigated for many years with much interest being shown recently. This has been aided by advances in genetic techniques. The realisation of the potential economic benefits of furthering our knowledge in this area has been a significant driving force. ... (Biology)

Figure 5.6  Professional layout of a review article assignment

student has based the layout of the assignment on that of the journal *Annual Review of Ecology, Evolution, and Systematics*.

Other review articles are more like essays but with headings that include an abstract and a conclusion:

*In conclusion ... The combination of lasers producing specifically desired and intense ultrashort pulse with developments in programmable pulse-shaping technology and learning algorithms control will continue to a rapid expansion in the numbers of fields where they could be fully applied. These technologies have generated a huge amount of interest both in the scientific community and the media, as the exciting possibilities of this new region of spectrum gradually becomes reality.*

(Cybernetics)

Swales (2004: 208) helpfully indicates alternative names for a review article: review, review essay, general article, report article and state of the art survey. He describes review articles as a type of research article, which is consistent with the fact that these assignments are generally formatted as if they were journal articles. We have opted to include the review article as a member of the Literature Survey genre family, however, in order to highlight its pedagogic role as a link in the genre chain towards an independent research project.

LITERATURE OVERVIEW

A rather different Literature Survey aims to develop a broad classification of numerous articles indicating the general position or focus of each. As one postgraduate student puts it, 'I have intended to produce a broad sweep of the most important literature on this topic over time from the late nineteenth century to the present'. In this assignment over 50 sources were itemised, and the writer reaches the following conclusion, demonstrating the ability to make sense of historical trends.

*It appears that the current state of affairs has the 'Ethnographic School' enjoying a numerical superiority over the Liar and 'Misinterpretation' Schools. Yet there are adherents for both of the older schools. The irony is that the tide may well have turned against the Liar School. ...For many modern scholars, ethnographic coherence is far more important than the practically impossible task of determining whether passages originate from Hecataeus or Herodotus.*

(Classics)

ANTHOLOGY

We also include anthologies in the Literature Survey family. In this type of assignment a theme is identified and explained, and examples of literature which illustrate the theme are included. As with other Literature Surveys, this involves selecting texts to include on the grounds that they meet certain criteria, and explaining what those criteria are with illustrations from the texts. For instance, one assignment explains the nature of Nonsense Poetry with reference to ten examples from authors such as Spike Milligan and Edward Lear. The examples are also included as part of the assignment.

LITERATURE SURVEY GENRE NETWORKS

The seven genres identified as members of the Literature Survey genre family do show some disciplinary leanings, for instance a typical Literature Survey for English is the anthology rather than the research methods review. Generally, however, their distinctiveness relates to their different genre networks. Thus, as Figure 5.7 aims to illustrate, the anthology and review article are modelled on professionally published anthologies and review articles and are situated in the top half of the figure alongside published genres. Bibliographies are found in both published and pedagogic contexts, and annotated and analytical student bibliographies are both similar to Exercises in terms of their preparatory, skill development focus. Research methods and literature reviews correspond broadly to chapters in planned Research Reports (dissertations or projects) and may be modelled on corre-

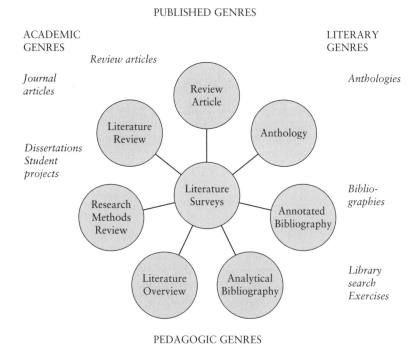

Figure 5.7    Literature Survey genre networks

sponding sections in published journal articles. In a similar way, student review articles may resemble professionally published review articles. These relationships highlight some of the influences and points of comparison between student genres and professional genres.

Despite this diversity, and the considerable variation in format and in the number of items surveyed, all seven genres of Literature Survey are the outcome of similar tasks. Literature Survey writers must conduct a library search, select appropriate entries, and summarise the relevance of those entries to a particular theme.

## Methodology Recounts

Just as Literature Survey assignments prepare students for the literature review chapter of a project or dissertation, Methodological Recount assignments prepare students for the methodology chapter of empirical projects. The central purpose of Methodology Recounts is to enable students to become familiar with experimental procedures and the ways in which findings are made in the discipline. This aim is reflected in the names given to such genres: lab report (Engineering), experimental report (Archaeology), field report (Meteorology), practical write-up, practical report, materials selection report (Engineering), and data analysis report (Economics). All tend to follow the IMRD progression, with a relative emphasis on the methodology. The following notes from an interview with an Engineering lecturer refer to the structure of a Methodology Recount assignment that the lecturer calls an 'academic laboratory report'.

*There is a standard structure: summary, introduction, literature review, description of what they've done, presentation of results, discussion, conclusions, references, appendices and so on. 'They have a layout of headings and a description of the sorts of things that would go under each of those headings, and they map whatever they've done into that.' Relatively constrained: they do a particular experiment and draw conclusions from that.*

(Engineering lecturer)

The following excerpt from an interview emphasises the way the four general sections (IMRD) of Methodology Recounts have distinct functions and language.

*The distinctive factor is that a report can be broken down into constituents. Some assessors give separate marks for separate sections, as the sections differ clearly in their rhetorical role. This can't be done with an essay. An essay would be seen as an integrated piece of work, wouldn't it?*

(Biology lecturer)

Essays in Psychology were described by one tutor as assignments where students write about other people's experiments, and thus address only a subset of the functions of the classic research article, e.g., introduction only, or discussion only. In other departments, including Chemistry, separate IMRD sections were set as formative assignments, to emphasise to students the importance of grasping the distinct purpose, rationale and language of each section. In the BAWE corpus introduction sections that occurred as distinct formally assessed assignments are generally classified as Literature Surveys, while interpretation of results sections tend to be classed as Critiques. This reflects what Swales calls the 'distinctive part-genre' nature of each of the IMRD sections (Swales, 2004: 216).

Methodology Recounts report work conducted in traditional science labs, in institutions, in natural settings and in virtual laboratories. Data analysis across the Sciences in the BAWE corpus was done using analytical software such as MatLab, which describes itself as 'a high-level technical computing language and interactive environment for algorithm development, data visualization, data analysis, and numeric computation' (www.mathworks.com/products/matlab). In these settings, students develop expertise in using the tools of the discipline, from questionnaire surveys to analytical frameworks to physical machinery and computational tools. These disciplinary differences are illustrated further in Section 5.3.

## 5.3  Demonstrating research skills across disciplines

Our discussion of Research Reports, Literature Surveys and Methodology Recounts has pointed to differences between disciplines not only in the genres preferred, but also in how the genres are conventionally realised. In this section we explore the way research skills are developed in writing across the disciplines.

If we compare macrostructures across selected disciplines, as in Table 5.8, we see that generally Engineering and Computer Science include a theory section, while Food Science includes a calculation section.

Many assignments have a second level of textual headings under Method. For example, Psychology assignments have participants, materials, procedure and data analysis. Some disciplines have second-level ideational headings, for example banana, ketchup and peanuts in a Human Nutrition assignment, with third- and fourth-level headings found occasionally in all the Sciences.

Table 5.8    IMRD variation across disciplines (Gardner and Holmes, 2009)

| Biological Science | Computer Science | Engineering | Food Science | Physics | Psychology |
|---|---|---|---|---|---|
| Abstract | Abstract | Abstract | Objective | Abstract | Abstract |
| Introduction | 1. Introduction | Introduction | Introduction | 1. Introduction | Introduction |
| – | 2. Theory | Theory | | – | – |
| Materials and method | 3. Design | Apparatus and methods | Method | 2. Experimental details | Method |
| Results | 4. Implementation | Observations and results | Results | 3. Results | Results |
| Discussion | 5. Results and analysis | Analysis of results | Calculation | 4. Discussion | Discussion |
| (Conclusion) (Future work) | 6. Conclusion | Discussion Conclusion | Discussion | | |
| References | References | References | References | References | References |

We now turn to the language used across disciplines to report research methods, design or experimental details in Research Reports and Methodology Recounts.

## 5.4  The language for displaying research skills

Having argued for grouping the three genre families in this chapter together on the basis of educational function, we now turn to explore how the distinctions among these three families are reflected in the language. From the figures in Chapter 2, we can see that the language of Literature Surveys is distinctive in being the most informational, the most elaborated and the least persuasive of all the genre families. Interestingly Literature Surveys are also relatively narrative, characterised by the use of the past tense and the third person pronoun when reporting other people's research, and relatively non-impersonal, indicated by a relative absence of agentless passives.

In contrast, Methodology Recounts and Research Reports do use agentless passives, and they cluster together as the most abstract and impersonal genre families. They also cluster with Explanations as informational, non-narrative and, after Literature Surveys, the least persuasive of the genre families. Methodology Recounts are considerably more situation dependent than Research Reports, however, with a greater focus on circumstantial details. Research Reports make greater use of relative clauses and nominalisation.

Table 5.9    Length of Research Reports, Literature Surveys and
Methodology Recounts

| | words | s-units | p-units | w/s | s/p | block quotes | tables | figures | formulae | lists etc. | abstracts |
|---|---|---|---|---|---|---|---|---|---|---|---|
| RR | 4158 | 170 | 52 | 22 | 3.6 | 1.5 | 2.5 | 4.1 | 6.5 | 3.9 | 0.5 |
| LS | 2346 | 92 | 25 | 28 | 4.7 | 1.0 | 0.3 | 0.7 | 0.1 | 5.3 | 0.1 |
| MR | 1813 | 88 | 40 | 20 | 2.5 | 0.2 | 2.5 | 3.1 | 9.7 | 3.8 | 0.3 |

Table 5.9 shows that Research Reports are long, with an average length in words (4,158) equal to the average for Literature Surveys and Methodology Recounts combined. Literature Surveys have long sentences (28 words per sentence), and Methodology Recounts have short paragraphs (2.5) particularly when compared to Literature Surveys (4.7 sentences per paragraph). Research Reports are most likely to include an Abstract; Methodology Recounts are unlikely to include block quotes, while Literature Surveys are unlikely to include tables, figures or formulae. The relatively high number of lists reflects the tendency to use bullet points, for example in analytical bibliographies.

This comparison of the multidimensional analyses and basic statistics of the language of the three genre families complements the genre analyses in Section 5.2 and supports expectations of clear linguistic differences between, for instance, the literature review and methodology. In the remainder of this section we briefly examine the keywords of Literature Surveys, then concentrate on the language of methodology sections, as these form substantial components of Methodology Recounts and project reports, and the development of a discipline-based understanding of methodology is a crucial stage in developing research skills.

## Keywords in Literature Surveys

Building on Kwan's (2006) move analysis of literature review chapters in Applied Linguistics doctoral theses, Flowerdew and Forest compare the same literature review data to the British National Corpus of general English. They suggest that the following are general (i.e., non-discipline specific) keywords for the literature review genre: *of, studies, analysis, research, study, chapter, example, knowledge, approach, approaches* and *discussion* (2009: 23).

In a comparison of the BAWE Literature Surveys with the British National Corpus the top keywords were numerals; specifically each of the years from 1994 to 2005. Words such as *University Press*, *Journal*, initials, *&*, *et* and *al.* were also key. The frequency of these features is due to the quantity of references to recent academic publications found in Literature Surveys in particular, but also in the BAWE corpus as whole.

The top 100 keywords identified (see Appendix 5.1) include *studies, methods, research, aspects, study, results, technique, analysis, effects, factors, differences, literature, sample* and *processes*, which suggests a more technical scientific orientation with less attention to *approaches, knowledge* and *discussion* than found in the Applied Linguistics theses.

While Flowerdew and Forrest found the collocations of *further research* and *little research* to be strongly associated with a move to indicate a gap in the research, these phrases are much less frequent in the BAWE Literature Surveys.

*It is clear therefore that* **further research** *is needed to find out whether the attendance legislation needs to be amended to take into account the child's age.*

(Health)

*... though* **further research** *of their genetics, anatomy and reproductive biology are considered necessary.*

(Anthropology)

*Further research* is found across the genre families (in all except Problem Question), particularly in higher level papers and in papers awarded a top distinction grade. In contrast, *little research* is very rare (three instances in the whole corpus), suggesting that students are not expected to be confident enough to indicate a research gap.

Compared to the BAWE corpus, the top ten general keywords in Literature Surveys relate to the texts being reviewed: *al, literature, whose, authors, survey, overview, et, paper, discover* and *search.*

| | | | |
|---|---|---|---|
| HTLM | lowest paid sector. However, Torrington (2002) *et al* | | suggested that people may be motivated |
| Agriculture | parents to buy organic food (Davies *et al* | | , 1995). In another study carried out in |
| Classics | produce a broad sweep of the most important | literature | on *this* topic over time from the late nineteenth |
| Health | prosecution of parents. (Zhang 2004). A thorough | literature | review on *this* subject has been carried |
| English | Introduces the concept of the "frigid heroine" | whose | reaction to the threat of sexuality is |
| Biological Sciences | . E. faecalis, a Gram-positive bacterium | whose | natural habitat is the mammalian gastrointestinal |
| Politics | 1851, only minority of males in factories | whose | working hours increased Even factory workers |
| Engineering | company to Asa Griggs Candler a businessman | whose | influencer ended up making it one of the |
| Law | . The selection *of* the cases reflect the | author | 's research skills, and ability to choose |
| Publishing | about the difficulty *of* selecting winning | authors | for the Man Booker Prize and the delight |
| Anthropology | lack of data does not seem to affect these | authors | from denominate their findings *of* a new |
| Anthropology | Journal of Primatology, 21, 537–555.The | authors | , researchers at Universities of Cambridge |
| Biological Sciences | exist within this line of research, but | papers | that have been reviewed all build upon |
| Law | he has undertaken a detailed research *to* | discover | the cases related to his statement; "The |
| Anthropology | tool can act *to* maximise the possibility of | discovering | new species within a region of interest |

| English | enjoyed. The pulling apart of nonsense *to* | discover | its structures may serve us to understand |
| Biological Sciences | repeats (VNTRs). Only four differences were | discovered | between the main chromosomes of the Florida |
| Health | been included in the final analysis. The | search | was then widened using Caredata and the |
| Health | included. The following data bases were | searched | in order to collect relevant papers. These |
| Publishing | Google Print is an online book and content, | search | engine. The Guild want to protect writers |
| English | rhyme as a parody of Lear, and a short | search | on the internet throws up dozens of parodies |
| Cybernetics & Electronic Engineering | incorporated other concurrently running | search | methods in addition to traditional GA search |

Further examples of these keywords in context are given in Appendix 5.2.

## Research decisions as elaborated or clipped text

While acknowledging that not all published Research Articles have a methods section *per se*, Swales argues that the major disciplinary differences in language lie not in the introduction and discussion sections, but in the methods and results sections (Swales, 2004: 219). These 'quite remarkable lower-level differences' involve the degree of elaboration of methods, and texts are characterised as 'fast' or 'slow'. Following the development of this concept by Bloor (1999), who pointed out that 'fast' texts can be slow to read, particularly by novices, as they are relatively dense and assume more background knowledge, Swales now refers to a continuum from 'clipped' to 'elaborated' texts (Swales, 2004: 220) as measured by nine specific features relating to whether background knowledge is assumed or provided, how acronyms are used, and the number of verbs per sentence. It is important to note here that Swales' definition of *elaborated* is quite distinct from Biber's (see Section 1.6 Dimension 3). While some differences may depend on how controversial the methods are, Swales also points to disciplinary differences:

The character of a Methods section in an experimental research paper ... would be clipped [fast] in areas such as physics, chemistry, biology and perhaps medicine; elaborated [slow] in education and psychology; and intermediate in areas like the language sciences, public health and the earth sciences.

(Swales, 2004: 223)

We will now explore whether such differences also apply to student writing. In particular, we focus on how explicit students are in their accounts of their methodology and the extent to which they justify decisions they make and what they do. This exploration will provide insights into how they construe the contexts in which they are writing in terms of what they can take for granted, what they need to explain and how they position themselves as actors and thinkers in the texts. Such construal is expected to reflect disciplinary differences and the specific methodology being described, as in the professional writing – in some studies there will be one recognised way of doing things that can be referred to, but needs little explanation or justification, while in others methodological decisions are expected to be clearly explained and justified. Such construal may also reflect the student apprentice role and the extent to which students feel they should explain and justify what they are doing to demonstrate for assessment puposes that they understand the disciplinary expectations.

We pay particular attention to ten features deemed to be characteristic of elaborated text in published research. The first nine are from Swales (2004: 220), while the tenth is lexical density, which Bloor (1999: 97) found to be a clear indicator, and more so than sentence length in words. It should be noted, however, that when these measures are calculated electronically, chemical formulae and acronyms are treated as short words (hence easy), although 'one formula may represent a complex nominal group incorporating long and specialist words' (Bloor, 1999: 98). Elaborated or slow text would:

1  include background knowledge
2  include subsections
3  use descriptions rather than citations to indicate the various aspects of methodology adopted
4  have all clauses with one finite verb
5  provide definitions, examples and illustrations
6  include justifications and rationales of the procedures adopted, sometimes placed in the marked subject position via a purpose clause
7  contain a number of *how* statements
8  contain one or more volitional verbs, such as in *we decided to focus on...*
9  tend to have a wide range of linking phrases (logical, temporal, spatial)
10  have relatively low lexical density

Starting with point (8) which focuses most directly on specific linguistic features, the results of a search for the lemma *decide* in disciplines with more than ten Methodology Recounts and / or Research Reports are shown in Table 5.10.

This initial measure suggests that the language of Linguistics is more elaborate, and that of Chemistry and Meteorology more clipped. To the disciplines in Table 5.10 we can add Computer Science, which has 24 instances of *decide* (tokens) across four of the five Computer Science assignments, and Sociology with 10 instances across two of the three Sociology assignments. Thus, Computer

Table 5.10    Lemma *decide* across disciplines in Methodology
Recounts and Research Reports genre families

|  | N tokens | N* texts | Tokens per text |
|---|---|---|---|
| Linguistics | 27 | 13 | 2.1 |
| Economics | 14 | 17 | 0.8 |
| Physics | 11 | 25 | 0.4 |
| Engineering | 20 | 87 | 0.2 |
| Psychology | 4 | 22 | 0.2 |
| Food Sciences | 7 | 62 | 0.1 |
| Biological Sciences | 7 | 60 | 0.1 |
| Chemistry | 1 | 52 | 0 |
| Meteorology | 0 | 13 | 0 |

*Disciplines with fewer than 10 texts omitted

Science and Sociology have an even higher number of tokens per text
(4.8 and 3.3) than Linguistics. The ranking of tokens per text bears
little resemblance to Swales' hypothesis and so warrants further
investigation. We shall start with Linguistics, Computer Science
and Sociology, then compare them to Psychology, Chemistry and
Meteorology.

In this Linguistics extract, which reports on a corpus linguistics
project, we see a number of linguistic features of elaborated text in
the Methods section, numbered here [1] to [9].

*1.0 Method*
*2.1 Samples used [2]*
*I decided to use two matches from each ... [+justification]*
2.2 Corpus construction
*In constructing the corpus I decided [8] to use AntConc as my concordancer
and Concapp to create wordlists. These are both freeware programs[3] and
although ... I felt they would be adequate.*
*2.3 Wordlist construction [2]*
*To determine how adjectives are used relating to the English football
team [6] I decided [8] to first build a wordlist using Concap for the
broadsheet and online news services samples as I felt this would allow me
an overview to evaluate my results [6] which would in turn give me the
opportunity to investigate any interesting features.[6] For clarification,[6]
I edited the results to show only adjectives. Both wordlists can be found in
section 5.1.*
*2.4 Concordances*
*With the wordlist in place, I then[9] decided [8] to divide the adjectives
into ...*

(Linguistics)

This extract generally has an elaborated feel. The writer does not simply say what she did, but she also describes the purpose, and provides reasons for doing so. Many of the nine features are evident: there are multiple subsections (2); no citations (3); all clauses have one finite verb (4); justifications and rationales are provided throughout, including initial purposes clauses (*to determine...*) (6); there is repeated use of 'I decided' (8); a narrative sequential organisation (*I **then** decided*) (9); and what might be seen as a rather loose justification (*as I felt...*) (6). Such explicit reliance on intuition combined with trial and error might be added as an additional feature of elaborated methodologies, and support for its use in corpus linguistics and other investigations of discourse is found in the literature.

On the one hand, there is growing acceptance that it is intuition – rather than database manipulation per se – which underpins successful exploration of a corpus (as it does any kind of discoursal material); on the other, in my own experience ... there seems to be a larger amount of trial-and-error involved than in more traditional approaches.

(Swales, 2004: 97)

In the Linguistics extract there is a sense that the methodology involves an individualised search for any 'interesting' findings. The narrative aspects of the text reflect the fact that the writer takes us through her decisions in chronological detail. This aspect of the elaborated methods section in Social Science texts is also found in published research articles in the Social Sciences (Bruce, 2008: 44). In the extract from Computer Science, in contrast, the use of 'decide' suggests that methodological decisions are presented as choices, for instance between software packages.

*3. Design*
*The design section discussed the equipment chosen for investigating pixel shape followed by some of the design ideas for the software and experiments.*
*3.1 Equipment*
*3.1.1 Graphics software*
*Currently there is no readily available hardware for displaying hexagonal or circular pixels. Therefore the best method to study pixel shapes is to simulate using computer graphics software. ...*
*Many software packages are available – some are easy to use, others provide the ability to control every aspect of an image or animation.*
*A graphics package will fall into one of two broad categories. The first type is the graphics software which is easy to use, ... However there is no high level control of what is being displayed. The second type of graphics package is fully customisable and ... However this type of package involves high level coding and ...*

*The main aim of the project is to control pixel shape. It is unlikely that an easy-to-use graphics package would provide such a high level of control. For this reason* it has been decided *[8]* to *investigate pixel shape using a graphics programming language.*
*3.1.2 Graphics Programming Language*

(Computer Science)

The Computer Science text goes on to evaluate programming languages and select a suitable language. While much of what is stated is presumably known to the tutor who assesses the assignment, it is important that decisions in the design are justified and made explicit. Unlike the methodological decisions in Corpus Linguistics which are based on intuition, the decisions here are based on text that shares features of Critique genres of software evaluation. These are used to explicitly justify the decisions made. Similar types of decision are found in Engineering.

In Sociology, methodological decisions can be imbued with discussion of ethics and references to the related literature.

*Methodology*
*In studying whether drug use within youth culture has really become normalised, I **decided** to perform a qualitative, semi-structured interview, with a … colleague … I was worried I may not get my subject to agree, especially as the respondent may want to be seen in a "favourable light".*[1]
*However, access was relatively easy to gain …*
*Nevertheless, …*
*Moreover, the illegality of the subject matter under discussion also brings about ethical questions. As a sociologist, I am responsible for the "social and psychological well-being of research participants".*[3] *I must protect the interests of my participant, and guard them from harm. Therefore it is very important I maintain his anonymity, and during this research I will be referring to him through a pseudonym; James. This concern for my research participant also led me to be as truthful and open to him as possible. I made James aware of his "right to refuse participation"*[4]*, informing him of his anonymity and also that this work would not be published. In addition, due to the overt nature of my research I avoided the "moral qualms, anxieties, and practical difficulties"*[5] *'covert' research has.*

(Sociology)

Here the student presents herself as a researcher, with specific ethical responsibilities which inform her methodological decisions. She demonstrates that her understandings are embedded in the literature through frequent citations, as indicated by numbered superscripts. Such references are not always included, particularly where knowledge about techniques is assumed, as in this example from Psychology, a notably less elaborated text.

*Data Analysis [2]*
*[6] In order to investigate whether self-esteem levels were lower and deviant eating behaviours were higher in first year university girls than a control group of non university girls, between subjects multivariate analysis of variance (MANOVA) and Pearson's correlation co-efficient were used to analyse data. [6] To check the assumptions of the MANOVA could be relied upon, a Mahalanobis distance identified one outlier, it was decided [8] to keep this in however [6] as one outlier is not going to effect the assumptions of the MANOVA. [6] To more fully investigate the effect integrating a new peer group may have on self-esteem levels, and therefore eating patterns, an independent samples t-test was carried out between the means for the experimental and control group for SERS. This time [9] however only the questions referring to "others" or "new friends" were included, 22 out of the original 40 questions. [6] This was to see whether self esteem levels relating to peers were significantly different between the two groups. One sample t-tests were also conducted [6] to investigate whether there was a significant difference between the experimental group and the normative values. A Pearson's product ...*

(Psychology)

The Psychology extract differs from the Linguistics and Sociology extracts in its impersonal stance (lack of first person mentions), and notably in its use of long pre-subject purpose clauses (in bold) in the first three sentences, followed by long nominal groups as grammatical subjects (underlined) which create high lexical density and a formal register. A third main difference reflects the certainty with which the tests are presented, without being explained or justified. The reader is expected to know this is an accepted test to perform in this study. In contrast to Swales' expectations of professional research articles, in our student assignments, Psychology seems to be towards the 'clipped' end of the continuum.

Swales had predicted that Chemistry, Physics and Biology would be more clipped. Here is an example of the methods section from a Chemistry lab report:

*Experimental*
*Four sets of boiling tubes were prepared as described below and placed in the thermostat to equilibrate at each temperature.*
Tube 1: *10 cm3 of 0.01 M phenol, 10 cm3 of the bromate/bromide solution (0.0833M Br⁻ and 0.0167 M BrO3), 4 drops of methyl red.*
Tube 2: *5 cm3 0.5 M $H_2SO_4$*
*When the solutions had reached the correct temperature, the contents of tube 1 was poured into tube 2 and shaken to mix. From when the solutions are mixed the time taken for the pink colour to disappear was recorded. The experiment was conducted at 5°C intervals between 20 and 70°C. The time taken for the pink colour to disappear was recorded.*

(Chemistry)

This is a relatively clipped text in that much knowledge is assumed, formulas are used, and there are sentences with multiple verbs (*were prepared and placed; was poured and shaken*). There are no definitions or examples; no justifications for methodological choices, and no volitional verbs. Unlike the preceding Psychology extract, there is no statement of purpose. The focus is on the techniques used. Here we get a sense of a methodology where experiments are conducted in order to find out what happens.

The one Chemistry example of *decided* brings to light a move in the results section that is unlikely to occur in professional research articles, namely apportioning responsibility.

*This is the chief source of error for this experiment, especially at higher temperatures where the reaction occurred very fast. In this experiment the same person decided the point at which the solution had turned colourless to minimise this source of error, however other groups may have had a different perception of when the solution was colourless.*

(Chemistry)

This error was not penalised, and indeed the awareness of the importance of certain decisions may have contributed to the top mark of distinction this assignment received.

If we look at the Physics examples, we see that, as in Linguistics, writers are not limited to one set method, but are allowed some room to act on their initiative, so that 'decisions' can be made.

*2- Experimental Details*
*2.1 General Points*
*[technical explanation with diagrams and theory of harmonic frequencies]*
*The harmonic frequencies were found in one of two ways depending on the particular investigation being carried out.*
*The first method, used for all investigations, was to slowly increase the oscillator output, noting the value at which the amplitude of the oscilloscope signal was a maximum whilst still remaining a pure sinusoidal wave. When using this method it was found that listening to the wire helped to locate this frequency, as the resonance of the wire at the harmonic frequencies, particularly when using the thin wire produced an audible hum. The y-divisions setting on the oscilloscope could be altered in order to make the trace appear larger, allowing the change in amplitude at the harmonic frequencies to be seen more clearly. If the trace was not a pure sinusoid, indicating a superposition of more than one harmonic frequency, then the amplitude of the oscillator output frequency was varied or the frequency itself was changed slightly in order to give the purely sinusoidal signal sought. The frequency was then evaluated using the frequency meter, with the range set so as to give the maximum possible precision of reading whilst still allowing readings to be readily taken.*

*Whilst testing the equipment* it was decided *to take the frequency readings using the frequency meter rather than the oscilloscope when using this method,* as it was felt that *the frequency meter would be more accurate. Using the oscilloscope required the estimation of the number of scale division that were equal to one wavelength of the trace, and* it was felt that *this would be inaccurate owing to the inherent thickness of the trace signal. Hence all values for the harmonic frequencies were recorded from the frequency meter.*
*The second method for finding the harmonic frequencies, used for the first investigation only, involved ...*

(Physics)

When the methodology sections are extracted it is particularly noticeable how many passives are used, though human agents are implicit – for example, *it was felt that, was evaluated.* This predominance of passives is perhaps what led a physics lecturer to comment that:

*Students find the style of scientific writing difficult. As a rule of thumb they say: if the MS/Word grammar checker "gives them all sorts of warnings, they know they're about right!"*

(Physics lecturer)

We shall conclude this snapshot of the language of methods by looking at two examples from Meteorology, where *decide* did not occur.

*3. Experimental Method*
*The platinum film resistance thermometer (PFT) and thermistor thermometer were immersed in a thermostatically controlled water bath. A precision platinum resistance thermometer was also immersed in the bath, and was used to record the 'actual' temperature of the water, required for calibrating the other two thermometers.*
*The PFT and thermistor thermometer were each connected to individual multi-meters, which displayed the resistance of the respective instruments. The resolutions of the multi-meters differed, with the meter connected to the platinum film thermometer having a resolution of 0.001 $\Omega$, and the meter connected to the thermistor thermometer having a resolution of 1 $\Omega$.*
*The temperature of the water bath was raised from 0°C to 50°C in approximately 5°C intervals. Resistance was recorded for the PFT and thermistor thermometer when the precision thermometer indicated that the water temperature was relatively stable (i.e. varying by only approximately 0.01°C $s^{-1}$). Resistance readings were taken simultaneously for both thermometers so as to avoid errors arising from differing lag characteristics.*

(Meteorology)

The lack of decisions explained here reflects the genre. This is a highly controlled lab experiment set by a tutor. Nevertheless, the methodology is made quite explicit.

In contrast, the following report on a Meteorology field weekend entirely assumes the methodology, and proceeds from aims to analysis with no methods section. In this example the analysis shows that although there are data collection methods (e.g., 'instruments' on the walk), how they work and how they are used is assumed rather than explained:

> 2. *Aims*
> *This report aims to both describe and explain the observed weather during the period 27th to 29th October 2006. It should link together observations from different sources to provide a coherent picture of the weather's evolution during this time.*
> 3. *Analysis ...*
> 3.1. *General situation and surface observations*
> ......
> *At approximately 1400UTC, a weak warm front passed over the region, bringing in exceptionally warm moist air (figure 2). As the air was already warm and moist, the front was too weak to cause precipitation. However, the relative humidity increased enough for fog to be recorded on one of the instrumented walks (Table 1, AB). The walk data also shows a drop in temperature and a peak in the wind speed at 1400UTC. However, geographical location needs to be taken into account, the 1400UT measurement was made on an exposed ridge at the highest elevation during the walk whilst the 1300UTC and 1500UTC measurements were made in more sheltered locations. Therefore it is more likely that local effects caused the readings rather than mesoscale events.*
>
> (Meteorology)

In this section we have seen, as Swales predicted, considerable variation in the way research methods are written. Our examples were elicited through a search for the lemma *decide*, which in some cases clustered with other features of elaborated methodologies as identified by Swales and by Bloor. The extracts provide insights into the nature of the methodologies: whereas students in Corpus Linguistics are looking for 'interesting' features of texts, in Psychology the focus is on judgements of human behaviour; in Chemistry the focus is on quantification and experimentation, and in Meteorology the focus is on the measurement of natural phenomena.

The differences observed may be attributed to the nature of the various projects (for example, a corpus linguistics versus an experimental linguistics study); to the section of the methodology (for example, a focus on materials selections or ethics) and to the genre (for example, lab report versus field report). For this reason it is important not to assume that all Linguistics methodologies, for instance, are elaborated, or that all Meteorology methodologies are clipped. Our investigation does show, however, much greater variety across disciplines than might originally have been anticipated.

## 5.5 Conclusion

This chapter has focused on genres that highlight the development of research skills, and has shown how assignments that require a literature review or the writing up of a set piece of empirical work are often precursors to assignments such as the undergraduate dissertation that give students the opportunity to conduct original research. Research Report genres include those which arise from a student-initiated question or issue, to explore with reference to relevant published literature, and also those which may be answered through empirical research, and which are intended to contribute to knowledge in the discipline. Seven main Literature Survey genres have been described, and their roles in preparing students and supervisors for the dissertation have been explained. Methodology Recounts have been differentiated from Research Projects according to their focus on the methodology at the expense of the literature review. We have seen how the methodologies of Methodology Recounts and Research Reports vary considerably across disciplines not only in terms of the sections and nature of inquiry, but also in terms of the more elaborated or clipped nature of the language. Some of our examples from Linguistics and Sociology were very elaborated; some of our examples from Computer Science and Physics were moderately elaborated, and some of our examples from Meteorology and Chemistry were relatively clipped.

In addition to Literature Reviews and Methodology Recounts, genres from other families can also play a role in preparation for a final year project. Skills developed through writing Explanation and Critique genres may be evident in the literature review and theory sections of project reports, while the ability to develop an argument may be evident throughout, and particularly in the discussion sections. In addition to all these possible opportunities to prepare for a major project, many courses also set a proposal assignment so that students can spell out exactly what their projects intend to achieve, and how their aims will be realised, before work on the project begins. Not all proposals are of an academic nature, however, as we shall see in Chapter 6 which explores those genres preparing students for specific professional practices.

## Notes

1. These statistics were calculated for the 61 Research Reports, 32 Simple Literature Surveys, and 345 Simple and mono-genre (e.g., MR + MR) compound Methodology Recount assignments.

## References

Alsop, S., & Nesi, H. (2009). Issues in the development of the British Academic Written English (BAWE) corpus, *Corpora*, 4(1), 71–84.

Basturkman, H. (2009). Commenting on results in published research articles and masters dissertations in language teaching. *Journal of English for Academic Purposes*, 8, 241–51.

Bizup, J. (2008). BEAM: A rhetorical vocabulary for teaching research-based writing. *Rhetoric Review*, 27(1), 72–86.

Bloor, M. (1999). Variation in the methods sections of research articles across disciplines: The case of fast and slow text. In P. Thompson (Ed.), *Issues in EAP writing research and instruction*, CALS: The University of Reading, 84–106.

Bruce, I. (2008). Cognitive genre structures in Methods sections of research articles: A corpus study. *Journal of English for Academic Purposes*, 7, 38–54.

Bunton, D. (2005). The structure of PhD conclusion chapters. *Journal of English for Academic Purpose*, 4(3), 207–24.

Flowerdew, J., & Forest, R. (2009). Schematic structure and lexico-grammatical realization in corpus-based genre analysis: The case of *Research* in the PhD Literature Review. In M. Charles, S. Hunston, & D. Pecorari (Eds.), *Academic writing: At the interface of corpus and discourse*, London: Continuum, 15–36.

Gardner, S. (2008). Mapping ideational meaning in a corpus of student writing. In C. Jones & E. Ventola (Eds.), *New developments in the study of ideational meaning: From language to multimodality*. In R. Fawcett (Ed.), *Functional Linguistics*. London: Equinox Publishing, 169–88.

Gardner, S., & Holmes, J. (2009). 'Can I use headings in my essay' Section headings, macrostructures and genre families in the BAWE corpus of student writing. In M. Charles, S. Hunston, & D. Pecorari (Eds.), *Academic writing: At the interface of corpus and discourse*, London: Continuum, 251–71.

Hoey, M. (1991). *Patterns of lexis in text*. Oxford: Oxford University Press.

Hyland, K. (2005). *Metadiscourse*. London: Continuum.

Kanoksilapatham, B. (2005). Rhetorical structure of biochemisty research articles. *English for Specific Purposes*, 24(3), 269–92.

Kwan, B.B.C. (2006). The schematic structure of literature reviews in doctoral theses of applied linguistics. *English for Specific Purposes*, 25(1), 30–55.

Lewin, B.A., Fine, J., & Young, L. (2001). *Expository discourse: A genre-based approach to social science research texts*. London: Continuum.

Lim, J.M. (2006). Method sections of management research articles: A pedagogically motivated qualitative study. *English for Specific Purposes*, 25(3), 282–309.

Loi, C.K. (2010). Research article introductions in Chinese and English: A comparative genre-based study. *Journal of English for Academic Purposes*, 9(4), 267–79.

Lores, R. (2004). On RA abstracts: From rhetorical structure to thematic organization. *English for Specific Purposes* 23(3), 280–302.

Peacock, M. (2002). Communicative moves in the discussion section of research articles. *System*, 30(4), 479–97.

QAA (The Quality Assurance Agency for Higher Education) (August 2008). *The framework for higher education qualifications in England, Wales and Northern Ireland*. Mansfield: QAA.

Samraj, B. (2008). A discourse analysis of masters theses across disciplines with a focus on introductions. *Journal of English for Academic Purposes*, 7(1), 55–67.

Swales, J.M. (1990). *Genre analysis. English in academic and research settings*. Cambridge: Cambridge University Press.

Swales, J.M. (2004). *Research genres: Exploration and applications*. Cambridge: Cambridge University Press.

Tribble, C. (2009). Writing academic English; A survey review of current published resources. *ELT Journal*, 63(4), 400–17.

Warschauer, M. (2002). Networking into academic discourse. *Journal of English for Academic Purposes*, 1(1), 45–58.

Williams, P. (1999). Results sections of medical research articles: Analysis of rhetorical categories for pedagogical purposes. *English for Specific Purposes*, 18, 347–66.

# 6 Preparing for professional practice

A graduate will have 'qualities and transferable skills necessary for employment requiring: the exercise of initiative and personal responsibility; decision-making in complex and unpredictable contexts; and the learning ability needed to undertake appropriate further training of a professional or equivalent nature.'

(QAA, 2001: Annex 1)

The framework for higher education qualifications in England, Wales and Northern Ireland states that university students must develop skills that are of value to employers, including the ability to act on their own initiative and make decisions. These requirements are relevant to all disciplines, and are particularly important in disciplines where the degree qualification is recognised by a professional body. This chapter will look at assignments that help students develop decision-making skills, and start to write more like professionals in their chosen fields. These assignments mostly belong in the Problem Question, Proposal, Design Specification and Case Study genre families. Following Spafford et al. (2006) we will refer to them as 'apprenticeship genres'.

## 6.1 The requirements of professional bodies

Many British university programmes are eligible for accreditation by what is known as a Professional, Statutory and Regulatory Body (PSRB). In some disciplines, such as Medicine, accreditation is essential, whereas in others, such as the Engineering disciplines, it can confer partial exemption from professional qualifications. Eligible departments generally regard accreditation as a worthwhile activity because it provides a means of quality assurance and enhances the employability of their graduates, for example by improving their prospects of practising their profession overseas.

Because of the benefits of accreditation, many university departments develop their programmes and curricula in close collaboration with PSRB members, although there may be some concern amongst lecturers about the need to balance the PSRB focus on practical professional skills against the academic requirements of a university education (LTS, 2007). PSRBs issue guidelines regarding course content, with an emphasis on the student's future working life outside the university. The academic accreditation guidelines developed by the Institution of Mechanical Engineers (2009), for example, emphasise the need to 'establish the relevance of engineering to real world problems', and the Chartered Institute for IT, or BCS (2007), requires that their accredited programmes should be 'influenced by research, industry and market requirements'.

When designing their assignment tasks, departments are also likely to bear in mind the role of PSRBs in post-experience career progression. For example, some of the accreditation schemes for practising solicitors organised by the Law Society require the submission of case reports. Law departments can teach future solicitors how to write these while they are still at university, before they qualify.

## 6.2 Genre families preparing for professional practice

Genres which prepare for professional practice discuss and seek solutions to practical problems. In some assignments students simply refer to a situation identified and described in the assignment task, in others they conduct some research to identify a problem or lacuna for themselves. Many of these genres involve a certain amount of simulation, the student may play the role of the professional, or report on their own workplace experience, writing as if addressing a client or a professional colleague. The arguments supporting the solutions the students propose thus reflect their understanding of the professional values of their field, for example usefulness, marketability, economy or aesthetic worth.

The simulated nature of these genres can create additional problems for students, however, because the motives and roles of writers of academic discourse differ from those of writers of workplace discourse, as Dannels (2000: 21) and Wardle (2009: 769) note. The 'customer' or 'colleague' in student simulations, for example, is really the person who will mark the assignment, and to please this person student writers often need to explain and justify the methodology they have chosen, provide evidence of their theoretical understanding, and distinguish between accepted facts and their own interpretation and opinion. At the same time they need to decide whether they can afford to neglect many of the complex requirements of real-world colleagues and clients. In professional contexts, on the other hand, details considered necessary in the academy are often deemed superfluous (Parks, 2001: 417; Yeung, 2007: 163), but the writer has to recommend a course of action to a range of different readers with different concerns and priorities (Dannels, 2000). In the workplace the professional writer's expertise will usually be assumed, and in any case the underlying theoretical knowledge will probably be shared by professional colleagues, and may be of little interest to other co-workers or clients who are focusing on the practical outcome (Yeung, 2007). In extreme cases, a professional genre demanded by the academy as an assignment task may not be required in the workplace at all. In a study by Parks (2001), for example, the francophone Canadian nursing students learned to produce patient care reports during their internships but reported that the regular staff nurses in the same hospitals never produced them, perhaps because they lacked the time. The same disjunct can be observed in the field of education, where trainee teachers produce full lesson plans, but many practising teachers do so only rarely. As Artemeva (2007, 2008) points out, each university writing task is perceived by the student as a goal in itself, requiring full and conscious attention. In professional life these thought processes become more automatic, and 'activities' and 'actions' become 'operations', in Leont'ev's terms (1981).

Genres which prepare for professional practice thus seem to be positioned at the crossroads, preparing students for both an academic future as writers of research, and a professional future as writers in the workplace. Genres which incorporate both academic and professional demands can be considered as 'boundary objects' (Popham, 2005; Star and Griesemer, 1989), acting as an interface between different communities of practice and fulfilling different purposes for different people. Maclean (2010: 180), for example, describes the tensions inherent in Level 1 Law students' attempts to reconcile the academic and professional communities; such students have to choose between a 'student' voice 'with an impartial, analytical, synoptic focus on interpretation of past events in terms of general categories', and a 'practitioner' voice 'with a partial, dynamic and specific focus on future action in a particular case'. As boundary objects, the broad range of apprenticeship genres in the BAWE corpus are characterised by such tensions.

## 6.3  Apprenticeship genres: Commonalities across disciplines

Our apprenticeship genres belong within the 'problem-solving' metagenre in terms of Carter's classification system (2007). According to Carter, problem solving is an activity which is shared by a range of disciplines but which manifests itself in different ways according to disciplinary preference. Carter claims that the emphasis in disciplines such as Agriculture is on solving problems by gathering data from sources, in disciplines such as Engineering on solving problems by designing a product, and in Science and Mathematics disciplines on solving problems by applying specialised knowledge.

The genres we have categorised as apprenticeship genres in the BAWE corpus belong within the Case Study, Design Specification, Problem Question and Proposal genre families, which seem to fit quite neatly into this system, although Carter does not identify the Proposal as a discipline-specific way of solving problems, perhaps because proposals tend to underlie all the problem-solving genres, as Bean (2011) suggests.

When categorising the apprenticeship genres, it is also useful to take into account the status of the ostensible reader and the problem to be solved. If we draw a cline from hypothetical to real, as in Figure 6.1, we find Problem Questions at the hypothetical end, invariably dealing with invented scenarios which lack extraneous circumstantial detail, and we find Case Studies at the other end of the scale, invariably dealing with real-life cases, and requiring the writer to take large amounts of contextual data into account. One of our business lecturer informants explained that there had been a change in the nature of tasks set in his department. Traditionally, assignments had been 'focused, technical, quantitative and intended to probe students' understanding and interpretative ability'. These sound like Problem Questions or Essays. More recently, with an eye to the development of transferable skills, students had been asked to 'confront and analyse complex, ill-structured problems'. These are Case Studies. Somewhere in the middle of this continuum we find Proposals and Design Specifications, which tend to address an authentic problem, but only in terms of one aspect, disregarding any messy peripheral issues. Design Specifications create an appropriate model, for example, but not a plan of how it should be put into practice. Proposals provide a plan, but do not test procedures.

Similarly we can distinguish between those genres which undisguisedly address the academic reader, and those which ostensibly offer advice to a client. Here the situation is more complex, as some Case

Problem Questions   ⇒   Proposals / Design Specifications   ⇒   Case Studies
   hypothetical                                                    real

Figure 6.1   The cline from hypothetical to real

Table 6.1   Distribution by Disciplinary Group

|  | Arts and Humanities | Life Sciences | Physical Sciences | Social Sciences | Total |
|---|---|---|---|---|---|
| Case Study | 0 | 91 | 37 | 66 | 194 |
| Design Specification | 1 | 2 | 87 | 2 | 93 |
| Problem Question | 0 | 2 | 6 | 32 | 40 |
| Proposal | 2 | 26 | 19 | 29 | 76 |
| Total | 3 | 121 | 149 | 129 | 403 |

Studies and Design Specifications simulate reports to an end-user, whereas others do not. As mentioned previously, writers of apprenticeship genres face the challenging task of establishing an appropriate relationship with the hypothetical and the real reader.

Table 6.1 shows the distribution of apprenticeship genres across the disciplinary groupings in the BAWE corpus. Case Studies are particularly common in the Life Sciences and the Social Sciences, reflecting their widespread use in the health and business disciplines. Design Specifications are common in the Physical Sciences because of the important role they play in Computer Science and Engineering, but are rare in other disciplinary groupings. Problem Questions are a particular feature of legal studies, and Proposals are produced across a range of disciplines, often in relation to the design and marketing of a product or service.

This spread of apprenticeship genres is wider than that suggested by Carter for the problem-solving meta-genre, and includes examples from disciplines where problem solving is not the main focus of activity. This may be explained by the fact that academics sometimes introduce new tasks which are not typical of their disciplines, for the sake of variety, or in response to the pressure to innovate (Nesi and Gardner, 2006: 109). Apprenticeship genres are not well represented in the Arts and Humanities component of the BAWE corpus, however, where PSRB accreditation is rare.

Bean (2011) discusses Carter's classification system in connection with Bizup's system for categorising types of source material (2008). Apprenticeship genres seem to be characterised by their use of two categories of material: in Bizup's terms these are 'Exhibit' or 'Evidence' sources such as data, field observations, images, cultural artefacts and natural phenomena, and 'Method' or 'Theory' sources, for example references to a standard procedure or paradigm.

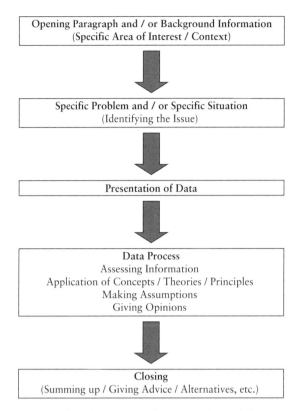

Figure 6.2    Hierarchical pattern of cases (adapted from Lung, 2008)

Most of the apprenticeship genres are broadly constructed as situation–problem–solution–evaluation texts (Hoey, 1983). The generic model for the discourse structure of cases proposed by Lung (2008: 429) can be applied to all the apprenticeship genre families, although it does not explicitly include the evaluation stage described by Hoey, which many of the BAWE assignments include. Lung's model is reproduced in Figure 6.2.

## 6.4  The Problem Question genre family

We will start with the Problem Question genres because they are the most pedagogical of all the apprenticeship genres, with no exact counterparts in the world of work or in the world of academic research. Although the given problem or scenario may resemble or be based on a real professional case, the task is designed solely to provide practice in applying the theory and methods of the discipline. Whereas Case

Studies often give scope for interpretations of complex human situations, and Design Specifications and Proposals require some sort of creative response, Problem Questions require a more convergent approach. However, as in all student assignments, the main focus is on the process of arriving at the conclusion rather than the conclusion itself, even if the application of the theory or method leads to a single correct solution. In Law Problem Questions, for example, this process will be 'how judges develop principles, and how they apply principles to facts' rather than what is decided (Lung, 2008: 436).

Like Exercises (Chapter 3), Problem Questions are particularly common as an examination genre. This is because they offer candidates the opportunity to demonstrate knowledge without requiring that they say something original (which might be an unfair demand under examination time constraints), and because Problem Question answers can usually be assessed objectively, with reference to the undisputed 'hard facts' of the discipline.

Most Problem Questions in the BAWE corpus are from the first two years of academic study, reflecting their essentially pedagogical nature. More than half are from the Law department or from law modules in other disciplines ('Legal and ethical issues in mental health nursing'; 'Introduction to business law'). As is well known, the Problem Question is 'the standard academic legal assignment' (Bruce, 2002: 322) and 'by far the most common type of examination in law school' (Candlin et. al., 2002: 305). However, although the answer to the legal Problem Question has its own unique procedure, examples from other fields are comparable to some extent.

## Problem Questions in Law

In the English and US legal systems, precedents set by previously decided cases are a major source of law. Bruce (2002: 329) explains that the law of precedent depends on finding an analogy between the facts of a new case and those of a past case 'whose ruling has come to represent the current state of legal interpretation in a specific domain.' Law students have to be trained to apply precedents to the facts of new cases, and it is for this reason that they work on cases of varying complexity presented in the form of Problem Questions. The general skills acquired through this procedure are 'key professional skills that lawyers will apply throughout their careers' (Bruce, 2002: 322).

Table 6.2 shows the structure of official law reports, based on analyses by Bhatia (1993), Badger (2003) and Lung (2008). These are the 'Theory' sources (Bizup, 2008) that Law students draw on when writing their Problem Question answers.

Table 6.2   The structure of law reports

|  | Main stages | Comments |
|---|---|---|
| 1. | identifying the case | a standard and formulaic title, e.g. *X vs. Y* |
| 2. | establishing the facts of the case | detailed information about the time, place and people involved |
| 3. | arguing the case | |
| 3.1 | history of the case | |
| 3.2 | presenting arguments | |
| 3.3 | deriving *ratio decidendi* | the legal principle that is applicable to the case |
| 4. | pronouncing judgements | |

The legal Problem Question usually requires students to consider the problem from the perspective of a defendant advising parties on the extent of their liability, or from the perspective of a plaintiff advising them of their chances of success in their legal action. The production of the Problem Question answer involves an IPCAC sequence (Bruce, 2002) where students first have to identify the relevant *issues, principles and cases* to cite in their answer, paying attention to any facts that lie open to argument, and then *apply* principles and precedent cases to the problem and draw their own *conclusion*. Conclusions may be positive (meaning that success is likely), or negative (meaning that success is unlikely). Bruce discusses whether it is better for students to present their argument first and draw a conclusion at the end, or to begin with the conclusion and proceed to justify it through factual argument. Howe (1990) recommends fronting the conclusion, but Bruce (2002) believes that this may give the false impression that the conclusion is invariably straightforward. He suggests that it may be better to delay the conclusion but signal the complexity of more problematic arguments in advance.

A further issue concerns the balancing of arguments for and against the client's case. Bruce (2002: 334) argues that facts which support the opposition must be included in the Problem Question answer, as they are likely to be used by the opposition to support their case. He advises writers to place counter-evidence first, as a concession, to be outweighed by the main point that the student wants to make.

A basic template for an answer to a legal Problem Question, using the IRAC structure (Issue, Rule, Analysis and Conclusion; Candlin et al., 2002: 303), is provided in Table 6.3. The analysis section is the most important part of the answer because it demonstrates

Table 6.3    Answer structure for a legal problem question

| Stage | | Comment |
|---|---|---|
| 1 | Issue | the facts and circumstances provided in the problem question |
| 2 | Rule | identification of the applicable point of law |
| 3 | Analysis | applications of the law likely to be raised by the opposition (concessions) |
| 4 | | applications of the law that are likely to be useful to the client (the writer's main arguments) |
| 5 | Conclusion | whether the client's case is likely to succeed or fail |

that the writer can apply the law to a specific set of circumstances; Stages 3 and 4 may be reiterated according to the complexity of the case.

We found that the hypothetical scenarios in legal Problem Question prompts included many small details, as in the example below. These details had been included intentionally and were in fact highly relevant, because any slight change of fact could change the issues of a case and thus raise a different rule of law.

*Laura, a 19-year-old law student, went to the Rotten Row Bus Station to catch a coach home to Sweet Valley. She had made this journey from time to time in the past. Above the ticket-office window of the Slowe and Wheezy Bus Company was a sign which stated that all tickets were issued subject to conditions displayed inside the coaches...*

(Problem Question prompt, Level 2)

This scenario goes on to describe how the driver accidentally broke Laura's mobile phone, and how the company refuses to accept liability. The student is instructed to advise Laura, stating the effects of relevant case law and statutes.

Three 2,000-word assignments in the corpus responded to this scenario. None of them presented their conclusions first, and all of them followed the pattern outlined in Table 6.4. Numerous precedent cases were used to support the arguments at each stage.

According to Finch and Fafinski (2007), Problem Questions should be broken down in this way into a series of points which are each discussed in turn. Other Problem Question answers in the corpus follow the same sort of structure, although questions do not always require the writer to represent a client, as in Tables 6.3 and 6.4, and in some cases reasoned analysis of the issues of the case in relation to relevant precedents and Acts is all that seems to be required.

Table 6.4    The structure of a Problem Question answer

| Section | Content | Stage (see Table 6.3) |
|---|---|---|
| Introduction | identifies the relevant field of contract law and the applicable statute law. | **Rule** |
| Incorporation | identifies the issue of <u>whether the contract incorporates an exclusion clause,</u> and discusses arguments that might be put forward by both sides. | **Issue** |
| Notice<br>Timing | discusses <u>whether</u> and <u>when</u> Laura might have <u>noticed the exclusion clause,</u> and evaluates the strength of arguments on both sides | **Analysis** |
| Incorporation | evaluates the strength of a possible defence argument that <u>Laura had had previous dealings with the company, and therefore knew about the clause</u> | |
| UCTA | Identifies a relevant <u>Act</u> and evaluates its usefulness | |
| 1999 regulations | identifies relevant <u>regulations</u> and evaluates their usefulness | |
| Conclusion | identifies <u>three valid arguments in favour of Laura's cause,</u> each one a fall-back if the previous argument fails | **Conclusion** |

The following examples show how students refer to participants but do not address them directly.

*In this case, **Albert could claim against the company** but since the company has gone into liquidation, the claim would be dismissed.*
(Introduction to Business Law)

*As a last resort, if all domestic avenues fail, **James can take recourse to the Human Rights Act 1998.***
(General Principles of Constitutional and Administrative Law)

***Laura must argue the EC is unreasonable** under either act.*
(Commercial and Consumer Contracting)

There are two cases of *I submit that* and *I suggest that*, but generally the writers do not identify themselves individually as an authority. Students rarely use the structure *I believe / feel / think that*, and instead favour the anticipatory *it* structure to project their own judgements about probability, as in the following examples. This gives the impression of greater objectivity, and reflects the logical process of case analysis in the manner favoured by the academy (Schleppegrell, 2004: 183).

*In refusing to consider the medical report, **it is arguable that** X was denied a fair hearing.*

> (General Principles of Constitutional and Administrative Law)

*... **it seems clear that** in punching Delia, Felicity commits an assault which satisfies the requirement that the action be 'unlawful'.*

> (Criminal Law)

***It is improbable that** the court would order ABC College to alter its drug-testing policy...*

> (General Principles of Constitutional and Administrative Law)

***It is unlikely that** Slowe and Wheezy could counter this argument very successfully...*

> (Commercial and Consumer Contracting)

## Problem Questions in other disciplines

Non-legal Problem Questions are sometimes used in Business and in Hospitality, Leisure and Tourism Management (HLTM) to provide simpler alternatives to Case Studies of real businesses, and enable the student to concentrate on a single issue, such as poor communication between departments, sales performance or hotel room bookings, without the distractions of a wealth of additional authentic data. Discipline-specific standard models of analysis are applied to the situation described in the scenario.

Legal Problem Questions in departments other than Law have much in common with Problem Questions in Law. Legal Problem Questions in Business, for example, examine hypothetical scenarios, discuss cases and reach conclusions with reference to precedents, but are shorter than those of Law students, and do not consider legal issues in the same degree of detail. A Health assignment for the module 'Legal and ethical issues in mental health nursing' also responds to a scenario, requiring the student to discuss the issues surrounding a decision to compulsorily admit someone to hospital under the Mental Health Act. However, the student evinces some uncertainty about the unfamiliar genre; he calls the assignment a Case Study, does not treat the problem as hypothetical, and seems unhappy with the fact that he does not know the patient:

*The client is not someone that I have nursed and so any hypothesis or conclusions which I have reached during this assignment are based on the limited information that I have about the client and the application of my*

*knowledge and reading around the subject of Mental Health law and ethics.
… I have presumed that, as is the accepted practice when writing a case
study, John is not the client's real name but has been changed to protect his
identity.*

(Health)

Law students are trained to isolate issues in the scenario that are perti-
nent to legal judgements, but, in Nursing, the more holistic approach
to patients' needs seems to be at odds with this approach. The student
discusses the case in terms of the Mental Health Act but does not
draw on precedents, instead much of the discussion relates to the
personal needs of the patient:

*It is essential that we try to understand the values that an individual holds
and try to accommodate these into the plan of care. As professionals, we
would not want John to feel he was being bullied into a hospital admission
and become more agitated – there are ways of explaining a situation to a
client without being threatening and this must be attempted even if one
thinks that the client is too ill to comprehend what is going on.*

(Health)

This assignment weighs up arguments in the same way as a Problem
Question in Law, and demonstrates awareness of the issues surrounding involuntary treatment, but it is written from the perspective of
someone who must justify their own professional behaviour in legal
and ethical terms, rather than from the perspective of someone who
must represent their client in court.

## 6.5  The Proposal genre family

Like other apprenticeship genres, Proposals 'define a problem,
establish parameters for a solution to the problem, generate possible solutions, and identify and justify a recommended solution to the
problem' (Carter, 2007: 396). However, whereas Problem Questions
converge on the best answer to a problem or dispute, Case Studies
identify and define problems and recommend future courses of action,
and Design Specifications create and evaluate an original solution,
Proposals focus on the planning stage of problem solving. This stage
occurs both before a solution is prepared and after a solution is evaluated, so a full length project might contain elements of various genre
families, with Proposals on either side of the Design Specification,
which in turn might embed an Explanation to identify and define the
problem, a description of the creation of the solution (which may
be likened to a Methodology Recount), and a Critique to evaluate
the solution. A full-length project might even contain a Narrative

Recount to reflect on the personal development aspects of the whole process (see Chapter 7).

In practice, these stages tend to become separated one from the other in academic assignments, and different problem-solving disciplines tend to favour different types of problem-solving genre. The Proposal genre family spreads across a fairly wide range of disciplines, as shown in Table 6.5, because those disciplines which do not conventionally prepare students for professional practice also use this genre family, but as a means of planning academic research rather than workplace strategy.

Some Proposals are plans for activities which can be completed within the duration of the writer's degree programme. Those which are most realistic – in the sense that they are most likely to be achieved by the writers who propose them – are Proposals for small pieces of research, such as Computer Science projects, or Proposals produced as part of Research Methods modules or in the therapeutic disciplines.

In many cases, however, it appears that the Proposal genre family is chosen because it offers students the opportunity to simulate the planning of an activity that they are not yet ready to perform in

Table 6.5    Distribution of Proposals by discipline and level

| Discipline | Level 1 | Level 2 | Level 3 | Level 4 |
|---|---|---|---|---|
| Agriculture | | 1 | | 5 |
| Anthropology | | | | 3 |
| Architecture | | | 1 | |
| Biological Sciences | | | | 3 |
| Business | | 1 | 1 | |
| Classics | | | | 1 |
| Computer Science | 1 | 1 | 3 | 1 |
| Engineering | 1 | 4 | | 5 |
| English | 1 | | | |
| Food Science | | | 3 | |
| Health | 3 | 10 | | |
| HLTM | 1 | 1 | 3 | 7 |
| Law | | | | 3 |
| Mathematics | | | | 1 |
| Physics | 1 | | | |
| Psychology | | | | 1 |
| Publishing | 2 | 1 | | 4 |
| Sociology | | | | 2 |

practice. Thus, a Masters student in the Biological Sciences writes a proposal asking for £1,600,000 to fund a six-year project.

All the research proposals have a certain authenticity, despite the ambitious nature of some of the plans, because the assessors who read them and assess them are part of the discourse community for whom they are ostensibly intended. In the professionally oriented disciplines, on the other hand, tensions arise between workplace and academic requirements. Most plans for manufacturing strategies and business ventures are not addressed to an external organisation, which makes it easier for writers to demonstrate their theoretical knowledge and methodological expertise without disrupting the flow of the document. Only a few Proposals are written as if for clients, in the style of company reports. A plan for the restructuring of a business, for example, is addressed to the board of directors, and a business proposal is accompanied by a letter to a bank.

Student writers of research proposals may well develop into postgraduate academic researchers, and some students in the Business and Technology disciplines will, presumably, go on to produce real proposals of a similar nature in their professional lives. Not all Proposal assignments seem to have been set as a rehearsal for later academic or professional writing, however. In some cases a Proposal genre is used to view a disciplinary issue from a different perspective. Thus, for example, publishing students are asked to write in the guise of authors proposing strategies for marketing their own work. This presumably encourages them to reflect on authors' wants and needs, while at the same time offering opportunities for the generation of creative new marketing ideas. Law students are required to write Proposals for legal reform, presumably as an alternative to the more standard Critique of legislation. The same professional knowledge and critical understanding is required of both genre families, but the Proposal genre is more decisive, as it requires a recommendation for change.

The language of Proposals will be discussed in more detail in Section 6.9.

## 6.6  The Design Specification genre family

The design of products and systems is a key academic task in technical and scientific disciplines. In the UK, some Professional, Statutory and Regulatory Bodies (PSRBs) make specific requirements regarding graduates' design skills: the Chartered Institute for IT, for example, requires that graduates in Computer Science and related disciplines should have the ability 'to specify, design or construct computer-based systems' (BCS, 2007), and the Engineering Council requires that mechanical engineers should be able to 'solve a wide range of applications-based engineering problems developed through open-ended design, make and test exercises, design and investigative project work' (Institution of Mechanical Engineers, 2009: 8).

Design tasks necessitate a real or invented user of the product or system, but there is great variation in how fully the writer's role and the customer's identity are constructed. Dannels describes an extended Mechanical Engineering design sequence at an American university, where 'students worked in project teams to design, construct, test and implement an actual product for industry' (2000: 10). She found that the students had a more sophisticated concept of the customer than the one presented to them in their curricular materials; they were aware of the professional designer's need to please a variety of stakeholders in addition to the end user, for example sales teams, management teams, safety departments, manufacturers, contractors and government agencies. Nevertheless she found that they neglected the process of consultation with real customers because of their more urgent need as students to please their teachers and get good grades. When questioned about this, one student commented, 'What do you mean, customer? We design for the prof; it is that simple' (2000: 22).

Design Specifications in the BAWE corpus demonstrate and develop design skills, and may occasionally include additional workplace-oriented documents such as user's manuals, budgets and schedules, as described by Zhu (2004a: 121–2). However, unlike the assignments examined by Zhu, most do not describe the organisations the specifications are created for, or discuss business models. The case for future implementation of the product or system is not argued as persuasively as in Proposals, and in many cases is merely implied as the consequence of a successful design process.

Although accounts of constructing and testing the model are the two main stages in Design Specifications, this genre family has the fewest narrative features, scoring -4 on Biber's Dimension 2 (see Section 1.6 and Section 2.3). This is because the constructing and testing phases tend to establish a standard procedure which might be applied in future, during manufacturing for example, rather than recounting what the student did. The design process is usually described in terms of calculations, computer code and diagrams; these are 'fast' or 'clipped' texts, like those described in Chapter 5, and they assume that the reader has prior knowledge of the technical procedures involved.

## The structure of Design Specifications

All but five of the 91 Design Specifications in the BAWE corpus are from the Physical Sciences, produced for modules in the Computer Sciences and Engineering. Typically, an introductory section explains the purpose of the report and the design specifications, a central section describes the model and provides a series of calculations, often made using computer applications such as MatLab and SimuLink, and a final section reviews the procedures previously described and notes that the stated specifications have been met. This cycle may be reiterated in longer projects. Thus Design Specifications embed a kind of Methodology Recount (see Chapter 5), in that they report on work undertaken in a computer laboratory, and also have some similarity to Case Studies, in that they are concerned with a real-world issue, and propose practical solutions.

For example, three assignments in the BAWE corpus written for the same 'Sustainable heat and power' module are concerned with the design of a primary school sheltered play area. They all use the same project design software packages (PVSyst and RetScreen) and discuss the practical issue of project cost, but one calls itself a lab report while the other two call themselves case studies. We class them as Design Specifications because the application of design methods leads to a replicable solution to a specific design problem, relatively isolated from its social and economic context.

A typical table of contents for a Design Specification is reproduced in Figure 6.3.

In this assignment, the 'theory' section provides information about the purpose of the system and its basic design rather than referring to methodological or theoretical issues. This practical focus is also apparent from the bibliography, which references textbooks rather

```
Table of Contents

1. Introduction
2. Theory
3. System Design
     3.1 Mechanical system
     3.2 Sensing elements
     3.3 Output system
     3.4 Overall system
4. Analysis and Discussion
5. Conclusions
6. Bibliography
```

Figure 6.3   Table of contents for a system Design Specification (Level 2, Engineering)

than academic research papers, and lists commercial websites for the manufacturers of measuring instruments.

The 'system design' section gives specifications for the system, making great use of equations, formulae and diagrams. As with technical Explanations (Chapter 3), many equations and other formulae are included in the clause structure of the sentences, and much of the information contained in diagrams is duplicated in the surrounding text. For example, the sentences preceding a diagram (labelled Fig.5) in the following extract explain its structure and function:

*This sensor is a transformer which comprises a single primary winding and two identical secondary windings wound on a tubular ferromagnetic former, it is shown as Fig. 5. The primary winding is excited by an a.c voltage ein, which is normally in the region of 400 to 50 KHZ to 10 V rms. The two secondaries are connected in series opposition so that the output voltage eout is the difference of the voltages induced between secondary coil 1 and secondary coil 2. A ferromagnetic core or plunger moves inside the former, while in an actual transducer, the core, primary coil, and secondary coils share a common axis, as shown in Fig. 5. As the core moves up or down, the mutual inductance between the primary and secondaries is changed.*

(Engineering)

The 'system design' section of the assignment explains how the system 'is', and also how it 'should be', with an eye on future replicability. This can be seen in the following excerpt, where we have italicised the features Hyland (2004: 17) calls 'research-focus directives'. Hyland describes this type of directive as standard in students' descriptions of procedures in the hard sciences.

*To ensure that the stylus can accurately trace the surface irregularities within the range of traversing speeds, the stylus, stylus beam, and transducer elements should be of minimum mass. And the stylus beam must be rigid, the knife edge pivot friction should be minimal.*

(Engineering)

The subsequent 'analysis and discussion' section goes on to suggest improvements conditional on changes to the design. We have italicised the features that signal the conditional *if...(then)* text pattern:

*If an A/D converter and a PC are to be used as a part of the instrument system, which means the output will be a digital form, it will make the system much better, and people can easily to read from the output, even print out the result to do further research.*

(Engineering)

The conclusion confirms that the design specifications have been met, but does not relate this to a wider context as a Case Study would. As

Turner (2010) points out, engineers tend to concentrate on components, or small systems, rather than the large and complex systems that society consists of.

## Design Specifications and the workplace

According to the Computer Science lecturers we interviewed, students are expected to 'write documents as menus for the user', and present them in a way that would appeal to customers. However, although most Design Specifications are attractive documents with sufficient signposting to guide technically informed readers to key information, on the whole they do not aim to simulate workplace texts. In some, the practical application of design is not made explicit; in other cases, the writer veers between the requirements of the workplace and of the academy.

In the following example from an 'e-business' assignment in Computer Science, the imaginary professional reader and the real academic reader are addressed alternately, within the same document. The introduction explains to the academic reader that the report will be directed at the professional reader:

*This report aims to inform the client of the steps taken to translate the designs, ideas, and foremost, the requirements identified during earlier stages in the project, and demonstrate how these designs have been implemented through the use of Microsoft Active Server Pages, VBScript, and HTML technologies to deliver an interactive, web-based E-Commerce solution.*

(Computer Science)

However, the reference list that follows this introduction includes textbook sources which a client would be unlikely to require (*ASP in a Nutshell*, *ASP.NET for Dummies* etc.), and, after a formal section which presents customer requirements, the final 'comment' section reflects on the 'slow and painstaking process' the writer underwent in order to complete the project. Similarly. the writer of another Design Specification assignment mentions 'our company' initially, but later records 'tutor interactions' with the website he has designed.

Tension between the requirements of a real-world client and the academic marker is also apparent in one of the Design Specifications for a sheltered play area. This assignment styles itself as a 'governors' report', but it seems highly unlikely that school governors would be able to make sense of the complex mathematical modelling the report contains, or would be interested in the methodological discussion surrounding the strengths and weaknesses of the two software packages the student used.

The two non-scientific Design Specifications in the BAWE corpus are evidence of attempts to approach discipline-specific topics from a different angle, by simulating tasks that students might eventually have to perform in the workplace. A Design Specification for a Publishing module is written as a short, informal, company-internal workplace document explaining fictitious design decisions concerning website content. A Design Specification for an Archaeology module explains the process of designing a label for a museum exhibit. The label is described and evaluated in terms of service provider values: the writer discusses the extent to which it is accurate, useful, accessible and comprehensible to a layperson. Such tasks look like innovative attempts to prepare students for professional practice, as an alternative to the more standard Essay and Critique genres.

## 6.7  The Case Study genre family

Case Studies usually deal with real-life cases, and are less clear-cut than Problem Questions or Design Specifications, because they require writers to consider the social and / or economic context in which the problem occurs. The use of the Case Study as an assessed task is widespread in Business (Zhu, 2004a), and in Medicine and Health (Hoekje, 2007; Méndez-Cendón, 2009; Schryer and Spoel, 2005).

Zhu discusses two types of writing task commonly used in an American business school (2004a: 120). In 'case analysis tasks' students use information supplied by the lecturer to 'apply business concepts, theory, and knowledge to the analysis of business problems and business decision making processes'. These sound like Problem Questions or possibly Critiques. In 'business reports', on the other hand, students gather some company information themselves, using primary and / or secondary sources. These sound as if they would fall into our Case Study genre family.

Hoekje (2007) includes the writing of 'case reports' amongst the tasks required of medical students, pointing out that the format of these reports is highly structured and that 'sanctions against violating institutional forms are strong' (2007: 335). Hoekje also mentions audio-taping case presentations, an oral genre which Schryer and Spoel (2005) describe as a 'scheduled, structured event in which upper-level students convey to their faculty mentors their analysis of a patient case' (2005: 260). By presenting cases orally and then reporting on the presentation in writing, students prepare for professional life both as medical practitioners and as academic writers. Many of the case reports in the *New England Journal of Medicine*,

Table 6.6   Distribution of Case Studies by discipline and level

| Discipline | Level 1 | Level 2 | Level 3 | Level 4 | Total |
|---|---|---|---|---|---|
| Agriculture | 4 | 4 | 4 | | 12 |
| Business | 6 | 8 | 10 | 7 | 31 |
| Chemistry | | 1 | 1 | | 2 |
| Computer Science | | | 2 | | 2 |
| Economics | | | | 1 | 1 |
| Engineering | 10 | 2 | 7 | 13 | 32 |
| Food Sciences | | | 2 | | 2 |
| Health | 2 | 5 | 1 | | 8 |
| HLTM (Hospitality, Leisure & Tourism Management) | 4 | 6 | 8 | 9 | 27 |
| Law | | 1 | | | 1 |
| Medicine | | | | 69 | 69 |
| Publishing | | 3 | | | |
| Sociology | | | | 1 | 1 |

for example, include a record of discussion indicating that they were originally presented orally to hospital doctors.

In the BAWE corpus the Case Study genre family contains texts which analyse an exemplar in order to demonstrate or develop an understanding of professional practice. They always include recommendations or suggestions for future action. The distribution of Case Studies in the corpus is indicated in Table 6.6. They are spread fairly evenly across levels of study in Business, Engineering and HLTM; in Medicine all the contributors were enrolled on a graduate entry programme (at Level 4). In Medicine, 69 out of the 84 texts submitted to the corpus were Case Studies, the majority of the remaining assignments were Essays. In other disciplines the Case Study accounts for a smaller proportion of assignments; only 27 out of 98 texts in HLTM are Case Studies, for example, and only 31 out of 146 Business texts.

## Case Studies in business and management disciplines

Yeung (2007) provides a generic model for full-length professional business reports, shown in Table 6.7, which compares them to research articles and textbook models of business reports.

The table indicates that decision making is the main feature distinguishing professional business writing from academic business writing. As Yeung (2007: 162) points out, 'rather than looking for a

Table 6.7    Comparison of report structures (Yeung, 2007: 165)

| Research articles | Textbook models | Business reports |
|---|---|---|
| abstract | executive summary | executive summary (optional) list of recommendations (optional) |
| introduction | introduction | introduction |
| methods | methods | methods (optional) |
| results and discussions | findings | topical sections containing findings and interpretations / conclusions |
| conclusion | conclusion | conclusion (optional) |
| recommendations for further research (optional) | recommendations for decision making | recommendations for decision making |

gap in theory and obtaining findings that facilitate the making of generalizations, business reports work towards specific answers for specific situations'. Both Lung (2008) and Yeung (2007) make the point that managers are not concerned with the theoretical significance of conceptual models, and tend to apply management concepts with reference to their own experience. Because of this lack of interest in theory and technique for their own sake, the methodology employed by the professional report writer may also be of little concern to the reader; clients are unlikely to care about the replicability of results, but do want the right solution to a possibly unique problem. However, the Business Case Studies in the BAWE corpus often refer to business and management theories – 'Method' sources in Bizup's terms (2008). One of the purposes of these assignments is to demonstrate the students' ability to apply the analytical procedures they have learned during their degree programmes, for example SWOT (strengths, weaknesses, opportunities, threats), PEST (political, economic, social, technological), and Five Forces (threat of new entrants; threat of substitutes; buyer's power; supplier's power; level of rivalry between competitors).

Nathan (2010) proposes a move structure for these kinds of assignments:

- orientation (optional); this includes summary and introduction sections
- methodology (optional)
- analysis (obligatory)

- options and alternatives (optional)
- advisory (obligatory)
- summary and consolidation (optional)
- reflection (optional)
- supplementary supporting information (optional)

The model does not differ greatly from Yeung's model for professional business reports; it allows for structural variation but does not provide the option to avoid making recommendations. The student reports also have an optional reflection move, however, indicating the genre's pedagogical role. Reflection would be out of place in a professional report to a client.

In the BAWE corpus, Case Studies which pretend to address a business or its shareholders, real or imaginary, are categorised as company reports. In these assignments the title often names the simulated addressee, for example:

- *Report to the Product Manager of Powermop*
- *Management Report for Chemimix Ltd. – Designing a Production Schedule*
- *CFS Insurance Executive Business Report*
- *Report to the Board of Compotech Industries Plc*

Company reports are often presented in the format of a workplace document, with a cover page as in Figure 6.4, which casts the author as a 'project manager'.

Some writers elaborate further on these simulated roles. A company report for an 'Understanding enterprise' module, for example, was submitted with a letter requesting payment:

*Please find enclosed the final report I have prepared on your company. If you wish to contact me to discuss any aspects of the report please contact me at the above address. The invoice will be sent through the post separately.*

(Business)

Similarly, a company report for the module 'Electrical machines' included some encouraging words for the imaginary reader:

*We would be pleased to answer any question that may arise after reading the report and would like to hear your comment. We wish you the best of luck in your future.*

(Engineering)

These documents suggest an overlap with Empathy Writing, discussed in Chapter 7. They reflect the students' interest in the real-life contexts in which Company Reports are written, but unlike Empathy

```
+-------------------------------------------------------+
|                         CONFIDENTIAL REPORT           |
|            For the attention of the Board of Directors |
|                                                        |
|                                                        |
|          CFS Insurance Executive Business Report       |
|                                                        |
|      Project Implementation Analysis & Recommendations |
|      for the restructuring of operations & the adoption of agent internet links. |
|                                                        |
|      IB3820 Project Management                         |
|                                                        |
|      Authorised by: Operations Manager                 |
|      Completed by: Project Manager                     |
+-------------------------------------------------------+
```

Figure 6.4    A company report cover page

Writing they would not have been evaluated for the appropriacy of their interaction with the client, and their inclusion would not have had any bearing on the overall assignment grade.

Case Studies which are concerned with business and management issues but which do not simulate workplace documents are categorised as organisation analyses. These are produced by Agriculture students after they have made farm visits, relating to the farm as a whole or from a particular management perspective such as health and safety or diversification. They are also produced by Tourism students with reference to the tourist industry, and by students studying Publishing, for example regarding the marketing of a new title or the launch of a new magazine.

Although organisation analyses do not directly address a professional readership, they may involve role play in the manner of company reports. Agriculture students contributing organisation analyses to the BAWE corpus wrote in the first person in response to the following hypothetical scenario:

*You are the owner and manager for a 180 ha farm in the county of Berkshire. The basis of its farming activities has been milk production, and at one time over 300 cows were milked. Latterly the number of cows have been reduced, but it remains a dairy farm. In addition to the dairy cows, there are also some sheep and some cereal production. Staff include a dairy herdsman, tractor driver, and your 19 year old son, currently at university, who helps out during his vacation.*

(Agriculture Case Study prompt)

Amongst other things, this scenario enabled the students to consider the skills required of a farm manager. Superficially, the resulting analyses looked like reflective assignments for personal development planning (see Chapter 7):

*As a farm manager I have to take on many different roles, I must plan, organise, lead, control and be responsible for the future of my farm. That in turn leads me to be responsible for the future of my workforce, to a certain extent. That puts a lot of pressure on me to make the right decisions.*

(Agriculture)

This assignment task required role play rather than reflection on the writer's own experience, however, and the primary emphasis was on business strategy and financial analysis rather than personal development.

When students simulate roles, discussion which focuses on the pedagogical purpose of the assignment is likely to be isolated in a separate section. Some assignments include an appendix which targets the real reader, the academic assessor. This enables the writer to evaluate methods and procedures and demonstrate understanding of management principles without compromising the imaginary writer–reader relationship established in the main body of the assignment. The following excerpt comes from an annexe to a company report, for example, but departs from the style of the main part of the report by reflecting on the process of self-evaluation:

*Because evaluation identifies whether the objectives have been achieved and the causes of problems and successes, it is an essential process to improving the efficiency and effectiveness of future projects. Managing learning processes is key to becoming a learning organisation.*

(Company report annexe)

Similarly, some Case Studies contain a 'lessons learned' section where writers can reflect on their own progress:

*Our behaviour and rationale for decisions evolved as we further understood the tools at our disposal and enhanced our knowledge of effective marketing.*

(Business)

Such sections would clearly be out of place in an authentic company report.

Genres which do not attempt to mimic the design and structure of workplace documents can more easily incorporate theoretical discussion and references to learning objectives. Some organisation analyses are explicit about their pedagogical role; a report including a recommendation to shareholders, for example, may also include in its executive summary the objective 'to learn how to calculate and interpret financial ratios'.

A third type of business and management Case Study is more overtly academic in style. The 'single issue' report looks not at one particular organisation but at an overarching theme which affects an industry or region, such as petrochemicals or hydropower. Although recommendations are made they are framed objectively in this type of report. As can be seen in the following examples, the 'single issue' report writer does not play a consultant role or assume any personal responsibility for the advice that is provided:

*For a sustainable future, China must broaden its thinking in giving agriculture the same importance as its newly developing industry, otherwise, the future of China's food security will be reliance on imports and a demise of the people who skilfully work China's productive land.*

(Business Studies)

*As a matter of practice, the Guidotti Rule suggests that the countries should hold external assets sufficient to ensure that they could live without access to new foreign borrowings for up to twelve months. This implies that the usable foreign exchange reserves should exceed scheduled amortization of foreign currency debts (assuming no rollover during the following year).*

(Business Studies student)

## Case Studies in Medicine and Health

The medical patient case report is 'one of the most popular text genres in medical academic prose' (Méndez-Cendón, 2009: 170). Versions of this genre are published in medical journals and Internet forums. The structure of case reports submitted to *The Lancet* is described by Bignall (1998: 1570):

There is a narrative leading to an implied question at the end of the first paragraph – what is the cause of the patient's illness? The question could also be – what do we do next? The second paragraph gives the answer and the outcome. The third paragraph discusses the implications of the case reported and may end with a recommendation.

(Bignall, 1998: 1570)

This problem–solution–evaluation structure (Hoey, 1983) is presented more elaborately in the template supplied to writers of case reports for the *British Medical Journal*, which uses the headings shown in Figure 6.5.

> TITLE OF CASE
> AUTHORS OF CASE
> SUMMARY *summarising the case presentation and outcome*
> BACKGROUND *Why you think this case is important – why you decided to write it up*
> CASE PRESENTATION *Presenting features, medical / social / family history*
> INVESTIGATIONS
> DIFFERENTIAL DIAGNOSIS
> TREATMENT
> OUTCOME AND FOLLOW-UP
> DISCUSSION *including very brief review of similar published cases (how many similar cases have been published?)*
> LEARNING POINTS / TAKE HOME MESSAGES *3 to 5 bullet points*
> REFERENCES *Vancouver style (Was the patient involved in a clinical trial? Please reference related articles)*
> Figure captions
> Copyright Statement

Figure 6.5    Case report headings for the *British Medical Journal*

According to Méndez-Cendón (2009: 171), journal case reports aim 'to convince the reader of the existence of an unusual syndrome or disease, to provide supporting evidence, to suggest an adequate treatment, and to make recommendations for further study'. This is the 'hourglass' research article structure (Gosden, 1992; Hill, Soppelsa and West, 1982; Swales, 2004), with a broader background section coming before the presentation of the case, and scope for generalisation in the final sections. Case reports submitted to Internet forums also aim to present uncommon cases, but they differ in that the writer appeals to other specialists for a diagnosis (Méndez-Cendón, 2009: 171).

Our Medical School informants told us that case reports produced for the workplace rather than for publication vary considerably in terms of style and structure. Some, written immediately after seeing a patient, may simply serve the doctor as an aide-memoire, in which case they will be short and may not follow an established structure. Even these, however, are open to scrutiny, and must be defensible in court in the case of litigation. Others are produced for fellow doctors or for outside bodies, following a referral or in a letter to an employer, for example. These will be longer and a standardised template may be used.

Parks (2001) describes nursing 'care plans' with sections for diagnoses, objectives and interventions in relation to a case history. Although these sections are similar to those of medical case reports, care plans are more forward looking in that they are intended to help nurses organise their ongoing work.

The majority of the 69 patient case reports in the BAWE corpus were written by medical students undertaking hospital attachments during the second phase of their degree programme, as part of a 'patient portfolio'. A few were produced by medical students prior to this workplace experience, during the first phase of study, and a few came from other therapeutic disciplines.

According to our lecturer informants, the reports produced by medical students before their hospital attachments were intended to demonstrate understanding of the patient's perspective. Half the marks were awarded for a description of the patient and the issues he or she faced, and the other half were awarded for a proposed management plan. The reports were first presented orally and were then written up for summative assessment. The focus throughout these reports is on the patient's attitude and state of mind, as can be seen from the following examples:

*P believes she is going to die and is frightened to deal with her illness. She uses self-coping skills, such as busying herself with household tasks, looking after the children and smoking to avoid thinking about her illness. The side effects of the treatment P received meant that she had to deal with an altered body image such as the loss of her hair, this made her feel unattractive.*

(Medicine)

*The patient seems unaware of her condition even though she has been told that she is very ill. If confronted with such fact, she promptly denies it.*

(Medicine)

*She discovered 'stoma care' following a severe infection of the stoma that required antibiotic treatment and was impressed by the care she received at that time, and by the ongoing stoma care provisions. However she still very much feels that when meeting new people, at least on first impressions, 'people look at the bag, not me'.*

(Medicine)

These reports are written in continuous prose without notes, lists, tables or figures. Medical terminology is used only sparingly, for example to identify suitable medications in the management plan.

When the students leave the Medical School and start their hospital attachments, however, there is a dramatic change in their reporting style. Their patient portfolio pieces are much more technical, and much more concerned with the patient's physical condition. The portfolio template is reproduced in Figure 6.6. It bears a strong resemblance to the case report template for the *British Medical Journal*

---

**PORTFOLIO CASE**
**Patient initials      Hospital number    Age                Gender**
Portfolio case presentation number
Course document objectives
Has the patient's permission, including for follow-up contact by telephone, been sought and recorded in the case notes?
**Referral information**
Source of referral and summary of key information
**History**
All ***relevant*** information gathered from the patient about the presenting illness, co-existing problems, current treatment, *significant* past medical history and the social and family background. The patient's view of the nature of the problem and their expectations for treatment.
**Analysis of history**
The most likely single cause of the presentation, other possible causes and reasons for these choices. The findings to be looked for on physical examination to help decide the cause
**Physical examination and mental state examination**
Highlight the findings most relevant to your clinical problem solving by underlining them
**Analysis of history and examination**
Reasons for your choice of the patient's problem and any other cause that still needs to be considered at this stage
**Formulation of the patient's problem(s)**
Encapsulate this in physical, psychological and social terms (the triple diagnosis)
**Management**
Use the framework of RAPRIOP to structure your proposed management.
**Outcome**
A description of the progress of the patient as far as possible. This should include consideration of further issues to be resolved.
**Evidence based care and issues for research**
A brief consideration of the evidence base required for the diagnosis and management of the patient's problem(s)
**Commentary**
A commentary on issues of health care delivery, ethical issues or disability relevant to the patient and / or problem
**Impact on your learning**
Describe what you have learnt from this case

---

Figure 6.6   Portfolio case report template

(Figure 6.5), with sections for presentation (analysis of history), investigation (physical examination and mental state examination), diagnosis (formulation of the patient's problem(s)), treatment (management), outcome (outcome), discussion (commentary) and learning points (impact on your learning). The 'impact on your learning' section is used to note procedural information, in the manner of journal contributors, rather than to reflect on personal development. This is in contrast to patient reporting practice in the other Health disciplines, where reflection plays a much more important role (see Chapter 7).

As can be seen from the template, patient portfolio pieces are structured in the manner of a situation–problem–solution–evaluation text (Hoey, 1983). Background information is provided in the 'referral information' section, and subsequent sections identify the problem, offer a solution (management) and evaluate it (outcome). The RAPRIOP framework referred to in the Management section is a standard procedure –RAPRIOP stands for Reassurance and explanation; Advice; Prescription / other medical intervention; Referral and team working; Investigation; Observation; Prevention. These elements are usually present but not in sequence in the student's response, as in the following example, which also demonstrates the writer's familiarity with hospital jargon:

**Investigations**
Bloods- FBC , U+Es , CRP. Imaging- CXR. Others- Peak flow measurement, ECG.
**Reassurance and explanation**
Mrs X was well-orientated in her illness, and asked questions when she felt unsure.
**Prescription / medical intervention**
Co-amoxiclav 750 mg po , + 1.2g stat i.v . Increase prednisolone to 30mg . Regular nebulisers . Regular PEFR . Repeat ECG .
**Observation**
Observed on ward for 4 days.
**Referral and team working**
Mrs X's care involved her GP , and the on-call team at the Hospital of XYZ
**Advice and Prevention**
Avoid people with respiratory infections . Have Influenza inoculation.

(Medicine)

The move in portfolio pieces away from the language and style of the layperson reflects the fact that the writers have become more advanced in their studies by the time they undertake a hospital attachment. It also marks a change of perspective away from the patient's personal experience. The template requires writers to record 'the patient's view of the nature of the problem and their expectations for treatment', and some writers provide quite detailed information in the 'mental state examination' section, especially when the patient presents a psychological problem. Nevertheless the standardised way in which the data is recorded provides some support for Hoekje's contention (2007: 335) that the template requirements of the hospital case report encourage doctors to use controlling questioning techniques with patients, extracting just that information which fits the form. According to Hoekje, 'in the hospital, recording information in the patient's medical record ... changes a patient from a subject to an object of inquiry and excludes the patient's voice'.

A particular feature of the medical portfolio Case Studies is the use of prefabricated or partly prefabricated expressions, also common in the published patient case reports examined by Méndez-Cendón (2009). A cluster analysis reveals that the longest strings repeat the language of the medical portfolio guidance notes. For example, there are 23 instances of *the most likely cause(s)*, 22 instances of *the most likely diagnosis / reason*, and many combinations of strings, including *on physical examination I will / it is important to look for / look out for / assess*. All of these expressions echo the wording in the 'analysis of history' section of the template. This heavy use of pre-fabricated language may be explained by the fact that the portfolio case report is the only genre in the corpus to be produced outside the university. Although the students would have had time to edit their writing before submitting it for assessment, the style reflects the time constraints of the busy hospital context in which they were originally created.

Patient case reports from health disciplines other than medicine focus on the problems of single (real) patients in different ways. Occupational therapy Case Studies are forward-looking plans of action, like the nursing reports described by Parks (2001), placing them on the cusp of the Proposal genre family. One Case Study is structured as a series of questions, for example:

- *What needs and strengths does Michelle have?*
- *What interventions are appropriate to meet her needs?*
- *Which frames of reference and approaches will you be using?*
- *What clinical reasoning is underpinning your decisions?*

(Occupational Therapy)

Another assignment plans an entire process of care treatment, including pre- and post-intervention interviews, under the headings:

- *introduction*
- *gather and analyse information*

- *define the problem*
- *plan and prepare intervention*
- *implement intervention*
- *evaluate outcomes*

(Occupational Therapy)

Other Case Studies develop arguments and have clear affinities to assignments in the Critique and Essay genre families (Chapter 5), as in the following extract:

*Throughout this case study, I will discuss the client's mental health problems and will attempt to evaluate whether the assessment and interventions that he has received have been appropriate and stem from a solid evidence base.*

(Mental Health Nursing)

In the following extract, the student writer is quite critical of standard clinical procedures:

*CPA is supposed to take a holistic approach and to be person centred but I feel that it actually tells me very little about this client other than his medical history.*

(Nursing)

Reflective techniques are often used to critique personal and / or current practice in this type of case study:

*I will be using Holm and Stephenson's (1994) model of reflection to guide my work and aid my reflection. I will also incorporate the module themes of personhood and values and assumptions which will be my main focus ... I will be discussing the assumptions of both the patient and the nurses including patient expectations versus what can be offered, patients' rights to access treatment and services, quality of care in relation to patient priorities and the concept of personhood and possible barriers to its provision.*

(Medicine)

In this respect such assignments are very similar to the reflective Narrative Recounts discussed in Chapter 7, and although they primarily discuss patient care they contain many references to personal professional development, as shown in bold in the following extracts:

*I was very nervous the first time Mary attended and trying to adjust to and understand the A&E department, although I had little confidence I was able to stay with Mary for most of the time until she was admitted because of my supernumerary status and was able to build up a relationship and rapport with her.*

(Medicine)

*Having discussed Jane's previous experience,* **I felt I was better equipped** to *provide her with more specific information regarding her decision to breastfeed.*

(Medicine)

**Upon reflection, I think that I judged** *his 'cheeky' behaviour in a positive light when in another child* **I may have considered it irritating.**

(Medicine)

## Other Case Studies

Most Case Studies in the BAWE corpus are reports of the kind we have previously described, on individual patients, organisations or business issues. Many of the exemplars from the Law, Economics, Chemistry and Engineering departments are actually company reports or organisation analyses produced for finance, marketing and management modules.

The site investigation report, however, is an engineering-specific genre. According to our Engineering informants it provides essential preparation for writing in the workplace, as professional engineers may be legally liable for their site investigation report recommendations. The examples in the BAWE corpus are cautious in their recommendations, suggesting that the writers are conscious of the legal implications of their decisions. Such caution is here indicated by bold type:

**There are several measures that would need to be taken if the site was to be used for its desired purpose.** *People must be made aware of the danger that the lake could potentially hold, this could be done by signposting...*

(Site investigation report)

**Overall it is hard to predict** *the behaviour of the pipe if it was replaced with a 6'* **without a full understanding of the flow properties** *of the pipe throughout the year, i.e. the air to water content of the fluid.*

(Site investigation report)

## 6.8 The language of apprenticeship genres

Lying as they do at the point where the requirements of professional academic writing and professional workplace writing often diverge, many writers of apprenticeship genres find a path between the 'hourglass' structure of the typical research article (Gosden, 1992; Hill, Soppelsa and West, 1982; Swales, 2004) and the 'funnel' structure of the professional report (Yeung, 2007). Both structures begin with general discussion of theory or models of practice and proceed to a more specific focus on findings, but whereas the research article uses these to draw broader generalisations in a concluding phase, the professional reports 'work towards specific answers for specific situations' (Yeung, 2007: 162). For students, the examination of a case or problem, or the design of a product or system, is usually only a means of demonstrating and developing professional understanding, and there is no expectation of putting the outcome into practice. For this reason it is sometimes beneficial to the student to consider broader implications in a concluding section. The apprenticeship genres vary in the extent to which the hourglass or funnel structure is adopted.

Many authors have noted the persuasive function of professional writing in Engineering and Business. Zhu found that engineering professors believed that professional engineers 'are almost always trying to sell their own ideas' (2004b: 35), and Yeung (2007: 165) considers professional business reports to be 'rhetorically oriented towards exhortation', although more objective and less emotive than other hortatory genres such as newspaper editorials and letters to the editor. Biber's (1988) multidimensional analysis scores for Dimension 4 (the persuasive dimension – see Section 1.6) were +3 for professional letters and 0 for published general academic writing. As discussed in Section 2.3, most BAWE genre families have negative scores, indicating that students make few overt attempts at persuasion. Literature Surveys score −3.4, for example, and Methodology Recounts and Explanations score −2.5 and −2.3 respectively. The scores for the apprenticeship genres, however, tend to fall somewhere between the typical scores for BAWE assignments and Biber's scores for professional correspondence, suggesting a move towards more professional academic and workplace writing styles. Case Studies and Design Specifications are almost neutral (−0.5 and −0.7 respectively), while Proposals (+1.3) and Problem Questions (+1.6) edge towards the persuasive (Nesi, 2009).

Whilst groups of linguistic features can reveal overtly persuasive tendencies, the design of the document can reveal more covert suasive effects. The BAWE apprenticeship genres are particularly rich in lists, bulleted items and visual devices for presenting information, intended to help the reader grasp the main points quickly. Tables 6.8 and 6.9 show the distribution of these features across disciplines and genre families[1].

In Table 6.8 clear differences are apparent between the more discursive Case Studies in the first phase of Medical School study and in the other health disciplines, which make little use of visual devices, and the more technical Case Studies in Engineering and in patient portfolios written during hospital attachments, which have shorter

Table 6.8    Comparative statistics for Case Studies

| Averages for: | w/s | s/p | tables | figures | formulae | lists |
|---|---|---|---|---|---|---|
| Engineering | 21.4 | 2.9 | 2.5 | 3.5 | 2.7 | 1.4 |
| Medicine: hospital attachment | 19.9 | 2.1 | 0.9 | 0.3 | 0.4 | 7.2 |
| Medicine: before hospital attachment | 19.7 | 4.0 | 0 | 0 | 0 | 0.3 |
| Health | 29.2 | 5.0 | 0 | 0 | 0 | 0.4 |

Table 6.9    Comparative statistics for other apprenticeship genres

| Averages for: | words | w/s | s/p | tables | figures | formulae | lists |
|---|---|---|---|---|---|---|---|
| Design Specifications | 2614 | 20.6 | 2.3 | 3.3 | 5.6 | 11.0 | 2.5 |
| Proposals | 2524 | 23.3 | 3.2 | 0.8 | 1.4 | 0 | 2.5 |
| Problem Questions | 2316 | 24.3 | 4.6 | 0.1 | 0 | 0.8 | 0 |

paragraphs and provide more information in tables, figures, formulae and lists.

The figures in Table 6.9 indicate the frequency of visual devices in most Design Specifications, and the more discursive style of most Proposals and Problem Questions[2].

Using Sketch Engine and the USAS system of semantic categorisation (Archer et al., 2002; see Chapter 1) we compared the frequency of some of the semantic categories within the apprenticeship genre families, and in the BAWE corpus as a whole. In Table 6.10 frequencies are compared for the major categories represented in the BAWE corpus. The figures for the apprenticeship genres are only for assignments representing a single text (non-compound assignments). All figures are standardised to 10,000 words.

Table 6.10 shows that all four families of apprenticeship genres have an above average number of words in Category X, mostly in the subcategories X6 DECIDING and X7 WANTING; PLANNING; CHOOSING. Proposals are particularly well represented in this category. The commonest words in each family belonging to Category X are listed in Table 6.11.

Table 6.10　Word frequencies for main USAS categories in the apprenticeship genres

| | B | E | L | N | S | T | X |
|---|---|---|---|---|---|---|---|
| Case Studies | 131 | 39 | 11 | 63 | 189 | 94 | 126 |
| Design Specifications | 7 | 33 | 5 | 65 | 90 | 72 | 104 |
| Proposals | 26 | 23 | 8 | 61 | 182 | 84 | 150 |
| Problem Questions | 20 | 36 | 30 | 38 | 177 | 45 | 129 |
| BAWE | 33 | 43 | 19 | 69 | 161 | 83 | 95 |

Letter key:

B = THE BODY & THE INDIVIDUAL

E = EMOTIONAL ACTIONS, STATES & PROCESSES

L = LIFE & LIVING THINGS

N = NUMBERS AND MEASUREMENT

S = SOCIAL ACTIONS, STATES & PROCESSES

T = TIME

X = PSYCHOLOGICAL ACTIONS, STATES & PROCESSES

Table 6.11　Words in Category X

| Case Studies | Design Specifications | Proposals | Problem Questions |
|---|---|---|---|
| project | project | project | decision(s) |
| strategy(ies) | required | strategy | policy |
| required | scheme(s) | target | required |
| plan | requirements | plan | intention |
| planning | chosen | planning | requirement(s) |
| target | decided | chosen | purpose |
| decision | selected | aim(s) | decide |

Case Studies, Problem Questions and Proposals also contain large numbers of Category S words, many of which belong in the subcategory S6, OBLIGATION AND NECESSITY: MUST; NEED(S); NEEDED; NECESSARY; SHOULD, or S8 HELPING / HINDERING: HELP; SUPPORT; SERVICE(S). Case Studies have a high number of words in Category B, belonging in the subcategories B2, HEALTH AND DISEASE and B3, MEDICINES AND MEDICAL TREATMENT: PAIN; DISEASE; SYMPTOMS; ASTHMA; INFECTION; WELL; ILLNESS; CANCER; INJURY; JAUNDICE; FRACTURE; STROKE; OEDEMA; DIABETES. As might be expected given the technical and numerical nature of most of the Design Specifications, many words in this family come from the subcategory N5 QUANTITIES: MANY; BITS; AGAIN; BIT; LOAD; FEW; ENOUGH; MUCH; OFTEN; GENERAL; ONCE; MASS; INDIVIDUAL; LITTLE; SERIES. Problem Questions have more words in Category L than the other apprenticeship genres. These mostly belong in L1, LIFE AND LIVING THINGS (terms relating to life and death), for example DEATH; MANSLAUGHTER; MURDER; LIFE; KILL; DIE; SUICIDAL; SUICIDE.

We also found that Case Studies and Proposals had an unusually high quantity of words in the USAS subcategory A5 EVALUATION. For Case Studies the most frequent words in this subcategory were: PERHAPS; MAYBE; LIKELIHOOD; ARGUABLY; PROBABILITY; EVENTUALITIES; CONCEIVABLY. For Proposals the most frequent were: QUALITY; QUALITATIVE; STANDARD(S); ASSESSMENT; EVALUATION; EVALUATE(D); EVALUATING; RATED; RANKS; RANKING.

Semantic tag searches identify semantic areas which are prominent in the apprenticeship genres as compared to the corpus as a whole. Keyword searches look for unusually frequent individual lexical items. The keywords listed in Table 6.12. were identified using WordSmith Tools, with the entire BAWE corpus as the reference corpus.

*Will*, *be* and *should* are indicators of the forward-looking and persuasive nature of apprenticeship genres. Most of the other keywords fall into the fields of commerce (*company, market(ing), management, business, cost, customer(s), sales, product, profit*) or health (*pain, examination, diagnosis, symptoms, patient, hospital, medication*). The occurrence of *your* and *Mr* on the keyword list point to the simulated nature of many apprenticeship genres. Writers may address a client directly, and use proper names to refer to other individuals, real or imaginary.

The keywords for each of the apprenticeship genres are compared in Table 6.13.

The keyword list for the Case Study subcorpus (554,842 words) is very similar to that of the apprenticeship genres corpus as a whole, although *should* and *will* are lower down the list.

The top 30 keywords in the Design Specification texts (230,329 words) indicate the technical nature of assignments in this genre. Almost all the keywords relate to computer data or calculations; this is technical lexis 'which has to be learned by definition, through language' (Martin, 2007: 41). There are no proper names or personal pronouns, but the presence of *the* as a keyword suggests that the texts are highly nominalised. A Sketch Engine search found 49 instances of *design* as a verb in Design Specifications, for example, but 530 examples of *design* as a noun.

Table 6.12    The top 30 keywords in apprenticeship genres

|    | Keyword | Frequency | Keyness |
|----|---------|-----------|---------|
| 1  | *will* | 5356 | 1491.9 |
| 2  | *project* | 1450 | 1119.8 |
| 3  | *company* | 1313 | 903 |
| 4  | *be* | 12357 | 869.86 |
| 5  | *market* | 1765 | 841.57 |
| 6  | *management* | 1309 | 819.33 |
| 7  | *business* | 1340 | 810.17 |
| 8  | *cost* | 1152 | 755.82 |
| 9  | *should* | 2381 | 704.66 |
| 10 | *customers* | 925 | 681.14 |
| 11 | *sales* | 678 | 640.09 |
| 12 | *pain* | 594 | 578.79 |
| 13 | *marketing* | 660 | 562.77 |
| 14 | *examination* | 530 | 552.87 |
| 15 | *appendix* | 773 | 515.81 |
| 16 | *user* | 546 | 512.58 |
| 17 | *customer* | 663 | 496.75 |
| 18 | *program* | 631 | 490.7 |
| 19 | *diagnosis* | 424 | 484.71 |
| 20 | *staff* | 630 | 468.43 |
| 21 | *product* | 1050 | 449.27 |
| 22 | *design* | 841 | 435.64 |
| 23 | *your* | 640 | 433.58 |
| 24 | *symptoms* | 424 | 433.18 |
| 25 | *mr* | 422 | 426.17 |
| 26 | *tourism* | 509 | 402.15 |
| 27 | *patient* | 538 | 377.56 |
| 28 | *profit* | 568 | 374.83 |
| 29 | *hospital* | 328 | 355.75 |
| 30 | *medication* | 242 | 355.63 |

The top 30 keywords in the Proposal texts (82,777 words) mostly relate to business and hospitality services. The names of countries, such as *Canada, Kenya* and UK indicate that proposals often concern international ventures. Many more countries and cities are named individually in the texts.

*Will* is the most significant keyword in Proposals, indicating their forward-looking nature, as in Figure 6.7.

Table 6.13    The top 30 keywords in each of the apprenticeship
genres

| Case Studies | Design Specifications | Proposals | Problem Questions |
|---|---|---|---|
| *management;* | *program; design;* | *will; market;* | *case; judicial;* |
| *pain; examination;* | *user; the; system;* | *be; customers;* | *contract;* |
| *market; project;* | *data; output;* | *marketing;* | *law; act; Ltd;* |
| *company; history;* | *array; shaft; code;* | *Canada;* | *decision; R;* |
| *business; diagnosis;* | *formula; input;* | *participants;* | *review; court; ex;* |
| *symptoms; patient;* | *signal; modulation;* | *business; research;* | *liability; offence;* |
| *Mr; should;* | *server; each;* | *project; Kenya;* | *Felicity; Laura;* |
| *cost; your; sales;* | *circuit; gear;* | *brand; hotels;* | *clause; Lord;* |
| *treatment; chest;* | *model; noise; bits;* | *HC; hotel; UK;* | *manslaughter;* |
| *tourism; referral;* | *number; file;* | *customer; service;* | *would; AC;* |
| *admission;* | *torque; enter; used;* | *company;* | *bias; ucta; panel;* |
| *medication;* | *function; gauges;* | *appendix; pmcs;* | *administrative;* |
| *customers; profit;* | *stylus; coding* | *zoo; Roma;* | *exam; liable;* |
| *no; patient's* | | *management;* | *hearing; Workwell;* |
| *respiratory;* | | *hand; study; local;* | *section; test* |
| *marketing; asthma;* | | *France; staff; sales* | |
| *surgery* | | | |

> We **will** study how the intracellular signalling of the T cell
>
> As services provided by the company **will** be more customised, a pricing variation policy can be
>
> These comparisons **will** be used to elucidate the signalling pathway and to
>
> Sun Company **will** pay more attention to new product introduction as a
>
> Indeed, the change of layout **will** provide new opportunities for everyone to promote

Figure 6.7    The use of *will*

The top 30 keywords in the Problem Question texts (96,208 words) are primarily words relating to law. Many of these are terms which have a very restricted technical meaning; Law students need to use these to demonstrate their knowledge of legal language. The proper nouns in the list – *Felicity*, *Laura* and *Workwell* – are used in scenarios for legal Problem Questions.

The Problem Question keyword *Lord* is used as a title, as in Figure 6.8. These concordance lines also illustrate the many different ways in which speech is reported in legal Problem Question answers.

|  |  |
|---|---|
| but as **Lord** | Denning said 'the rules of natural justice vary |
| in the seminal GCHQ case, **Lord** | Diplock usefully classified the ways in which a |
| to the requirement of reasonableness, **Lord** | Greene asserted that the decision-maker 'must |
| However, **Lord** | Hoffmann has stated that 'almost all the old |
| **Lord** | Hope's analysis could also encompass the teacher |
| This too, according to **Lord** | Hope, is in the interests of a democratic society. |
| Quoted in **Lord** | Irvine of Lairg – 'Judges and Decision-Makers: the |
| However, **Lord** | Irvine warns against judges straying into a review of |
| in Page v Smith we find, as per **Lord** | Lloyd, that a duty of care is owed if psychiatric |
| **Lord** | Oliver indicated that to exclude judicial review on |
| Those four conditions were laid down by **Lord** | Oliver from Hedley Byrne v Heller (1963) and as the |
| First noted by **Lord** | Parker, CJ in Re HK (an infant) [1967] 2 QB 617, |
| the general principle asserted by **Lord** | Reid that, 'a man is not to be dismissed for |
| **Lord** | Reid identified a number of errors of law that went |
| **Lord** | Wilberforce stressed in Ailsa Craig that 'one must |
| We should nevertheless bear in mind **Lord** | Woolf's stipulation that 'the evidence [regarding |

Figure 6.8    Examples of reported speech in Problem Questions

In the concordance lines in Figure 6.8, Lords *say, classify, assert, state, warn, indicate, lay down conditions, note, identify, stress* and *stipulate*, amongst other things, and their pronouncements are referred to by the expressions *as per* and *according to*.

The range of reporting verbs used in legal Problem Question texts is an indication of the linguistic demands of this genre. Verbal dexterity counts for more in Law than in Engineering or Medicine, and the Problem Question answer offers students the opportunity to display this skill.

## 6.9 Conclusion

As we have seen, the apprenticeship genres offer students the opportunity to practise writing the kinds of texts they will produce in their professional lives. Whilst earlier chapters examined the ways in which, through writing, students develop their ability to explain, argue and conduct research, this chapter has looked at the ways in which students balance the requirements of the workplace with the requirements of their university degree programmes. The next chapter will also look at writing which does not belong in the 'essayist' tradition (Lillis, 2001), but the genres discussed will address important topics in a different sort of way, on a personal rather than a professional level. Reflective and creative writing tasks enable students to revisit what they have learned, and make sense of it in terms of its human impact. This kind of writing thus provides a foil for the factual information and logical deductions on display in the apprenticeship genres. Both mind-sets are necessary in the world of work – we need to engage with the data and the procedures relating to our professions, but we also need to engage with attitudes and aspirations in response to this information, as experienced by ourselves and others.

## Notes

1. Statistics were calculated only for assignments that contained a single text (see Section 1.4).
2. Statistics were calculated only for assignments that contained a single text (see Section 1.4).

## References

Archer, D., Wilson, A., & Rayson, P. (2002). *Introduction to the USAS Category System*. Lancaster, UK: University Centre for Computer Corpus Research on Language, University of Lancaster; http://ucrel.lancs.ac.uk/usas/usas%20guide.pdf.

Artemeva, N. (2007). Becoming an engineering communicator: A study of novices' trajectories in learning genres of their profession. In C. Bazerman, A. Bonini & D. Figueiredo (Eds.), *Genre in a changing world*, 253–65. Parlor Press Online http://wac.colostate.edu/books/genre.

Artemeva, N. (2008). Toward a unified social theory of genre learning. *Journal of Business and Technical Communication*, 22, 160–85.

Badger, R. (2003). Legal and general: Towards a genre analysis of newspaper law reports. *English for Specific Purposes*, 22(3). 249–63.

BCS (the Chartered Institute for IT) (2007). *Accreditation criteria*. Available at: www.bcs.org/upload/pdf/criteria.pdf.

Bean, J. C. (2011). Backward design: The writing in the majors project at Seattle University. In M. Deane & P. O'Neill (Eds.), *Writing in the disciplines*. Houndmills: Palgrave Macmillan.

Bhatia, V.K. (1993). *Analysing genre: Language use in professional settings.* London: Longman.

Biber, D. (1988). *Variation across speech and writing.* Cambridge: Cambridge University Press.

Bignall, J. (1998). 3 years of Lancet case reports. *Lancet* 352 (9140): 1570, 14 November 1998.

Bizup, J. (2008). BEAM: A rhetorical vocabulary for teaching research-based writing. *Rhetoric Review*, 27(1), 72–86.

Bruce, N. (2002). Dovetailing language and content: teaching balanced argument in legal problem answer writing. *English for Specific Purposes* 21(4), 321–45.

Candlin,C., Bhatia, V.K. , & Jensen, C.H. (2002). Developing legal writing materials for English second language learners: Problems and perspectives. *English for Specific Purposes*, 21(4), 299–320.

Carter, M. (2007). Ways of knowing, doing, and writing in the disciplines. *College Composition and Communication*, 58(3), 385–418.

Dannels, D. (2000). Learning to be professional: Technical classroom discourse, practice, and professional identity construction. *Journal of Business and Technical Communication*, 14(1), 5–37.

Finch, E., & Fafinski, S. (2007). *Legal skills.* Oxford: Oxford University Press.

Gosden, H. (1992). Discourse functions of marked theme in scientific research articles. *Applied Linguistics* 14(1), 56–75.

Hill, S., Soppelsa, B., & West, G. (1982). Teaching ESL students to read and write experimental research papers. *TESOL Quarterly* 16,333–47.

Hoekje, B. (2007). Medical discourse and ESP courses for international medical graduates (IMGs). *English for Specific Purposes*, 26(3), 327–43.

Hoey, M. (1983). *On the surface of discourse.* London: George Allen & Unwin.

Howe, P. (1990). The problem of the problem question in English for Academic Legal Purposes. *English for Specific Purposes*, 9(3), 215–36.

Hyland, K. (2004). Patterns of engagement: Dialogic features and L2 undergraduate writing. In L. Ravelli & R. Ellis (Eds.), *Analysing academic writing*, London: Continuum, 5–23.

Institution of Mechanical Engineers (2009). *Academic accreditation guidelines.* Issue 1, 06/10/09. www.imeche.org/NR/rdonlyres/17701440-D714–4743-B3EE-DE5D1195301E/0/AcademicAccreditationGuidelines2009working documentV1.doc.

Leont'ev, A.N. (1981). The problem of activity in psychology. In J.V. Wertsch (Ed.), *The concept of activity in Soviet psychology*, Armonk, NY: Sharpe, 37–71.

Lillis, T. (2001). *Student writing: Access, regulation, desire.* London: Routledge.

LTS (Learning and Teaching Support) Initiative (2007). *Interacting with Professional, Statutory and Regulatory Bodies (PSRBs).* Report of LTS Lunch 11: Monday, 30 April 2007. University of Cambridge. www.admin.cam.ac.uk/offices/education/lts/lunch/lunch11.html.

Lung, J. (2008). Discursive hierarchical patterning in Law and Management cases. *English for Specific Purposes*, 27(4), 424–41.

Maclean, R. (2010). First-year law students' construction of professional identity through writing. *Discourse Studies*, 12(2), 177–94.

Martin, J.R. (2007). Construing knowledge: A functional linguistic perspective. In F. Christie & J.R. Martin (Eds.), *Language, knowledge and pedagogy*. London: Continuum.

Méndez-Cendón, B. (2009). Combinatorial patterns in medical case reports: An English–Spanish contrastive analysis. *The Journal of Specialised Translation*, 11, 169–90.

Nathan, P. (2010). *A genre-based study of pedagogical business case reports*. PhD thesis, Birmingham, UK: University of Birmingham.

Nesi, H., & Gardner, S. (2006). Variation in disciplinary culture: University tutors' views on assessed writing tasks. In R. Kiely, G. Clibbon, P. Rea-Dickins & H. Woodfield (Eds.), *Language, culture and identity in applied linguistics* (British Studies in Applied Linguistics, Volume 21), London: Equinox Publishing, 99–117.

Nesi, H. (2009). A multidimensional analysis of student writing across levels and disciplines. In M. Edwardes (Ed.), Taking the measure of applied linguistics: Proceedings of the BAAL Annual Conference, University of Swansea, 11–13 September 2008. London: BAAL / Scitsiugnil Press.

Parks, S. (2001). Moving from school to the workplace: Disciplinary innovation, border crossings, and the reshaping of a written genre. *Applied Linguistics*, 22(4), 405–38.

Popham, S.L. (2005). Forms as boundary genres in medicine, science, and business. *Journal of Business and Technical Communication*, 19, 279–303.

QAA – Framework for Higher Education Qualifications in England, Wales and Northern Ireland – January 2001. Available at: www.qaa.ac.uk/academicinfrastructure/FHEQ/EWNI/default.asp [Accessed 3 June 2008].

Schleppegrell, M. (2004). Technical writing in a second language: The role of grammatical metaphor. In L. Ravelli & R. Ellis (Eds.) *Analysing academic writing*, London: Continuum, 172–89.

Schryer, J., & Spoel, P. (2005). Genre theory, health-care discourse, and professional identity formation. *Journal of Business and Technical Communication*, 19, 249–78.

Spafford, M., Schryer, C., Mian, M., & Lingard, L. (2006). Look who's talking: Teaching and learning using the genre of medical case presentations. *Journal of Business and Technical Communication*, 20, 121–58.

Star, S., & Griesemer, J.R. (1989). Institutional ecology, 'translations' and boundary objects: Amateurs and professionals in Berkeley's Museum of Vertebrate Zoology, 1907–39. *Social Studies of Science*, 19, 387–420.

Swales, J.M. (2004) Research genres: Exploration and applications. Cambridge: Cambridge University Press.

Turner, J.D. (2010). Putting the world back in working order. *Times Higher Education*, 29 April 2010.

Wardle, E. (2009). "Mutt Genres" and the goal of FYC: Can we help students write the genres of the university? *College Composition and Communication*, 60(4), 765–89.

Yeung, L. (2007). In search of commonalities: Some linguistic and rhetorical features of business reports as a genre. *English for Specific Purposes*, 26(2), 156–79.

Zhu, W. (2004a). Writing in business courses: An analysis of assignment types, their characteristics, and required skills. *English for Specific Purposes*, 23(2), 111–35.

Zhu, W. (2004b). Faculty views on the importance of writing, the nature of academic writing, and teaching and responding to writing in the disciplines. *Journal of Second Language Writing*, 13(1), 29–48.

# 7 *Writing for oneself and others*

> Some futurists and radical thinkers consider that the concepts of 'qualifications' and 'professions' may become obsolete. Instead, people will continually build their own personal portfolios of learning and development and access other learning in an open way on the internet. Each person will have a learning plan and 'qualifications' will become incidental markers along the way for those who need them.
>
> (The Higher Education Academy, 2005)

The kinds of assignment considered in this chapter enable students to monitor their own development or practise communicating with a readership beyond their own field. Narrative Recounts narrate a series of fictional or factual events. Empathy Writing, a term coined by Lea and Street (2000: 39), mimics non-academic genres ostensibly intended for non-experts.

If Explanations and Exercises (Chapter 3) and Problem Questions (Chapter 6) lie at one end of the convergent–divergent scale, many Empathy Writing and Narrative Recount tasks lie at the other. Explanations, Exercises and Problem Questions are favoured for examination papers because they can be objectively assessed for facts, procedures and logic, but Narrative Recounts and Empathy Writing often require greater creative effort on the part of the writer, and this can only be assessed with a certain amount of subjectivity. Moreover it may be unclear to both the writer and the assessor whether an Empathy Writing text which is effective on its own terms, for example for its potential appeal to the hypothetical reader, should be penalised if it fails to meet some more standard departmental criterion, for example regarding the referencing of sources. Problems with assessment may explain why some of the Empathy Writing and Narrative Recount genres in our corpus were written as part of multi-genre compound assignments, and accompany Case Studies, Essays, Explanations, Methodology Recounts, Problem Questions and

Proposals. The assignment task required that they should be included, but it may have had little impact on the assignment's overall grade.

Like the writing in the other genre families we have discussed in this book, Empathy Writing and Narrative Recounts demonstrate knowledge of the field of study, critical thinking, and the ability to apply appropriate methods of enquiry. In many cases they also showcase the employability skills demonstrated in the apprentice-ship genres (see Chapter 6). These accomplishments are not displayed as part of an overt attempt to convince the reader of the writer's expertise or good judgement, however. Instead they may be carried lightly, perhaps as a prerequisite for the communicative activity the writer is undertaking, but not, apparently, as an end in themselves. Both genre families ostensibly bypass the academic reader; the more personal Narrative Recounts are inward-looking and present them-selves as tools for self-discovery or self-development, while Empathy Writing looks beyond the immediate need for academic success and professional qualifications to address an imaginary reader with other, nonspecialist, communicative demands.

Because Narrative Recounts are often ostensibly written for the lay reader, and Empathy Writing can be used as a means of self-expres-sion, the boundaries between the two genre families are sometimes blurred. A reflective letter telling a friend about an Occupational Therapy course is classed as Empathy Writing even though it recounts the student's experiences during the first week of term. On the other hand a sample chapter for a crime thriller is classed as a Narrative Recount because it is fiction, even though it demonstrates the ability to communicate with non-academic readers.

Both types of writing also occur on the periphery of other types of writing task. Chapter 6 mentions the existence of role-play letters which accompany students' reports to hypothetical clients. These types of text are really short pieces of Empathy Writing, although they are not identified as such in the corpus holdings. In Section 7.5 of this chapter we discuss reflective paragraphs embedded within longer assignments from other genre families. These elements share many of the distinctive features of Narrative Recounts, and are included in our Personal Development Planning (PDP) subcorpus.

## 7.1 Narrative Recounts and Empathy Writing in the BAWE corpus

Both Empathy Writing and Narrative Recounts are produced at all four levels of study in the BAWE corpus, and in all four disciplinary groupings (see Appendix 7). They are spread thinly and widely in the corpus, and apart from the slightly higher numbers of texts received from the final year of undergraduate study (Level 3) no particular distributional pattern emerges.

Most Narrative Recounts are recounts of historical events or personal experiences, or pieces of creative writing. Empathy Writing in the corpus mostly consists of letters or texts which engage with the media in some way. Assignments in both genre families tend to be shorter pieces – our examples from both families are on average well under 2,000 words – and this length may suit those within higher education who have recently called for the introduction of shorter and more frequent writing tasks, as Leedham (2009: 194–5) points out. They are sometimes set as alternatives to more conventional Critique or Essay genres, and can be applied across the same broad range of disciplines; one can write a newspaper article, for example, with reference to any academic topic, and a narrative of any kind of activity.

Empathy Writing and Narrative Recount tasks may be valued by some academics simply because they depart from convention. Nesi and Gardner (2006) discuss the increasing emphasis on teaching and learning innovation in British universities, also noted by Evans and Abbott (1998: 115), Lea and Stierer (2000) and Leedham (2009). There are few, if any, prizes for the excellent implementation of established educational practice, but the successful introduction of new practice is rewarded by the media (for example, the *Times Higher Education Innovation Awards*), the professions (for example, the *Royal Academy of Engineering / BNFL Education Innovation Awards*), and public services (for example, the *Higher Education Innovation Fund*). The value placed on innovation in higher education was evident in the interview comments of academic staff who considered essays to be too 'traditional' (Sociology) and 'limiting' (English).

Lecturers were often keen to draw our attention towards experimental assessment practices in their departments, even if these were the exception rather than the norm. For example, the academic staff we interviewed were proud to tell us about their exciting new ideas for a crime fiction assignment in a Sociology module, and for a Law assignment in the form of a play script of a legal case. In Computer Science, our interviewee spoke of her reputation for setting 'completely whacky' tasks, and in English Studies another spoke of her course as a 'freak module' because of its unusual creative writing assignments. Theatre Studies lecturers said that they encouraged students to 'write dangerously', and lauded the work of a student who analysed 'King Kong as a Wagnerian Opera'.

Not many assignments of this type found their way to us, however, and although the corpus does not claim to represent the spread of genres in a proportionate way, we assume that such assignments were not produced by large numbers of students. This apparent unwillingness to answer highly innovative assignment questions may be due to the risk involved. It is surely difficult to express one's own creative ideas and appeal to a hypothetical nonspecialist reader, while at the same time meeting the needs of a real and powerful assessor. All forms of student writing are occluded to a certain extent, but there is bound to be particular uncertainty concerning the style, form and content of a completely new assignment type.

Empathy Writing and Narrative Recount genres are well suited to the affordances of the new media, and often mimic new-media presentation styles. Our staff interviewees mentioned assignments involving blogs (Narrative Recounts) and multimedia installations (Empathy texts) which we could not include in the corpus, either because they were not deliverable to us in the requisite form, or because they were too situation-dependent (one idea depended on the placement of the texts in various physical locations). We anticipate that future student assignments will become increasingly multimodal and hypertextual, and that this may result in more experimentation with the Narrative Recount and Empathy Writing genres. The effects of the new media on students' writing are already being investigated, for example via the seminar series 'New forms of the doctorate', funded by the UK Economic and Social Research Council (2008–2010), and events organised by the British Association for Applied Linguistics (BAAL) 'Multimodality' Special Interest Group[1].

## 7.2  Empathy Writing

Most of the Empathy Writing in the corpus comes from the Sciences, and particularly the Life Sciences, and much of it is produced for modules which have the primary aim of preparing students for professional engagement outside the academy, for example 'Communicating science' (Physics), 'Communication, dissemination and professional issues' (Psychology), 'Preparation for practice' (Architecture), 'Professional issues and skills' (Computer Science), 'Publishing today' (Publishing) and 'Starting and running a business' (Engineering).

Because there are so many possible types of non-academic audience, and so many possible contexts for public engagement, these assignments do not follow any one particular pattern. Nevertheless three main formats can be identified: letters, newspaper articles and expert advice interviews. A fourth type of Empathy Writing consists of report-type texts, addressed for example to policymakers, but this is a very mixed bag, representing idiosyncratic approaches to assignment tasks which other students might have tackled more conventionally as Case Studies or Critiques.

In all the Empathy Writing tasks there is a clear requirement for content accuracy and clarity. Writers do not usually have to construct an argument or demonstrate new reasoning, but they do need to engage with their hypothetical readers or listeners, and translate an existing body of knowledge into layperson's terms. Thus Empathy Writing tasks enable students to develop and demonstrate communication skills and content knowledge, and may also serve to motivate students, raising their awareness of both the intrinsic fascination of their field of study and the contribution it can make to society.

Some pieces of Empathy Writing are simply short cover letters, accompanying a more elaborate assignment belonging to another genre family. Longer letters explain to clients the process of applying for planning permission (Architecture) or the process of publishing a book (Publishing). These letters clearly belong with the apprenticeship genres discussed in Chapter 6, as the writers role-play the part of a member of their future profession and engage in typical professional writing activities.

A letter-writing task set for a 'History of mathematics' module asks students to make a greater imaginative leap, but has a similar focus on content accuracy and clarity:

*Imagine it is the early 1830s and you are writing a letter of advice to a very good student of yours who is about to go to travel abroad to study Mathematics. Describe recent developments in EITHER the theory of functions of a real variable OR in the topic of complex functions and complex integrals.*

From a pedagogic perspective the task serves the same purpose as an Explanation, but writers seemed to have entered into it with particular enthusiasm, as the following examples show. The tone is much more personal and informal than in an Explanation; writers use first and second person pronouns, colloquial expressions such as *our profession is really taking off*, and evaluative language (*interesting; intriguing; valuable; new and exciting*).

*We are living in an interesting time for mathematics and I feel our profession is really taking off. My advice to you would be to continue your work on pure mathematics but also consider applied mathematics which the French are becoming more concerned with. Base yourself in France if you can as I feel the focus of mathematics is shifting there. Continuity is an intriguing subject at the moment…*

*During my time studying here, at L'École Polytechnique in Paris, I have come into contact with undoubtedly one of the most gifted mathematicians of our time, Augustin-Louis Cauchy. Through his lectures and published work I have been given a valuable insight into many new and exciting developments in the theory of functions of a real variable...*

Empathy writing allows and often encourages this more personal and lively response, of the kind that the writers might one day appropriately convey in the classroom, in the lecture theatre, or in a radio or television programme, to inspire the enthusiasm of others for their subject.

All the expert advice interviews in the corpus emanate from the Department of Food Sciences. In these the student poses as an expert, communicating with a media representative or directly with a member of the public, as in the following task prompts from the module Nutrition in Health and Disease:

*Donna Spencer is a journalist and wants to write an article on obesity for a newspaper. She has the following questions for you.*

*Valerie Bash is 30 years old and pregnant with her first child. She has the following questions:...*

These tasks have a ready-made structure in the form of a series of questions provided by the lecturer. The format is that of an exam paper requiring a number of short answers to problem questions, but the introduction of a hypothetical reader (or listener) makes the activity more meaningful, and also requires the student to adapt the explanation so that the language is less technical than that of the textbook sources.

Newspaper and magazine articles often adopt the authentic format of the genre. In an assignment written by a Masters level psychology student, for example, the heading, font and layout all mimic those of a magazine article, and there is an accompanying photograph which catches the eye but does not contribute to the information content of the piece. In accordance with the conventions of magazine journalism, the reader will understand that the photograph is staged, and that the girl in a photograph illustrating the incidence of mental illness amongst students probably does not have mental health problems herself, and may not even be a student. This contrasts with other genre families where visual images are only included if they convey factual information more effectively than is possible through text alone.

Like historical recounts, Empathy Writing draws heavily on background sources. These sources often remain unacknowledged, however, in order to maintain the integrity of the genre. Empathy Writing newspaper reports and letters ignore normal academic referencing conventions, although Empathy Writing transcripts of spoken discourse can include bibliographies and footnotes; the Food Sciences expert advice interviews refer to sources such as the Scientific Advisory Committee on Nutrition, for example, and 'a case for the prosecution of Freudian theory', produced by a Level 1 Psychology student, refers to biographies of Freud.

Empathy Writing's departure from conventional academic practice is both a strength and a weakness in pedagogical terms. Empathy Writing tasks signal to students the relevance of their discipline outside the academy, and they can also give scope to students' creativity and design flair. On the other hand these kinds of task are riskier for all concerned; students and tutors may not share the same views regarding the communicative requirements of the hypothetical audience, and the audience's requirements will always differ from those of the university department. One student's own assessment of his Empathy Writing article, ostensibly intended for 'the mechtech [Mechanical Technology] section' of the *New Scientist*, reflects a desire to excite and inform his readers in equal measure:

*The strengths of the article are an interesting introduction and amusing end, with good use of images and comparisons to other "hot" topics to interest the reader. The weaknesses of this article are the short length and lack of in-depth discussion of the topic.*

In this case the module leader had made clear the assessment criteria, but in some cases students may be left in doubt as to whether there are more marks to be gained for *"hot" topics* or for *in-depth discussion.*

## 7.3 Narrative Recounts

Narrative Recounts are so named because they recount a temporal sequence occurring in the past. Typical temporal sequences are the stages in a simulation game, as in the first of the two following examples, or the application of a research technique, as in the second.

*Before starting this level we calculated break even analysis which came 3000 units every week so that we may not again miss the opportunity of utilizing capacity and pay the fixed costs. We became proactive rather than reactive since our demand was fluctuating. In the trend there was a rise in the demand and the peak period comes gradually with modest peak in third week followed by highest peak in fourth week. In order to meet this demand we decided to build up stock to buffer against supply problems and finished goods stock to buffer against fluctuations in demand keeping in view the next peak period.*

(Logistics and operations management)

*At points my status as a disabled person, and my ability to use BSL (even in a limited capacity) united me with certain members of the group. Indeed, my experiences of my disability together with my motivations for taking up sign language were frequently brought up by members of the group as 'conversation-starters', and this common ground enabled me to conduct reasonably in-depth interviews and build a sense of rapport with certain members.*

(Research methods)

Past actions are usually recounted in the past tense, but apart from in one or two creative writing pieces there is little evidence of the Labovian narrative structure (Labov, 1972) which requires not only a temporal sequence but also a complicating action and a resolution. Reflective writing in the Narrative Recount family often describes a process of triumph over adversity, but even in this type of Narrative Recount the narrative is not fully developed; the writer simply progresses from a state of insecurity and unhappiness to a state of security and happiness. Thus our Narrative Recounts are not narratives in the Systemic Functional schools genre sense (as described, for example, by Christie, 1999), and in all but a few cases our student writers' primary aim is to report events in a truthful and accurate way, rather than to amuse, entertain or keep their readers in suspense.

Broadly speaking, there are two types of Narrative Recount in the BAWE corpus: those written in the third person (impersonal narrative recounts), where the writer describes a historical or fictional process, and those written in the first person (narratives of personal experience).

## Impersonal narrative recounts

Historical recounts, which describe for example the lives of famous scientists or processes such as the spread of a disease, were produced for modules in Agriculture, Biological Sciences, Engineering, Maths and Physics. They contain no self-reference, and their purpose, as with Explanations (Chapter 3) is to demonstrate knowledge, translating into a new form of words information that has already been documented elsewhere.

Because historical recounts retell a sequence of events that the writer has not personally experienced, and can only have discovered by reading other texts, they largely draw on 'background' rather than 'exhibit' sources. Typically these are introductory textbooks, reference books, government reports and organisation websites. An account of the 2003 space shuttle accident, for example, refers to the *Columbia Accident Investigation Board Report*, and an account of the development of particle accelerators refers to the CERN website.

Some historical recounts are close to Empathy Writing. They resemble their encyclopaedic and textbook sources in style, and although the intended readership is not made explicit, attempts may be made to engage with the reader in ways that are not typical of other genre families, for example by including pictures for decorative effect. Historical recounts might also be considered as a type of Explanation (Chapter 3). They pose the same kind of challenges in that their writers have to explain complex events clearly, and decide what information from their various sources to include and what to omit. Some historical recounts have affinities with Case Studies (Chapter 6) although the case under consideration in the narrative is always firmly in the past, so problems are addressed by identifying past failings, as in the following example, rather than by recommending future action.

**Conclusions as to how the accident could / should have been avoided**
*In the short term, to prevent this accident a number of additional checks should have been carried out before the launch and once the shuttle was in orbit. A visual inspection should have been carried out…*

In addition to historical recounts the corpus also contains one or two examples of impersonal narratives that are fictional, some of which are accompanied by reflective personal narrative recounts describing the process of their creation. These pieces appear to be the result of free writing, but are in fact responses to tasks designed to encourage focus on specific writing skills. One of our English lecturer informants described how she required students first to select texts to form an anthology, then to analyse these in terms of their linguistic features, and finally to write a new text inspired by their selection, accompanied by linguistic analysis and a discussion of the writing process. She reported some resistance to this, especially from young British students who had 'come through the English literature critical review route'. They complained on the one hand that the approach was too low level and 'primary school', but also that they found the task difficult and threatening. She described the process as 'risky', both for herself and for her students, because it departed from established practice.

## Narratives of personal experience

Many of the departments represented in the BAWE corpus asked their students to reflect on their own personal experiences. We might expect

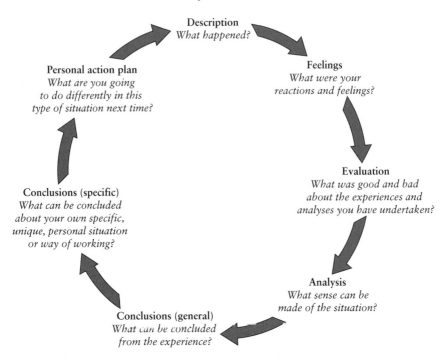

Figure 7.1    The experiential cycle (after Gibbs, 1988)

this kind of writing to be more prevalent in the applied disciplines; self-appraisal in relation to classroom practice has long been a requirement for student teachers, for example, and models such as Gibbs' experiental cycle (1988, see Figure 7.1) and Johns' model for structured reflection (1994, 1995) are widely used in Nursing to encourage professional development, as noted by Jasper (2003) and others. As Squires points out, 'the professions differ from other disciplines in being concerned primarily with acting rather than knowing' (2005: 130). Events in the professions are unpredictable and irreversible, and as there are no controlled conditions for experimentation, apprentices are asked to reflect on their past performance in order to improve their future practice. Nevertheless, even if their degree programme does not aim to prepare them for a specific profession, there is always scope for students to reflect on their progress. This is because all disciplines require students to acquire study skills, choose learning pathways and ultimately seek paid employment.

The majority of Narrative Recounts in the corpus review and reflect on the writer's personal experiences during an academic or workplace activity. In most genre families, students learn the concepts and methods of their disciplines while writing. This is true of Exercises and Problem Questions, where the text maps the writer's reasoning processes while progressing towards a solution, and of Critiques and Essays, where the task is the means by which the writer develops skill in argument construction. Students also have to record their experimental process during Methodology Recount and Design Specification tasks, and most, if not all, Case Studies are constructed from notes taken while engaging with the case. Narrative Recounts which reflect on personal experience tend to be different in this respect, because the activity has been undertaken prior to writing the assignment, is not replicable, and was an important event in its own right in terms of the acquisition of relevant disciplinary concepts and methods. The post-event recount may provide the student with a further opportunity to review techniques practised during the activity, but it is mainly important for other reasons: for the student as a means of reflecting on the significance of what happened, and for the assessor as proof that the student actually did undertake the activity. The assignment thus focuses on the way that the activity has impacted on the actor, in contrast to the 'essayist' approach to writing which seeks 'academic truth over personal experience' (Lillis, 2001).

Many of the narratives of personal experience in the corpus relate to a real or simulated work experience. Tutors usually have no other means of knowing the details of what went on during a student's work placement or project team meetings, so these kind of activities are difficult to assess except in terms of the student's own commentary. Such narratives are not necessarily entirely reliable reports of what went on, however, because writers are likely to cast themselves in a favourable light and shift responsibility for problems onto others. They may be a better indicator of a writer's ability to learn from experience. Usually, discussion of problematic issues concerning team management, as illustrated in the first of the following two examples, or a problematic incident in the workplace, as illustrated in the second, leads the student to state an intention to alter his or her practice. (A quarter of all occurrences of the word *hindsight* in the corpus occur in Narrative Recounts.)

*If I was to be involved in a similar group setup in the future, I would choose to allocate a group leader to ensure structure to the meetings, and that all other group members had their say, and to make decisions on how to undertake the required task, taking into account what the rest of the group feel.*

(Partnerships in practice)

*I had never appreciated that other nurses could be the third party you would be attempting to influence in triadic advocacy (Wheeler, 2000) or the conflicts that this can cause (Hamer & Collinson, 2005) and had not considered how the lack of autonomy of nurses and nursing can affect the achievement of patient autonomy (Tschudin, 2003a). I am also more aware of the many potential conflicts of duties that are present in ethical reasoning and will aim to acknowledge these in my future practice.*

(Ethics in health and social care)

Narratives of personal experience are also used in the creative arts disciplines, to communicate the nature and aims of the students' artwork, and their reflective analysis of the creative process. According to our academic informants, such assignments can be written prose narratives or be submitted in other formats, for example via audio or video footage, as a webpage, or as an appendage to a play script. In the BAWE corpus there are just a few Narrative Recounts in which students reflect on their own creative processes. In these cases the focus is on the student's creative fulfilment and personal improvement as a writer or director:

*The whole process of presenting Mulan, from choosing a story to tell to finalizing our product on stage, is like a journey of treasure hunt to me. The more I look back on the journey, the more I grow fond of being a storyteller.*

*This re-writing has been a new and enriching experience. First it allowed me to revisit a myth, Robinson Crusoe, and to remould it. Secondly, it entitled me to realize what I have often wished to do.*

The role of reflective writing in the creative arts is well documented, for example by Gray and Malins (2004), Evans (2007) and Walters (2008). It is intended to inform and enhance the student's artwork, situate it in a given context, and constitute evidence of the acquisition of disciplinary knowledge, not necessarily proven by the success of the artwork itself. Additionally, a written narrative of the creative process may help to validate creative studies as bona fide university disciplines, and creative work as research, although what research in the creative arts actually consists of remains a matter for debate. Gray and Malins (2004) argue that, from the academy's perspective, it is a means of contributing to knowledge, whereas from the students' perspective it is a means of improving their own practice. This may lead to some confusion about the identity of the target reader, as discussed by Paltridge (2004). Supervisors may think that the students' discussions of their creative output are aimed at subject experts, but students may have a more general reader in mind, and one very successful student interviewed by Paltridge claimed that she had written her MA art and design exegesis only for herself.

The question of who the assignment is written for must affect the narrative style, and the extent to which the writer is willing to risk exposure and admit to faults. Evans (2007: 75) emphasises the importance of students being honest when they reflect on their performance; he is suspicious of writing that seems too 'polished', because it is possible that 'tidying up uncertain situations and unassociated ideas may be indicative of a failure to deal with the complexity of the world, and a desire to assert the self, rather than reveal / discover it'.

Other narratives of personal experience in the corpus describe the process of undertaking a literature search, or of following qualitative approaches such as interviewing, observation or ethnography. These tasks are oriented towards research in the conventional sense, but acknowledge the importance of the individual researcher. They include reflective self-evaluation, as shown in the following examples.

*However much I probed my informants for 'juicy' information I found that it was really hard for them to say anything shocking or what I didn't already think I knew about them.*

(Anthropology)

*My first intention was to observe activity and interaction in a second hand book shop, paying special attention to variables such as gender and age, and their potential relation to areas of interest. This, as we will see, proved to be difficult.*

(Sociology)

Qualitative research methods are interpretative, and require a full acknowledgement of the researcher's presence within the environment that is being studied, but there seemed to be mixed views about the recounting of personal experiences in the Sociology and Anthropology departments where assignments of this type were set. One informant from Anthropology preferred essays to personal narrative assignments, on the grounds that essays prevented 'waffle', and another Anthropology lecturer reported that she particularly disliked to see students 'using their own experience of life' in their writing, 'with no evidence of reading'. A colleague in the same department, however, set a variety of non-traditional tasks including a take-off of the 'Ready Steady Cook' television programme (a daytime cooking show broadcast in the UK by the BBC) as discussed in Leedham (2009). This same lecturer assigned a practical task accompanied by a 5,000-word reflective commentary as an alternative to the traditional Masters dissertation.

Hemphill (2004) describes how students taking degrees in Exercise and Sport Science at an Australian university built on an experience-based piece. What was first produced as a 750-word 'descriptive and reflective first person written account of a signifi-cant personal experience' was gradually developed through input from lectures, readings and tutor feedback to become a 2,000-word 'philosophically informed research paper', including references to independently gathered sources and a discussion of how the origi-nal narrative could inform professional practice generally. Hemphill's students produced both pieces of work during the first semester of their first year of university study; the method was introduced partly in response to the finding that research papers written by such stu-dents at the end of their first semester typically contained a great deal of undigested material, copied uncritically from source texts. One of the purposes of Hemphill's approach was to encourage the stu-dents to think independently and critically about their topics. Gocsik (2006) advises film students to develop their writing skills in a similar way, by taking their own response to a film as a starting point, and then refining this response through critical thinking processes until it bears more resemblance to a conventional academic text. Gocsik sees the personal narrative as a first stage towards scholarly writing, but warns students that they have to develop beyond this stage:

'[A]dding something of your own' is not an invitation to bring your own personal associations, reactions, or experiences to the reading of a film. To create an informed argument, you must first recognize that your writing should be analytical rather than personal.

(Gocsik, 2006: 2–3).

In our corpus and interview data there is some evidence of students following a similar pathway from the first person Narrative Recount to the third person Essay or Critique. Our lecturer informants in English Studies took the long view of their students' progress, start-ing in Level 1 when they 'unlearned' the essayist tradition as it had been taught at school. In Level 1 rewriting and commentary tasks, the tutor was keen for students to discard 'the filter of secondary reading' and engage with the primary source, in this case their own and others' creative work. In later years this personal response was expected to be increasingly tempered by disciplinary knowledge:

*By the third year you expect them to engage with the debates in the field and make their standpoint on the basis of what they understand about the field in general.*

(English Studies lecturer)

In the BAWE corpus first person reflective recounts are distributed across all four levels of study, however, and clearly not all departments regard them as tasks only suitable for beginners. The role of this kind of writing depends on departmental and disciplinary responses to the question 'What is research?' In applied and creative disciplines there are many who regard improvement in personal practice as a valid research objective.

In Bizup's terms (2008), the writers of narratives of personal experience base their writing on authentic data ('exhibit' sources). They may not refer to any sources other than their own personal experience, or they may refer to procedures and analytical techniques ('method' sources) in order to explain their own and others' behaviour. For example, narratives of personal experience from Level 2 of the 'Starting and running a business' module in Engineering contain no references to sources, drawing solely on the writers' own experiences, whereas narratives of personal experience from a Level 2 practice module in Health each list between eight and twelve sources of the following type:

Belbin UK. (2005). *Belbin team-roles*
Bennis and Shepard (1956) *A theory of group development*
Bion (1996) *Experiences in groups*
Boaden, N. & Leaviss, J. (2000). *Putting teamwork into context*
Cottrell, S. (2003). *The study skills handbook*
Gibbs, G. (1988). *Learning by doing. A guide to teaching and learning methods*
Levin, P. (2005). *Successful teamwork!*
Miller, C, Ross, N and Freeman, M. (1999). *Shared learning and clinical teamwork: new directions in education for multiprofessional practice.*
Payne, M. (2000). *Teamwork in multiprofessional care*
Stanton, N. (2004). *Mastering communication*
Tuckman, B. (1965). *Developmental sequence in small groups*

Most of these sources are not discipline-specific, and none of them provide information about medical treatments. Clearly the assignment focuses on social practice and personal development rather than nursing scholarship.

## 7.4  Reflective writing for personal development

Almost any writing task might serve as a means to improve text organisation and language accuracy, and any argumentative or critiquing task might serve as a means to improve critical thinking skills. However personal narratives do sometimes target competencies that are neglected in other types of academic writing activity. Other types of writing task may involve reader awareness, and possibly interaction with a tutor, but personal narratives often pay additional attention to the social dimension; students may discuss their own performances as team members, for example. This kind of reflective writing calls into play the metacognitive skill of self-evaluation, and it may also address the affective dimension if students record their own emotions as part of this evaluative process. Science students taking a course described by Kathpalia and Heah (2008), for example, were encouraged to express their feelings using the first person, and their progress was partly measured in terms of their ability to make heard their own 'voice'.

In recent years much has been made of the need to measure student achievement in new ways which will help employers select suitable job candidates from the growing pool of graduates with very similar qualifications (Varnava, 2008). Some sort of record system which provides a 'means by which students can monitor, build and reflect upon their personal development' was originally proposed to UK higher education institutions in the Dearing Report (1997, Recommendation 20), and the requirement was reiterated in the QAA for Higher Education *Guidelines for HE Progress Files* (2001) and in the Burgess recommendations (Universities UK, 2004). It resulted in widespread initiatives to support Personal Development Planning (PDP) in British universities.

PDP requires learners to set targets, act on plans, record achievement, and interpret and evaluate what they have recorded (Varnava, 2008). It is supposed to lead to greater independence and a more proactive approach to academic study (LTSN, 2002), and also to help students present their achievements more explicitly, thus making it easier for employers to recognise them during the graduate recruitment process. The following examples, taken from job application forms, demonstrate how the labour market requires evidence of reflective practice of the kind students engage in during PDP:

Please describe any formal / informal leadership positions that you have held including details of how you may have mobilised support, had a positive impact on others or brought out the best in a team member. (300 words)

Tell us about an experience and feedback, which you feel significantly impacted on your development....

Give us an example of when you have worked successfully as part of a team or in a partnership. In your example explain clearly the relationships and interactions that took place....

Describe for us a time of complex change when you were expected to take on new tasks and responsibilities....

(British Gas Centrica Finance Graduate Programme, 2009)

Please describe a specific situation that demonstrates how you go about understanding customer needs and expectations and go on to exceed them.

Describe a time when you had to persuade a person or group to accept a decision they were initially reluctant to consider.

How do you think your skills, knowledge and experience can contribute to your chosen part of the business i.e. HR, Finance or Marketing, Sales & Customer Services?

(Royal Mail Group Graduate Programme, 2009)

Describe one example, not necessarily clinical, that has increased your understanding of team working. Describe your role and how you contributed to the team. What have you learned and how will you apply this to working with colleagues as a foundation doctor?

Describe a situation, not necessarily clinical, where you personally felt challenged and under pressure. Describe how you responded. What did you learn from this experience and how will this benefit you as a foundation doctor?

Describe one of your non-academic achievements. Explain clearly why this was an achievement for you. What did you learn from this achievement and how will this influence your approach to patient care?

(Foundation Applicant's Handbook, 2008)

One difference between PDP and job applications, however, is that the application form questions invite applicants to present a positive view of their past achievements, whereas reflective writing tasks at university often seem to encourage students to consider learning deficits, mistakes, or problems, as well as achievements.

## Issues with the assessment of Personal Development Planning

Although reflective writing is sometimes undertaken on a voluntary basis it is often incorporated within degree programme assessment systems, as this helps departments gather consistent evidence of PDP activity, and also motivates students to take part. As Williams and Ryan (2006: 175) point out: 'If it's not assessed, I don't know the take-up and commitment you'd get towards it, that's the problem'. Departments may feel compelled to assess their students' PDP output for this reason.

However Williams and Ryan claim that time-pressed lecturers often only glance at reflective pieces, to check whether the task has been attempted. It is also possible that some departments lack the appropriate assessment criteria, as many of the features which contribute to the success of reflective writing flout academic conventions within the Western higher education 'essayist' tradition. Reflective writing is primarily concerned with the expression of affective responses to events that the writer has personally experienced, and that are often of a social and collaborative nature. Moreover these responses are often complex and are likely to alter over time. The essayist tradition, on the other hand, prioritises:

...logic over emotion; academic truth (published theory and research) over personal experience; linearity over circularity; explicitness (a form of) over evocation; closing down of possible meanings rather than open-endedness; certainty over uncertainty; formality over informality; competitiveness over collaboration.

(Lillis, 2001: 81)

Thus, although there is much promotion of PDP within higher education, the assessment of self-reflection is clearly not a straightforward task. Many lecturers may feel on safer ground when assessing logical consistency, theoretical knowledge, and explicit statements of proven fact, and some, like Ecclestone and Hayes, may resent PDP as a facet of a burgeoning 'therapeutic' approach to university education which 'takes us away from the business of developing subject knowledge' (2009: 102).

Some students are doubtful about the assessment of reflective writing too, perhaps due to prior academic conditioning which has discouraged displays of personal feeling, or because of the risk entailed in admitting mistakes and personal weaknesses in the context of grading. Kathpalia and Heah describe the reactions of a group of Science students who were initially daunted by the affective aspect of self-reflection: 'They were uncomfortable about expressing their attitudes and feelings towards writing and they preferred to write in the third person' (2008: 311). Wickens and Spiro found that some informants rejected grading while acknowledging the benefits of reflection:

It's a vehicle to teach you the process of reflection, I think there would be tension if it was graded... it's a pass fail module if it was graded (...) you are running the risk of grading the content of somebody's personal life story.

(Wickens and Spiro, 2010)

A more extreme reaction is reported by Ecclestone and Hayes in a section entitled 'Sarah learns to become a therapeutic lecturer'. In the following excerpt, 'Sarah' speaks about her embarrassment and suspicion when group work required the sharing of emotional experiences:

...I was thinking I can't believe I just disclosed all that to strangers. It wasn't what I wanted to do – I'm happy saying that stuff to friends – and I wished I hadn't done it...It's just the same with the reflective statement we have to do; I've got 2,500 words to write, I've left it till the last minute and it's being assessed. It's the way they write the questions: it's a horrible mix of NVQ[2]-style competences, develop a portfolio of evidence, and questions about that invite you to write about how you feel not what you think or believe. It's really insidious.

(Ecclestone and Hayes, 2009: 103–4)

This kind of resistance to the aims of the reflective assignment can be sensed in some of the writing in the BAWE corpus. Contributors did not always write about their feelings or evaluate their own performance when the writing task seemed to require this sort of response, and perhaps their assessors did not expect them to do so. It is also sometimes impossible to judge from the corpus evidence whether or not students were fully engaging with PDP. Some apparently reflective writers may not have disclosed their true feelings, perhaps in order to protect their privacy or because they did not wish to present themselves in a negative light. Putting a positive spin on past achievements might, of course, be regarded as good practice in self-promotion, something that the graduate job market apparently requires.

## *The PDP subcorpus*

The PDP subcorpus is made up of most of the reflective narratives of personal experience in the BAWE corpus, and excerpts from assignments in any other genre family which contained evidence of Personal Development Planning. This amounts to 86,795 words in 59 files. The texts range in length from 6,748 words (an HLTM portfolio submission) to about 200 words (the concluding paragraphs of some Health and Computer Science assignments). 'Reflective narratives of personal experience in health', the biggest sector in the subcorpus, range from just over 500 words at Level 1 to about 4,000 words at Level 3. The texts come from 12 of the 30 major disciplines represented in the BAWE corpus, and also include one piece from Education, classed as 'other' because Education was not a department targeted for data collection.

Of course all utterances are in some way value judgements, and as Römer (2008: 115) points out, 'expressions of what we think of what we talk or write about' are everywhere to be found in academic texts. Reflection in its broadest sense is also characteristic of successful academic writing generally, and occurs throughout the BAWE corpus, in every genre family. Most assignments, however, demonstrate the ability to evaluate and reflect on entities, propositions or the behaviour of others, and draw on external evidence such as experimental data or academic readings. The PDP subcorpus does not contain this

Table 7.1    The PDP subcorpus and genre families

| Discipline | Case Study | Critique | Essay | Exercise | Explanation | Methodology Recount | Narrative Recount |
|---|---|---|---|---|---|---|---|
| Archaeology | | | | | | 1 | |
| Architecture | | | | | | | 1 |
| Business | 1 | 1 | | | | | 3 |
| Chemistry | | | | | | | 1 |
| Computer Science | | | 1 | 3 | | | 1 |
| Cybernetics | | | 1 | | | | 1 |
| Education | | | | | | | 1 |
| Engineering | 1 | 1 | 1 | | | | 6 |
| English | | | | | | | 2 |
| Health | | | | | | | 18 |
| HLTM | | 1 | | | 1 | | 4 |
| Linguistics | | | | | | | 5 |
| Medicine | | | 1 | | | | 2 |

kind of reflective writing, but only those texts which draw on personal feelings and experiences in order to evaluate the self. Such texts may focus solely on past, present or future events, or may present the entire reflective cycle, from retrospection to future planning.

Table 7.1 shows the distribution of PDP reflective writing in the subcorpus. It can be seen that most is in the Narrative Recount genre family; belonging within the subset of Narratives of Personal Experience. It is also particularly common in Health. However it is quite likely that reflective writing in higher education is more widespread than Table 7.1 suggests, and that examples from other disciplines and genre families were simply not submitted to the BAWE corpus.

Table 7.2 shows the distribution of PDP reflective pieces across levels. As we have seen, reflective writing can serve as a preparation for applications to many types of graduate position, and the sharp rise in numbers in the final year of undergraduate study seems to point to this link between reflection and employability. Students at Level 4 (Masters level), on the other hand, are more likely to be taking a career break sponsored by their existing employer, or planning employment in another country which has other types of application requirement. All assignments in Medicine are at Level 4, because all the students on the programme were graduates.

A considerable amount of the writing in the PDP subcorpus is in diary form, recording and reflecting on learning processes over

Table 7.2   The PDP subcorpus and levels of study

| Discipline | Level 1 | Level 2 | Level 3 | Level 4 |
|---|---|---|---|---|
| Archaeology | | 1 | | |
| Architecture | | | | 1 |
| Business | | | 5 | |
| Chemistry | | | 1 | |
| Computer Science | 3 | | 2 | |
| Cybernetics | 1 | | 1 | |
| Education | | 1 | | |
| Engineering | | 6 | 2 | 1 |
| English | | | | 2 |
| Health | 6 | 4 | 8 | |
| HLTM | 1 | 2 | 2 | 1 |
| Linguistics | | | 4 | 1 |
| Medicine | n/a | n/a | n/a | 3 |

a period of time, for example during a series of practical sessions (Archaeology), teamwork sessions (Business, Health), overseas visits (Engineering, Medicine), coursework (Business, HLTM) and patient care (Health). Other types of reflective writing in the subcorpus include self-appraisals relating to work performance (HLTM), interviewing technique (Health) and career prospects (Business), and commentaries on the process of producing other non-reflective texts submitted for assessment, for example literature reviews (Health) and creative writing (English).

Although all the complete assignments in the PDP subcorpus are narratives of personal experience, belonging to the Narrative Recount genre family, the subcorpus also contains self-reflection sections from assignments classified as belonging to other genres, and the headings of these sections may or may not indicate their reflective nature. For example, an Explanation written for HLTM includes a section entitled 'Personal career plan and reflective commentary', while a Business Critique contains a final 'Learning process' section. Likewise a highly reflective 'Feedback' section is annexed to a Computer Science Essay. In other cases, the reflective content of a given section is not signalled in any way, but may be found in a paragraph or two at the beginning or end of the assignment.

On the other hand, whilst there is PDP writing in the corpus that is not overtly signalled as such, there are also assignment sections which are labelled in ways which indicate reflective practice, but which turn out not to be concerned with personal experience or planning. In these cases it would appear that the academic department endorses a different interpretation of reflective practice. The Medical School patient portfolio template, for example (see Chapter 6), contains a section labelled 'Impact on your learning', which requires the student to 'Describe what you have learned from this case'. This section is almost always used to note key information relating to disease and treatment, as in the following example. We assume that this sort of response is acceptable to tutors in Medicine in the context of the Case Study.

*Presentation, complications and management of Down's Syndrome, differential diagnosis of wheezy breathlessness in infants, presentation and management of bronchiolitis.*

(Patient portfolio)

On the few occasions when the 'Impact on your learning' section of the patient portfolio template was used to explicitly evaluate impact, as in the excerpt below, it is the medical case that is reflected upon, rather than the student's own performance:

*This case has provided an opportunity to study infective endocarditis in much greater detail. In particular it has highlighted the difficulties which may arise in diagnosing the condition due to its diverse and non-specific clinical presentation. The value of the Duke criteria when trying to confirm a diagnosis has also been exemplified. Furthermore it has allowed the management and possible complications to be studied.*

Such an approach to reflection prioritises the formal assertion of academic truth, in accordance with the essayist tradition, but it does not prepare GPs for the reflective writing required of them when they apply for their first job (see the Foundation Year application form), nor does it prepare them for the yearly PDPs they will be required to write throughout their careers (see, for example, the National Association of Primary Care Educators' *Introduction to GP Appraisals*). Case Studies in the corpus for the other Health professions do not contain a similar 'Impact on your learning' section, but students of nursing and related subjects do produce a great deal of reflective writing in other formats, frequently referring to scholars who have theoreticised reflection such as Schön (1987, 1991) and Gibbs (1988).

The dividing line between self-reflection and other types of evaluative writing is sometimes thin, but is evident when comparing superficially similar assignments written for different modules. An account of a literature survey from Anthropology, for example, is

a narrative of personal experience, written in the first person, but simply summarises the process and outcomes of the activity, as can be seen in the following excerpt:

*Through this project I have been able to gain information on five journal / books based around my essay title. These articles would enable me to write a lengthy, in-depth essay about the importance of witchcraft in African society. I have been able to do this firstly by choosing the appropriate search database to me, then narrowing down the search using a variety of techniques to gain the correct articles for my essay title.*

This can be contrasted with a narrative of personal experience from Health, which explains the writer's motivation for conducting a literature review, and is cast as 'a reflection on the ways I can improve my time management and reduce my anxiety and stress levels':

*Seeley et al (2003) list the long-term physiological and psychological changes caused by stress. Secretion of cortisol suppresses the immune system and secretion of adrenaline and noradrenaline increases heart rate and blood pressure. Exposure to stress and anxiety over long periods can therefore have very serious physiological affects. One of the psychological responses noted by Howard (1998) is change in cognitive ability. He argues that individuals who are stressed find their concentration span decreases, their problem solving abilities are reduced and they move from task to task but never complete tasks. This is how I feel when I try to juggle meaningful patient interaction, observations rounds, medication rounds, discharge planning etc. I decided to focus on time management and prioritization as tools to overcome my anxiety.*

The same differences in approach can be found in reflections on business simulations. The following excerpt is from an Engineering Business Management module. The writer was told to 'Discuss the importance of the marketing strategy decisions made by your team during the Marketing Game', and asked, 'What do you consider to be the main learning points of the game?'. The response is an objective account of the team's performance, and although the assignment contains plenty of evidence of reflection on marketing strategy, there is no explicit indication of self-evaluation:

a. *The disappointing results of year 3 showed us that there was no point targeting segments that were not our strength, especially where one team is overwhelmingly dominant. (Fantastic 4 with 66% market share with managers)*
b. *Underestimating the importance of advertising had proved costly for Innotech 2, especially compared to other teams who were spending more on advertising and doing better.*

In contrast the response to team work in the following piece, a Narrative of Personal Experience written for a 'Starting and running a business' Engineering module, is much more formative on a personal level:

*We all struggled halfway through because we all had one or two more group projects going on at the same time and they had more pressing deadlines. So we let things slack until one week before the elevator pitch, when we all did some intense work, and discovered almost all of us like working under pressure. I really enjoyed being stressed before the pitch and then seeing it all come together. I was a bit worried when we did not get plenty of questions, and I felt that I had failed my group. I was concerned that we were not well prepared. On hindsight, I should not have let things slide in the weeks preceding the upper level pitch, and made sure we stayed on track, and not done things last minute.*

In view of this apparent difference in communicative purpose, the Anthropology Narrative Recount and the excerpt from the Engineering Case Study referred to above were not included in the PDP subcorpus, while the Narrative Recounts from Health and for the 'Starting and running a business' Engineering module were included.

More difficult inclusion decisions had to be made when writing contained oblique indications of personal reflection and growth. In the following account of the Business simulation 'Winning margin', for example, there is some indication that the writer learned from problems encountered during teamwork, but it is difficult to tell the extent to which he takes responsibility for the team's actions. The assignment was excluded from the PDP subcorpus.

*The cash management was poor. The team aimed to win as many as possible orders in year 1, and the author succeeded in it, after persuading the team to invest $14 m in Engineering & Quality. But on trying to complete the won orders, the team came to realise that it was short of cash; the team had failed to take into consideration other costs such as market, product and supplier development and stock expenses. The easy solution was to make discounts to customers and have bank loans to cover current liabilities. But both of them deteriorated team's cash position; although the team was achieving high sales, it could not make profit! That is when the team realised the importance of effective cash management.*

## 7.5  The language of writing for oneself and others

Narrative Recounts and Empathy Writing are different from all the other genre families in terms of their multidimensional scores, as discussed in Chapter 2. Narrative Recounts are outliers on Biber's Dimensions 1 (involved vs. informational) and 2 (narrative vs. non-narrative), 3 (elaborated vs. situation-dependent) and 5 (non-impersonal v. abstract and impersonal), and although closer to the norm, Empathy Writing displays similar register features. It should be noted, however, that although Narrative Recounts and Empathy Writing are comparatively more involved, situation-dependent, concrete and persuasive than the other BAWE genre families, they still exhibit many of the features of formal academic prose when compared to genres such as conversation.

Most writers of Narrative Recounts and Empathy Writing texts are concerned with engaging their readers on a personal or professional level, and they work hard to create writer–reader dialogues, foregrounding interpersonal meaning. These texts have relatively high scores at the 'involved' end of the involved-informational continuum, suggesting that they contain relatively high quantities of first and second person pronouns, counted as 'engagement features' by Hyland (2004). Hyland found that expert academic writers used more engagement features generally than student writers, for example they asked more questions and directly addressed their readers more often than students did. Perhaps this is because such strategies place an imposition on the reader, and students are not powerful in relation to the tutors who read their work. We might expect different behaviour from student empathy writers when they pose as experts and address a different hypothetical readership. Of course, the expert texts that empathy writers emulate are not research articles, and some of the functions of questions listed by Hyland, such as 'establishing a research niche' and 'suggesting further research', would be irrelevant in typical Empathy Writing texts such as business correspondence, magazine articles and media interviews.

If we take question marks as an indicator of the question function, most of the genre families in the BAWE corpus contain more questions per 10,000 words than either Hyland's student project reports (4.3 questions) or his research article corpus (5.0 questions). Empathy Writing contains the highest number of question marks of all the genre families in the corpus, more than double the amount in Explanations, as shown in Table 7.3.

Many of the questions in Empathy Writing occur as structuring devices in section headings, predicting the content of the forthcoming section. In the expert advice pieces from Food Sciences, questions are provided with the assignment task; each one is used to signal a new topic, as in the following example:

Table 7.3   Distribution of question marks (per 10,000 words)

| Genre family | Question marks |
| --- | --- |
| Empathy Writing | 28.6 |
| Explanations | 11.1 |
| Proposals | 9.8 |
| Essays | 8.0 |
| Narrative Recounts | 6.6 |
| Problem Questions | 4.7 |
| Case Studies | 2.8 |
| Design Specifications | 1.7 |

*Q. Does obesity run in families?*
*A. Looking at some families, you would probably comment that; 'yes obesity does run in families'. However whether this is down to genes or lifestyle (nature vs. nurture) has been the cause of much debate over recent decades…*

In other cases, students create their own question headings, as in the case of a leaflet produced for an Agriculture module which lists the following questions on its front cover, and on later pages repeats each question in turn with accompanying information:

*What are roundworms?*
*What are the symptoms?*
*What is the life cycle of the parasites?*
*What are the organic regulations?*
*How do you control them?*
          (An organic farmer's guide to biological roundworm control in sheep)

This leaflet's front cover attracts the eye with a decorative picture of a sheep, and the whole text is designed to convey a small amount of practical information as accessibly as possible. The interpersonal section heading style contrasts sharply with the style of headings typically used in the Sciences in other genre families; these convey textual rather than interpersonal meanings, for example introduction, method, results and conclusion, or use letters and numbers to construct a hierarchy of text divisions (Gardner and Holmes, 2009).

## Grammar and lexis in the PDP subcorpus

The keyword lists in Table 7.4 were created by comparing word frequencies in the PDP subcorpus (86,795 words in 59 files) with frequencies in the entire BAWE corpus. Words which occurred

Table 7.4   The top and bottom 30 keywords in the PDP subcorpus

|    | Positive keywords | Keyness | Negative keywords | Keyness |
|----|-------------------|---------|-------------------|---------|
| 1  | *I*               | 6587.87 | *the*             | −486.64 |
| 2  | *my*              | 2828.23 | *of*              | −286.40 |
| 3  | *me*              | 957.58  | *is*              | −247.05 |
| 4  | *team*            | 550.35  | *its*             | −97.14  |
| 5  | *group*           | 480.68  | *law*             | −75.80  |
| 6  | *had*             | 448.15  | *economic*        | −72.93  |
| 7  | *feel*            | 445.26  | *by*              | −62.22  |
| 8  | *we*              | 416.09  | *women*           | −60.74  |
| 9  | *work*            | 354.75  | *system*          | −60.70  |
| 10 | *our*             | 349.52  | *human*           | −56.29  |
| 11 | *skills*          | 305.29  | *between*         | −54.46  |
| 12 | *am*              | 300.01  | *state*           | −51.56  |
| 13 | *learning*        | 297.95  | *model*           | −44.75  |
| 14 | *was*             | 275.18  | *war*             | −42.12  |
| 15 | *interview*       | 270.70  | *ibid*            | −40.19  |
| 16 | *felt*            | 246.91  | *data*            | −39.58  |
| 17 | *rails*           | 241.06  | *power*           | −39.20  |
| 18 | *nurses*          | 231.89  | *results*         | −38.83  |
| 19 | *myself*          | 228.08  | *nature*          | −38.62  |
| 20 | *about*           | 226.57  | *control*         | −37.51  |
| 21 | *Crusoe*          | 225.39  | *countries*       | −36.53  |
| 22 | *learnt*          | 219.85  | *are*             | −35.86  |
| 23 | *nursing*         | 208.57  | *international*    | −35.74  |
| 24 | *bed*             | 204.11  | *there*           | −35.16  |
| 25 | *to*              | 196.84  | *society*         | −34.87  |
| 26 | *Thompson*        | 196.53  | *government*      | −33.67  |
| 27 | *think*           | 192.92  | *world*           | −32.95  |
| 28 | *have*            | 190     | *effect*          | −32.92  |
| 29 | *rewriting*       | 187.24  | *policy*          | −31.70  |
| 30 | *communication*   | 186.04  | *public*          | −31.54  |

significantly more frequently in the subcorpus were considered positively key, while words which were unusually rare were considered negatively key.

The positive key words give a good picture of the main themes of PDP writing. Emphasis is on the first person (*I, my, me, we, our, am, myself*) and on affective and cognitive mental processes (*feel / felt, learning / learned, think*). *Crusoe* appears on the list because English Studies students wrote narratives of personal experience about their rewriting of parts of the novel *Robinson Crusoe. Thompson* is the name of an author frequently cited in Health students' narratives of personal experience.

The negative keywords indicate that reflective writing is not about models, systems, affairs of state or society at large, all themes which are common in other genres of academic writing. The list contains more nouns and prepositions, and is dominated by *the* and *of*, two words which frequently form a collocational framework for nominal groups. *Women* and *human* occur in the negative list because they are used to refer to people en masse; rather than to the individual.

Keywords can tell us a lot about corpus topics, but although *good, difficult, better, confident, improved, comprehensible, surprised, uncomfortable, lonely, enjoyable, easier, worried* and *helpful* were all positive in the PDP subcorpus at lower levels of keyness, none of the keywords listed in Table 7.4 seem particularly expressive of attitude.

Römer (2008) examined methods of identifying the linguistic features which indicated evaluative meaning in a three million word corpus of book reviews. She found that 5-grams were far more useful than key words as a means of finding evaluative elements. Most of the most frequent 5-grams in her corpus were either evaluative or described the structure of the book under review. The 86,795-word PDP subcorpus, being considerably smaller than Römer's corpus, generated only eight 5-grams which occurred five or more times, and only two of these occurred in five or more texts (*I will be able to* and *the rest of the group*). We therefore generated a list of 4-grams; Table 7.5 presents all those that occurred five times or more, in five or more different texts.

Many of the clusters in Table 7.5 are similar to those identified by Wickens and Spiro (2010), who examined a small corpus of reflective writing produced for a Masters programme in Education. Their top 4-grams include *I would like to, I feel that I, to be able to, it is important to*, and *will be able to*.

As in the studies by Römer (2008) and Wickens and Spiro (2010), only a small number of the clusters are topic-related (*health and social care* and *the upper level pitch*). The remaining 4-grams in the table mostly reflect genre-specific but not discipline-specific characteristics

Table 7.5     4-grams in the PDP subcorpus

|  | Cluster | Frequency | Texts |
|---|---|---|---|
| 1 | *to be able to* | 21 | 10 |
| 2 | *I was able to* | 18 | 13 |
| 3 | *the rest of the* | 18 | 14 |
| 4 | *health and social care* | 12 | 5 |
| 5 | *the upper level pitch* | 11 | 5 |
| 6 | *at the same time* | 10 | 7 |
| 7 | *I would like to* | 10 | 7 |
| 8 | *will be able to* | 10 | 8 |
| 9 | *I will be able* | 9 | 7 |
| 10 | *I feel that I* | 8 | 7 |
| 11 | *I feel that this* | 8 | 6 |
| 12 | *I will try to* | 8 | 6 |
| 13 | *in order to improve* | 8 | 5 |
| 14 | *member of the group* | 8 | 5 |
| 15 | *the end of the* | 8 | 8 |
| 16 | *at the beginning of* | 7 | 5 |
| 17 | *it is important to* | 7 | 5 |
| 18 | *on the other hand* | 7 | 7 |
| 19 | *rest of the group* | 7 | 5 |
| 20 | *we were able to* | 7 | 6 |
| 21 | *a better understanding of* | 6 | 5 |
| 22 | *at the end of* | 6 | 6 |
| 23 | *I have learnt a* | 6 | 5 |
| 24 | *I will reflect on* | 6 | 5 |
| 25 | *the purpose of the* | 6 | 6 |
| 26 | *to focus on the* | 6 | 5 |
| 27 | *a wide range of* | 5 | 5 |
| 28 | *have learnt a lot* | 5 | 5 |
| 29 | *it would have been* | 5 | 5 |

of reflective writing. Some seem to have a metadiscoursal framing function (*it is important to, the purpose of the, to focus on the*). Others are concerned with temporal order (*the end of the, at the beginning of, at the end of*). Time sequence is frequently referred to in PDP writing, as in the following examples, because it typically recounts a series of events, in bold here:

*Member D was an envisioner: he had excellent ideas **at the beginning of the project**, but he struggled in developing these ideas **after** the Upper Level Pitch.*

***During the year** the chemistry meetings held were very useful to my project, any issues that came up could be discussed with more experienced chemists and advice on any action to take was given.*

*I had to spend two or three hours every night studying Arabic but **by the end of the first fortnight** I was able to take a basic history in Arabic.*

*I also helped with the 'organiser' role, especially **nearer the end of the process** when we were not being as organised as I liked so therefore took matters into my own hands and organised the group myself.*

The most frequent clusters also reveal the extent to which reflective writers look towards the future, in keeping with the aims of PDP. Several of the contexts for *I will be able to* relate to employment prospects:

*I have spent 10 sessions in each section. They have taught me **lessons that I will be able to use** in the future, in my career in the hospitality industry.*

*I hope that in future **I will be able to creatively engage** in professional work.*

*I am acutely aware of the increased expectations of third year students and the impending expectations of qualifying and hope that by focusing on a personal characteristic I feel needs attention **I will be able to develop** both personally and professionally.*

On the other hand *I will try to* tends to be used with reference to more immediate cognitive and communicative goals:

*Through reflection **I will try to explain** why I found this particular situation challenging and what I have learned from it.*

*Anyway, I will be preparing for the BA case next week for Orchestrating Knowledge, so I will have an opportunity to practice this image then. **I will try to understand** the images by reading the textbook.*

*Rather than focusing on individual projects or on project stages as defined by RIBA Plan of Work, **I will try to indicate** how each of the mentioned skills developed through my involvement in various projects.*

Apart from one instance of use as a temporal marker, *at the same time* functions contrastively in the PDP subcorpus, like *on the other hand*. Both were regarded by Römer as having 'strong evaluative potential' (2008: 122), and she notes that in book reviews *on the other hand* is likely to precede a negative comment. This is also true in the PDP subcorpus, as can be seen from the following examples:

...*members' willingness to participate and suggest solutions helped the team's effort in completing the task in a satisfactory way.* **On the other hand, the team's main weakness** *was the difficulty faced coming up with a truly innovative product.*

*We have achieved to understand better by helping each other.* **On the other hand it was challenging** *as each of us were given different sources approaching the topic with different ways.*

Römer also noted that *at the same time* tended to precede positive evaluations in her corpus. In the PDP subcorpus, however, what follows is sometimes positive, sometimes negative:

*Learning Persian was a* **difficult but at the same time interesting** *experience, because it was the first time that I tried to learn a foreign language not by means of my mother tongue.*

*I managed to provide* **some good comments but at the same time realized that I missed out** *some key points.*

Another frequent and evaluative cluster in both the PDP subcorpus and in Römer's corpus was *it would have been*. There are 14 instances of the '*It * have been*' construction in the PDP subcorpus, and most are used to reflect negatively on the unsatisfactory outcome of a past action, as the following examples show:

*I found the experience challenging because Death and Dying was taught in five hours over two weeks and I felt that* **it should have been accorded more time and importance.**

*It could be argued that by using the word 'dispute' we immediately made the interviewee feel anxious and* **it may have been better for us to be more general about the content of questions** *we were going to ask.*

*This sometimes meant that three of us worked and then we informed the rest of the group about what we had discussed, when instead* **it should have been the group discussing it all together.**

*Ideally* **it would have been beneficial** *to record the interview on a camcorder*

*Also at the beginning of the interview* **it would have been better** *to state how long it was likely to last.*

All but the first of these examples can be interpreted as indirect admissions of responsibility which could be more directly expressed by *I should have* or *we should have*. These constructions are rarely used by student writers, however. *I should have* in particular is a risky claim, and there are only 11 instances of this in the entire BAWE corpus, seven of which come from the PDP subcorpus, and five of which were produced by the same writer. The following examples all include some mitigating element which lessens the burden of culpability. The first *I should have* in the first example actually points the blame at others, the second offers an excuse (*I lacked the practice*) and the last is only a partial admission (in some cases the writer apparently 'did "say no"'):

*I should have been told about the quick lunch, but equally I had heard that the quick lunch menu was on, so I should have asked who prepared it.*

*Personally, I have to admit that, because of the fact that I lacked the practice that input and output offers to a learner, I should have invested more time and effort to the learning process.*

*I will reflect on and evaluate my progress following every situation where I should have or did 'say no'.*

*We should have* seems to require less mitigation, probably because the burden of blame is spread amongst group members. There are still only 13 examples in the entire BAWE corpus, however, five of which come from the PDP subcorpus, the product of four different writers:

*This was possibly an issue we should have addressed early in order to maintain some professionalism and structure to the group.*

*In hindsight we should have mentioned the noise levels during our interview.*

*I feel that before actually carrying the interview out we should have carried out further research into carrying out interviews.... I also feel we should have picked a more confident person to carry out the actual interview.*

*A customer didn't want caraway seeds on their carrots, but all the portions had been made with caraway seeds. We should have considered that a customer may not like caraway seeds.*

*I would have*, a more common construction in both the main corpus and the subcorpus, is usually found in contexts where the writer does not take responsibility for a problem, although it is occasionally used to acknowledge personal error, as in the following examples:

*... had I thought about all the different issues and influences of stressors at the beginning of my care for them I would have done some things differently.*

*In retrospect I would have requested that all team members within the first week made a short list of their talents and interests.*

Most of the remaining clusters listed in Table 7.5 are 'oral' fragments of declarative mental process clauses: *I would like to, I feel that I, I feel that this,* and *I have learnt (a lot).* Nominalisation, a process which tends to make claims more value neutral, does not seem to have taken place to such an extent in these texts as in other academic genres, and the unusually verbal nature of the reflective pieces also suggests a more spontaneous and conversational style, in keeping with the personal topics under discussion.

## Appraisal in the PDP subcorpus

As evaluation plays such a major role in PDP writing, the APPRAISAL system developed by Martin (2000) and Martin and White (2005) was an appropriate tool for examining PDP writers' stance. APPRAISAL is concerned with emotions (AFFECT), ethics (JUDGEMENT) and aesthetics (APPRECIATION), and it is the first of these that is most distinctive in the PDP subcorpus.

Martin and White consider six factors when classifying AFFECT:

1. Whether it is positive or negative
2. Whether it is internally experienced or manifests itself externally (mental 'disposition' or a behavioural 'surge')
3. Whether it is an undirected mood or a reaction to a 'trigger'
4. Its position on a cline of intensity
5. Whether the emotion has been experienced (*realis*) or relates to future dis/inclination (*irrealis*)
6. Whether it has to do with un/happiness, in/security or dis/satisfaction.

(Martin and White, 2005: 46–52)

The contributors to the PDP subcorpus tend to balance the negative and the positive, often reporting initial negative feelings leading to a 'happy ending' and an overall positive evaluation of their experience. In this they may be influenced by common discourse patterns: the problem solution structure (Hoey, 1983) and the narrative, with its 'complicating action' and 'coda' (Labov, 1972). A concluding positive evaluation also seems to be a good preparation for the job application form, which invites applicants to provide an upbeat appraisal of their past experiences.

The following example briefly summarises the writer's progress from insecurity to security and happiness:

*Moving into the world of full time work after my first year at university was*
**quite a shock** *[AFFECT: insecurity]. The first few weeks were busy with me*
*settling into a new job and new town. I soon discovered that* **I enjoyed the**
**set routine** *[AFFECT: happiness, security] that comes with a full time job*
*and knowing that time outside work was my own.*

The emotions in the PDP subcorpus tend to be internally experienced, and are expressed through mental and relational rather than
behavioural processes. In mental processes the 'trigger' that causes
the affective reaction can be expressed as a clause participant, the
'Phenomenon' (Halliday, 2004), but triggers in relational processes
are expressed as propositions. This is illustrated by the following
examples:

*I was a bit nervous* [relational AFFECT: security -: disposition] **because**
**we were the first group to go,** *and I felt slightly disadvantaged* [relational
AFFECT: security -: disposition] *because* **I like** [mental AFFECT: happiness -:
disposition] *learning from other people's mistakes* [Phenomenon], *rather*
*than making mine.*

*I was upset* [relational AFFECT: happiness -: disposition] *that the person*
*who was supposed to work on that aspect* [circumstantial] **didn't look into**
**it.**

*I found it very frustrating* [relational AFFECT: satisfaction -: disposition]
*that she didn't contribute* [circumstantial] **to group communications,** *even*
*though we did all we could to encourage her.*

The PDP aspect of reflective writing also results in a balance between
*realis* and *irrealis*, as writers balance their feelings about past and
present experiences against feelings about events that have yet to
occur. Past experiences are more likely to be presented in a negative
light, most commonly in terms of the writer's feelings of insecurity in a
new situation, or distress in response to the behaviour of other people:

*Term 2 was a shock to me* [AFFECT: insecurity]. *It was an intellectually*
*confusing phase* [AFFECT: insecurity] *and it shook my beliefs and raised*
*plenty of doubts.* [AFFECT: insecurity]

*Beginning my first third year placement I can honestly say that I felt more*
*apprehensive and nervous* [AFFECT: insecurity] *than at any other time*
*during my course.*

*Joe was in charge of the finances; Ben was all over the Design. Apart*
*from this, the other two didn't really do much. I was quite disappointed*
[AFFECT: dissatisfaction] *that they wouldn't get more involved.*

Generally, the story is one of triumph over adversity, however, and
future events are always anticipated with hope rather than dread:

*This assignment has left me with a genuine interest* [AFFECT: satisfaction] *in the area of international strategies and strategic thinking, which I would like to explore further.* [AFFECT: **irrealis** inclination]

*With better time management I hope to overcome my anxieties* [AFFECT: **irrealis** inclination +] *and find the time to provide the care described by Fordham and Dunn.*

*By mapping out my experience, I became aware of my limited skills related to legal issues or project management. Obviously, I am hoping to develop these* [AFFECT: irrealis inclination] *once I go back to work.*

As we have seen, the subcorpus contains many strongly evaluative words. *Surprised, uncomfortable, lonely, enjoyable* and *worried* are key, but students also describe themselves as becoming *desperate, enthusiastic* or *upset*, and write of *alienation, anger, anguish, anxiety, confusion, fear, frustration, humiliation, passion* and *stress*. This kind of language can be used to express personal feeling (AFFECT) or to evaluate entities or behaviour (APPRECIATION, JUDGEMENT). Writers who express APPRECIATION refer to products or performances in terms of the values society places on them. Writers who express JUDGEMENT refer to society's beliefs about the way people should or shouldn't behave. Thus APPRECIATION and JUDGEMENT are reworkings of the spontaneous AFFECT response, a transformation of 'common sense' into the institutionalised knowledge we acquire as members of society (Martin, 2000).

APPRAISAL theory identifies two types of JUDGEMENT, that concerned with social sanction and that concerned with social esteem. Martin (2000) describes social sanction as involving praise and condemnation. Negative social sanction often has legal implications; failure to conform to the social norms of 'propriety' and 'veracity' can result in contravention of the law. Social esteem, on the other hand, generally lacks legal implications; it involves admiration and criticism of social behaviour in terms of its 'normality', 'tenacity', and 'capacity'. Writers contributing to the PDP subcorpus are concerned with social esteem rather than social sanction, and especially with the capacity of themselves and others to fulfil task requirements. The emphasis on capacity is apparent from the list of frequent 4-grams in Table 7.5, which contains many clusters with *able*.

Typically, the writers judge themselves or members of their group. Judgement is frequently preceded by *I think*, or *I felt*, perhaps serving to signal the departure from the norms of the essayist tradition, which favours objective evaluation supported by evidence, rather than anecdote.

*Having only had a week to prepare for this presentation, my group was forced to gel quickly which* **I felt we did with a reasonable degree of success.** [JUDGEMENT: capacity]

**I think I felt that she was not seeing the bigger picture** [JUDGEMENT: incapacity] *and was making more work for us all.*

**I think** *that after doing this coursework, I have* **a much more mature and experienced view of programming in Caml** [JUDGEMENT: capacity]*, and find it easier to see how problems can be tackled in a functional way.*

As we have already seen, writers of reflective pieces often shift personal responsibility for outcomes that are less than satisfactory, either by writing on behalf of the group *we should have...*, or depersonalising the process *It would have been better if....* In the expression of JUDGEMENT, negative self-evaluations are often mitigated, as in the following example, where the writer provides an excuse for her mistake and also uses the passive to disguise her agency:

*It is not envisaged that any specification changes would be necessary, but it is possible (as the author has little previous experience in these areas) that the time required* **has been underestimated** [JUDGEMENT: incapacity] *and therefore that these phases may take longer than anticipated.*

APPRAISAL theory identifies three types of APPRECIATION, concerned with 'reaction' (Did it grab me? Did I like it?), 'composition' (Did it hang together? Was it hard to follow?) and 'valuation' (Was it worthwhile?) (Martin, 2000: 160). In the following examples, the expression of APPRECIATION rather than JUDGEMENT has enabled negative self-evaluation to be even more disguised. The choice of subclass of APPRECIATION is open to interpretation, but the cases that follow seem to express 'reaction' (Did I like it?), 'composition' (Was it hard to follow?) and 'valuation' (Was it worthwhile?). As Martin and White point out (2005: 57) there are strong semantic links between 'reaction' and AFFECT; however whereas AFFECT construes an emotion that is felt by someone, 'reaction' ascribes something with the power to trigger this emotion. In the following example the writer reacts negatively to an 'area', judges negatively the capacity of some unspecified agent, and only obliquely refers to her own lack of ability.

**One area I found difficult** [APPRECIATION: negative composition and reaction] *was that sometimes* **too much was expected of me** [JUDGEMENT: incapacity] *in terms of my ability.*

In the next example, however, rather than passing judgement on her own lack of team-working skills the student judges positively a contrasting quality in herself (a quality which makes her 'special') and evaluates positively the interview activity which is helping her to improve.

*I feel the interview also gave us an opportunity to build on our team building skills and organisational skills. I however, **feel that I am a very independent person** [JUDGEMENT: normality] and I work better on my own. Yet within this profession it's not possible to work on my own and so **it has helped me** [APPRECIATION: positive valuation] to try and improve my skills and confidence of working within a group and learning to listen to other people's opinions.*

Similarly, in the following examples writers seem to react to the difficulty of the task they have been set rather than passing negative judgement on their own capacity:

**I found the objectives of the book reviews fairly obscure.** [APPRECIATION negative composition and reaction]

**Providing feedback has been a difficult task for me.** [APPRECIATION negative composition and reaction]

In the next example the language becomes indistinguishable from that of a Critique, and it is impossible to tell whether the writer is obliquely appraising her own personal capacity, or whether the intention is to evaluate the complexity of the framework.

**Johns' framework is slightly more difficult to access** [APPRECIATION negative composition] *than others such as the Gibbs reflective cycle (Gibbs 1988) since it encourages the practitioner to consider events from many different angles and reflection therefore takes longer.*

The construal of emotion as APPRECIATION (*the framework is difficult*) rather than JUDGEMENT (*I can't understand the framework*) or AFFECT (*I feel confused by the framework*) seems to require critical thinking rather than personal development skills. It therefore sits much more happily within the essayist tradition, and is likely to be the preferred tactic of those who have been well schooled in this tradition, and discouraged from expressing in writing their untrained responses to human activity.

Thus the PDP corpus writers demonstrate mastery of a wide range of linguistic resources in order to present themselves in an appropriate light, and many of them balance the resources of APPRAISAL quite cleverly. Personal voice, indicative of sincerity, is conveyed through AFFECT, but the emotions writers attribute to themselves tend to be positive ones, suggestive of willingness and enthusiasm, or ones that are likely to arouse the reader's sympathy (*I was a bit nervous*; *I was upset; I was quite disappointed*). JUDGEMENT is used to show-case positive personal attributes of capacity and tenacity; negative JUDGEMENT often being reserved for the behaviour of others, so that the role of the writer is obscured (*sometimes too much was expected of me in terms of my ability*). Negative APPRECIATION of complex composition (*a difficult task*) is used to shift the onus of responsibility from the writer in cases where expressions of AFFECT or JUDGEMENT might be more revealing of personal inadequacy. Positive APPRECIATION of the value of the activity again creates the impression of willingness and enthusiasm, reinforcing expressions of positive AFFECT (*Posting on fora is not something I tend to do, but it was strangely enjoyable*).

Writers who follow a reflective cycle of the sort outlined by Gibbs (1988, Figure 7.1) reserve their negative appraisals for past actions, and conclude on a positive note. *Hindsight* and *hope* are both positively key in the subcorpus, and writers are keen to show that they are capable of learning from experience, and moving on. How closely their accounts reflect their true feelings, however, especially in the tumultuous final undergraduate year (Level 3), with looming exams and stiff competition for graduate employment, is anybody's guess.

## 7.6 Conclusion

This chapter has identified some academic writing genres that are often neglected in academic writing classes, and which are testimony to the diversity of the demands placed on student writers. It is striking to consider that the same students in the Social Sciences who produce emotionally charged, involved narratives of personal experience also produce highly informational Case Studies and Proposals, and that the same students who produce texts on scientific and technical topics to appeal to a popular audience, also produce abstract and impersonal Design Specifications and Methodology Recounts.

Personal or literary writing is no easier to produce than detached, third person, objective writing, as Hemphill (2004) points out, and Narrative and Empathy Writing assignments place particular demands on students because they operate outside an exacting but familiar academic context. It is certain, however, that in their future careers students will need to call upon the resources of both codes in order to achieve their own communicative ends.

## Notes

1. For example the BAAL Multimodality SIG event 'Changing communication: New technologies and their impact on meaning making and pedagogy', held at the Open University, Milton Keynes, 26 November 2010.
2. National Vocational Qualifications (NVQs) are work-based awards intended to provide evidence of a candidate's ability to perform a particular job role.

## References

Bizup, J. (2008). BEAM: A rhetorical vocabulary for teaching research-based writing. *Rhetoric Review*, 27(1), 72–86.

Christie, F. (1999). Genre theory and ESL teaching: A systemic functional perspective. *TESOL Quarterly* 33(4), 759–63.

Dearing Report (National Committee of Inquiry into Higher Education) (1997). https://bei.leeds.ac.uk/Partners/NCIHE.

Ecclestone, K., & Hayes, D. (2009). *The dangerous rise of therapeutic education*. London: Routledge.

Evans, M. (2007). Another kind of writing: reflective practice and creative journals in the performing arts. *Journal of Writing in Creative Practice*, 1(1), 69–76.

Evans, L., & Abbott, I. (1998). *Teaching and learning in higher education*. London: Cassell.

Gardner, S., & Holmes, J. (2009). Can I use headings in my essay? Section headings, macrostructures and genre families in the BAWE corpus of student writing. In M. Charles, S. Hunston, D. Pecorari (Eds.), *Academic writing: At the interface of corpus and discourse*, London: Continuum, 251–71.

Gibbs, G. (1988). Learning by doing: A guide to teaching and learning methods. Further Education Unit. Oxford Polytechnic: Oxford.

Gocsik, K. (2006). *Writing about movies* (supplement to Barsam, R., *Looking at movies: An introduction to film*). London: W. W. Norton and Company.

Gray, C., & Malins, J. (2004). *Visualising research: A guide to the research process in art and design*. Aldershot: Ashgate Publishing.

Halliday, M.A.K. (2004). *Introduction to functional grammar*. (3rd ed., with C.M.I.M. Matthiesson). London: Arnold.

Hemphill, D. (2004). Putting it into words: Experience-based writing and pedagogy. *Journal of Hospitality, Leisure, Sports and Tourism Education*, 3(2), 15–24.

The Higher Education Academy (2005). *Connecting PDP to employer needs and the world of work*. www.heacademy.ac.uk/assets/York/documents/resources/resourcedatabase/id71_connecting_pdp_to_employer_needs.pdf.

Hoey, M. (1983). *On the surface of discourse*. London: George Allen & Unwin.

Hyland, K. (2004). Patterns of engagement: Dialogic features and L2 undergraduate writing. In L. Ravelli and R. Ellis (Eds.), *Analysing academic writing*, London: Continuum, 5–23.

Jasper, M. (2003). *Beginning reflective practice: Foundations in nursing and health care*. Cheltenham: Nelson Thornes.

Johns, C. (1994). Guided reflection. In A. Palmer, S. Burns & C. Bulman (Eds.), *Reflective practice in nursing. The growth of the professional practitioner,* Cornwall: Blackwell Science, 110–30.

Johns, C. (1995). Framing learning through reflection within Carper's fundamental ways of knowing in nursing. *Journal of Advanced Nursing ,* 22(2), 226–34.

Kathpalia, S., & Heah, C. (2008). Reflective writing: Insights into what lies beneath. *RELC Journal* 39 (3), 300–317.

Labov, W. (1972). The transformation of experience in narrative syntax. In W. Labov (Ed.), *Language in the inner city: Studies in Black English vernacular.* Philadelphia, PA: University of Philadelphia Press, 354–96.

Lea, M., & Stierer, B. (2000). Editors' introduction. In M. Lea & B. Stierer (Eds.), *Student writing in Higher Education: New contexts.* Buckingham: The Society for Research into Higher Education and Open University Press, 1–14.

Leedham, M. (2009). From traditional essay to 'Ready Steady Cook' presentation: Reasons for innovative changes in Higher Education assignments. *Active Learning in Higher Education,* 10(2), 191–206.

Lillis, T. (2001). *Student writing: Access, regulation, desire.* London: Routledge.

LTSN Generic Centre (2002). *Guide for busy academics No.1: Personal Development Planning.* www.heacademy.ac uk/resources/detail/resource_database/id66_guide_for_busy_academics_no1.

Martin, J.R. (2000). Beyond exchange: APPRAISAL systems in English. In S. Hunston & G. Thompson (Eds.), *Evaluation in text.* Oxford: Oxford University Press, 142–75.

Martin, J.R., & White, P.R. (2005). *The language of evaluation: Appraisal in English.* Basingstoke: Palgrave Macmillan.

National Association of Primary Care Educators (2005). *Introduction to GP appraisals.* PDP Toolkit www.pdptoolkit.co.uk.

Nesi, H., & Gardner, S. (2006). Variation in disciplinary culture: University tutors' views on assessed writing tasks. In R. Kiely, G. Clibbon, P. Rea-Dickins, & H. Woodfield (Eds.), *Language, culture and identity in applied linguistics* (British Studies in Applied Linguistics, Volume 21). London: Equinox Publishing, 99–117.

Paltridge, B. (2004). The exegesis as a genre: An ethnographic examination. In L. Ravelli & R. Ellis (Eds.), *Analysing academic writing: Contextualized frameworks.* London: Continuum, 84–103.

Quality Assurance Agency (2000). *Policy statement on a progress file for Higher Education.* www.qaa.ac.uk/academicinfrastructure/progressFiles/archive/policystatement/default.asp.

Römer, U. (2008). Identification impossible? A corpus approach to realisations of evaluative meaning in academic writing. *Functions of Language,* 15(1), 115–30.

Schön, D. (1987). *Educating the reflective practitioner: Toward a new design for teaching and learning in the professions.* San Francisco: Jossey-Bass.

Schön, D. (ed.) (1991) *The Reflective Turn.* New York: Teachers College Press.

Squires, G. (2005). Art, science and the professions. *Studies in Higher Education,* 30: 127–36.

Varnava, T. (2008). *PDP update: Policy and practice*. The Higher Education Academy www.ukcle.ac.uk/resources/pdp/varnava.html.

Walters, D. (2008). Developing reflective practice through patchwork writing. Paper presented at the 12th Writing Development in Higher Education (WDHE) Conference, 25–27 June 2008, University of Strathclyde, Glasgow, UK.

Wickens, P., & Spiro, J. (2010). Reflecting on reflection: Identity and discourse on a reflective professional development module. Paper presented at the 43rd Annual BAAL Conference, 9–11 September 2010, University of Aberdeen, UK.

Williams, S., & Ryan, S. (2006). Identifying themes for staff development: The essential part of PDP innovation. In C. Bryan & K. Clegg (Eds.), *Innovative assessment in Higher Education*. Routledge, 171–9.

# 8 Networks across genres and disciplines

In this book we have described the linguistic features and the social purposes of assignments produced by university students. Our descriptions have identified different genres within 13 genre families, and have indicated the central stages through which these genres unfold across and within specific disciplines. In this final chapter we will consider the methodologies we have used, and review our major findings in relation to the broad social purposes of student writing, to genre families, genre networks and registers. We will then identify some of the ways in which these findings can be applied to the teaching and assessment of academic writing. The chapter concludes with suggestions for further research, both in the UK and internationally, and information about how to access the BAWE corpus and related resources.

## 8.1 Our location among research on student writing

The landscape of research on university student writing is broad and diverse. In this section we identify where the contribution of this book is located in relation to other research in this area, which we view as complementary and mutually beneficial.

Our aim has been to develop a classification of university writing, and in this respect our research is similar to research that examines university writing tasks. Studies of university writing tasks are motivated by the desire to improve the relevance of university entrance examinations or programme syllabuses; they draw on questionnaire or interview data using university teachers as informants (Jackson, Meyer and Parkinson, 2006; Rosenfeld, Courtney and Fowles, 2004) and / or they refer to course documentation, such as assessment plans, module descriptors and assignment rubrics (Carter, 2007; Cooper and Bikowski, 2007; Gillett and Hammond, 2009; Hale et al., 1996; Melzer, 2009; Moore and Morton, 2005; Zhu, 2004). They usually result in classifications of task types, together with hypotheses about

254

the writing students might produce in response to these tasks. Our research has also drawn on interview data and course documentation to develop our concepts of the social purposes of genres, but importantly our main focus has been on examining and classifying the writing students produce, rather than the tasks university teachers set.

Our classification has been shaped by the broad social purposes that we have identified: demonstrating knowledge and understanding (Chapter 3), developing evaluation and argumentation (Chapter 4), conducting independent research (Chapter 5), preparing for professional practice (Chapter 6) and writing for oneself and others (Chapter 7). Because these purposes are grounded in the national context of the writing we examined, collected from four universities in England, we have focused on a broad understanding of social processes across the academy, rather than on individual texts and writers.

Our focus has been on social processes rather than the more cognitive writing processes associated with research that examines how individual writers develop ideas and shape them into finished texts. Such studies of the way students write within a university context are more concerned with empowering writers or improving methods of writing instruction. Data is gathered directly from writers, and / or by studying their notebooks and user logs, observing them while they are composing, and comparing successive drafts of their work (Stapleton, 2010; NCTE, 1982, 2008).

The social processes are associated with writer positions – as students, as apprentices, as researchers – but we have not explored the situated nature of individual writers or the many discourses that shape and position writers in the academy. An investigation of these issues requires engagement with the politics of writing (Clark and Ivanič, 1997), academic literacies (Lea and Street, 1998; Lillis, 2008), and critical discourse analysis (Benesch, 2001). Ha (2009: 134), for example, takes a critical discourse approach when following a writer's 'struggles to sustain identity … while accommodating the demands of the university'.

Beyond classification, we belong to a research tradition that aims to better describe and explain the nature of collections of university students' work. Such collections vary in size from a few texts to substantial corpora, although before the development of the BAWE corpus these collections were usually made purely for personal research, and featured just one or two genres, levels or disciplines at a time, for example PhD theses (Thompson, 2005), undergraduate dissertations (Hood, 2004) or essays in specific disciplines such as Geography

(Wu, 2007), the History of Science (North, 2005), Management (Loudermilk, 2007) or Sociology (Starfield, 2004). Studies of the functional and linguistic features of student writing can inform curriculum and syllabus design (as in Gruber, 2005), methods of teaching and learning (as in Charles, 2007; John, 2009) and university entrance test design (as in Sharpling, 2010).

Finally, and as should be evident throughout this volume, we draw extensively on the traditions of genre analysis (Coffin, 2006; Martin, 1992; Swales, 1990) and of corpus linguistics (Biber, 1988; Scott, 1997). We identify genre families not only through their social purposes, but also through the stages in which they unfold. Differences between genre families, between genres, and across disciplines have been identified, and these classifications and differences have been supported by the results of various techniques of corpus linguistics, most notably multidimensional analysis and keyword analysis, both of which provide a window on the lexicogrammar of registers of student writing.

## 8.2  Our contribution to research on university student writing

Our broad classification of university student writing provides an overview of genres across programmes of study. It can be used to inform assessment practices, and to enrich understanding of student progression. We identify five broad social processes and thirteen genre families, each of which embraces half a dozen or so distinct genres (as summarised in Section 2.2). Our contribution here has been to highlight the diversity in student writing assignments while making an understanding of such diversity more manageable. For instance, lecturers looking for new ways to assess students' familiarity with prior research might find inspiration in the range of Literature Survey genres identified in the corpus, while those considering a move away from 'traditional essays' might find alternatives among the Narrative Recount or Empathy Writing genres.

This genre family classification has been embedded within the BAWE corpus, which includes a relatively large number of assignments fairly equally distributed across disciplines and levels of study (as described in Section 1.4). The embedded information will enable researchers, here and in future, to investigate student academic writing from various perspectives of genre and register.

In terms of vocabulary, the comparison of keywords in the BAWE corpus with those in larger corpora of general English has created a new kind of academic word list (see Appendix 1.4). Throughout, we have examined keywords for genre families and for genres across disciplines in ways that were not possible before the existence of our corpus.

## 8.3  The networks that link genres and genre families

The findings reported in this book reveal many different purposes for student writing: educational, academic, professional and social. In Figure 8.1 we have mapped these globally, but this diagram belies the complex networks that link genres across and beyond the academy. We have discussed elsewhere (Nesi and Gardner, 2006) the way that traditional student assignments are viewed as primarily pedagogic, research-academic or professional, and the influence of recent trends concerned with everyday life and the general development of the individual in society. Viewed from a genre network perspective, we can thus see that student writing is subject to four major forces, and responds to writing in four distinct domains.

These four domains are represented in Figure 8.1. In the bottom right quadrant are Essays, Exercises and Methodology Recounts, primarily 'pedagogic' genres intended to help students learn how to think, act and reason in the ways of the chosen discipline. Pedagogic genres are the most occluded genres because they are written to be assessed and then discarded; published examples are rare. It is remarkable that although the majority of assignments in the BAWE corpus are Essays, most students have very limited exposure to examples of the Essay genres, and some may only have read those Essays that they themselves have written.

In the bottom left quadrant of Figure 8.1 we have the 'everyday' genres belonging to the Empathy Writing family. Creative writing assignments belong to this 'everyday' domain, as do assignments written for the purpose of personal development or public engagement. Linguists such as Myers (1990) and Nwogu and Bloor (1991) have identified the changes in register that scientific information undergoes when it is transferred from research journals to teaching materials and popular science magazines. The same sort of register transformation seems to have taken place in some Empathy Writing assignments which re-express in more ordinary language information derived from academic sources. The difficulties such genres pose are less to do with the construction of argument or the justification of decisions and more to do with finding an appropriate register to communicate with a non-academic readership. Narrative Recounts also fall into this quadrant because their central purpose is to record a sequence of events, perhaps in the manner of the creative writer or the journalist.

ACADEMIC
GENRES
       *Research articles*
         *Research proposals*   *Work plans*
*Review articles*

*Book reviews,
film reviews,
product
reviews*

*Encyclopedia
entries*

*Letters*

*Leaflets*

EVERYDAY
GENRES

PROFESSIONAL
GENRES
      *Patient case reports*
   *Company Reports*

*Tenders*

*Legal cases*

*Textbooks*

PEDAGOGIC
GENRES

*Stories Diaries*

Figure 8.1    Genre network potential

Moving towards the 'academic' genres, assignments in the Explanation genre family often bear some resemblance to entries in encyclopaedias and other reference works, while Critiques of certain kinds may be seen as corresponding to book and product reviews in newspapers and technical magazines. Critiques generally have a less persuasive purpose than published reviews, because expert reviewers aim to influence choice, rather than simply indicate strengths and weaknesses to demonstrate their evaluative skill.

Along the top of Figure 8.1 we find expert genres. On the left are review and research articles published in research journals and written by professional academics for an audience of peers. In our interviews with academic staff we learned that some disciplines, such as Physics and Psychology, present experimental research journal articles to students as models. Across disciplines we have found examples of genres which are formatted as experimental or review articles, complete with abstract, page numbers, columns and other formatting associated with specific journals in the discipline (see example in Section 5.2). In such cases, the genre networks are made explicit to students, although it is important to note that dissertations, theses and assignments in the Research Report genre family normally include more elaborate literature surveys and fuller explanations of their 'workings out' than can be found in published research articles. To convert student research writing to a published article not only involves reducing the length and summarising the highlights, but also repositioning the writer in the (inter)national rather than university discourse community, and as an expert rather than as a novice (Pramoolsook, 2008).

The most explicit genre networks are between genres produced in the workplace and those belonging to the apprenticeship genre families (Proposals, Case Studies, Design Specifications, and, to a lesser extent, Problem Questions). In the top centre of Figure 8.1 are research proposals, written by academics, and work plans, produced in a range of other professions. These correspond to assignments in the Proposal genre family, although student proposals usually remain at the planning stage and lack the practical detail required of a workplace proposal. Some student Case Studies replicate professional genres very closely; patient case reports written during hospital attachments follow hospital reporting practices, for example, and engineering site reports are evaluated by the same rigorous legal and ethical criteria that bind actual site reports on the basis of which companies would invest significant sums of money. These assignments, then, have the highest face value, and appear to assess students' preparedness for life in a particular profession. Paradoxically, the 'everyday' genres, which do not appear to be either academic or professional, are also often designed to prepare students for future employment. They provide unusual opportunities to display disciplinary knowledge and understanding without regard for some of the standard academic conventions, and to develop the practical writing and communication skills which employers value.

These networks between the student and non-student genres are complex, and not all members of each genre family make the same connections. Paltridge suggests that 'a text may belong to more than one genre category, such as a book review being used as an advertisement' (2006: 89). We prefer to take a position similar to Askehave and Swales (2000), however, viewing each genre as having complex or multiple purposes. This is what makes writing for assessment a complex endeavour. Students have to somehow demonstrate knowledge and understanding, show that they can perform in ways approved by the discipline, and yet also sustain and develop their own identity so that they can make an original contribution to topics and issues deemed relevant to the course of study.

## 8.4  Register and genre families

In Chapter 2 we mapped the genre families in the BAWE corpus along Biber's 1988 dimensions and characterised the register of student writing in general as highly informational, impersonal, non-narrative, elaborated, and lacking overt features of persuasion. We also noted specific ways in which certain genre family registers are similar, and ways in which they are distinct.

Narrative Recounts emerged as outliers, followed closely by Empathy Writing. These genre families have *relatively* high scores along the involved, narrative, situation-dependent and (non)abstract dimensions, using first person, past tense, specific place references and concrete nouns. Literature Surveys and Proposals, on the other hand, are highly informational and elaborated.

The results of multidimensional analysis reported in Chapter 2 provide an overview of the registers used, and subsequent chapters indicate the range of variation that occurs within each genre family. Our analyses in Chapters 3 to 7 also indicate that register varies across the stages of each genre. Within every genre we would expect some variation in lexical density and grammatical metaphor; introductions and conclusions, for example, tend to be denser than other sections. In some families the register of other stages is also distinctive. For instance, the language of the final persuasive or inferential recommendation stage in Case Studies tends to contrast along several dimensions with earlier sections which detail past events and analyses. Even where the same tokens are used, there can be differences in meanings according to the disciplinary context. For instance, in Chapter 4 we saw how pronouns such as *I* and grammatical constructions such as IF–THEN construed distinct meanings in specific contexts. In the case of *I* the referent was different; in the case of IF–THEN, the logical force of the warrant, or the meaning of the construction, was interpreted in disciplinary terms.

Disciplinary variation also accounts for some register variation beyond the expected differences in content (or field). We saw in Chapter 4 how the language of Essays in the Sciences is influenced by the predominance of scientific report writing, with its extensive use of headings and absence of the first person (*I*). Conversely, we saw in Chapter 5 how the methodology sections of Arts and Social Sciences reports are more elaborated or more 'essay-like' than the language of similar methodology sections in reports in the Life and Physical Sciences. Further evidence (Gardner, 2009) of the effect of discipline on register shows that whereas genre has a greater influence than disciplinary grouping on scores for Dimension 4 (the overtly persuasive dimension), disciplinary grouping has a greater influence than genre on scores for Dimension 1 (informational) and Dimension 2 (narrative). Methodology Recounts use less overtly persuasive language than Critiques, which in turn use less persuasive language than Case Studies, but writing in the Life Sciences is more informational than writing in the Social Sciences, which in turn is more informational than that in the Arts and Humanities. Also writing in the Arts and Humanities has more narrative features than writing in the Physical Sciences.

## 8.5 Genre knowledge for teaching and learning

Several studies have drawn attention to the inability of expert academic writers to specify the conventions that they follow, for example Lea and Street (1998), Norton (1990) and Turner (2011). When we asked university tutors about the desirable characteristics of student writing (Nesi and Gardner, 2006) they spoke of the importance of argument and structure, and expressed appreciation of clarity and originality, but they did not provide any detail of how these characteristics could be recognised, or realised in text. This is perhaps understandable, as academic writing skills have traditionally been acquired through prolonged exposure rather than explicit instruction, a process described by Turner as 'the pedagogy of osmosis' (2011: 21).

In some contexts this process of osmosis may be successful, especially if the student body is fairly homogeneous and already shares some tacit knowledge of the social conventions of the academy. The educational contexts we describe in Chapter 1, however, are characterised by diversity, a consequence of widening participation policies and increased student mobility. In these contexts it is probably unrealistic to expect all or even the majority of students to absorb without explicit instruction the writing knowledge that the academy requires.

Differentiating and describing the genres that students need to write is an important step towards explicating the tacit knowledge that the initiated possess. We think that most student writers will benefit from acquiring explicit knowledge of the genres they are attempting to produce, in terms of their functions, their components, and the way they differ one from the other. Merely locating an assignment genre within one of our thirteen genre families may be sufficient to provide a writer with a sense of direction. Structural appropriacy, clarity and originality all depend on a clear understanding of the social purposes of the writing task.

Our genre descriptions are not only useful to writing tutors and students for the purpose of task identification, but can also help subject lecturers to create more relevant and diverse assignment tasks, and more meaningful assignment prompts. A further use for the descriptions relates to materials design. Academic writing course materials often concentrate on Essays or research genres relevant to thesis and dissertation writing, to the exclusion of other genre families. Tribble's review of 27 popular academic writing textbooks, for example, complains of their focus on the development of 'essayist literacy' (2009: 114), and Gillett and Hammond draw attention to the lack of advice in study skills manuals regarding 'the purpose and function of the wide range of academic activities demanded of students' (2009: 112).

Our analysis of the BAWE corpus shows that although Essays are a most important genre in many disciplines, all 13 genre families occur in at least seven of the major departments represented in our corpus, and 11 are found in all four disciplinary groupings (see Table 2.10). Students have to learn to move between genres in response to the demands of different tasks, and to craft their writing for the varied purposes of argumentation, evaluation, professional communication, public engagement and personal reflection. Tutors and materials developers could choose to apply our wider range of genres to exercises of the type first developed by Swales and Feak for use with research students (2000, 2004, 2009). There is also scope to explore and compare the genres and genre families we have described by means of the data-driven learning techniques pioneered by Johns (see for example Johns and King, 1991).

## 8.6  The BAWE corpus, genres and future research

The BAWE corpus contains student writing from four English universities, and although these were chosen to represent a broad spectrum of disciplines and institutional types the corpus is unlikely to contain examples of every possible genre that university students produce. Further comparisons of genres from other departments, other institutions and other countries are needed. Within the UK, for instance, comparisons with institutions in Scotland where four-year undergraduate degrees are the norm, or with institutions in Wales where there is bilingual provision, would indicate the effects of local differences in educational provision.

A number of Masters dissertations and Doctoral theses have already compared BAWE assignments with those produced in other contexts. These include comparisons with undergraduate Economics assignments from Pakistan (reported in Gardezi and Nesi, 2009), with Biotechnology and Environmental Engineering dissertations from Thailand (Pramoolsook, 2008), and with English Literature Essays from Syria (Fakhra, 2009). The closer the genre families and disciplines match with those in the BAWE corpus, the greater the explanatory power of any comparisons made.

The descriptions of the registers of genres across disciplines in this volume are intended to capture the essence of the writing. Much work remains to be done to provide more extensive and detailed accounts of the language features and general nature of student academic writing. The research mentioned in the previous paragraph and other investigations with the BAWE corpus have extended the range of features associated with the genres, the disciplines and the levels of study.

The BAWE corpus was developed to complement the BASE corpus of Spoken Academic English, which in turn is styled as a companion to the Michigan Corpus of Academic English (MICASE). BAWE has most in common with the Michigan Corpus of Upper-level Student Papers (MICUSP), however, as this has been developed along similar lines to BAWE, although, as its name suggests, it only contains assignments written by final year undergraduates and graduate students. MICUSP is also a smaller corpus, containing around 830 texts and 2.6 million words (http://micusp.elicorpora.info). All four corpora, BAWE, BASE, MICASE and MICUSP, are similarly (but not identically) stratified according to four disciplinary groupings, facilitating comparisons between British and American academic speech and writing.

There is also increasing scope for comparison with other types of academic corpora. For example the English as a Lingua Franca in Academic Settings (ELFA) corpus (www.helsinki.fi/englanti/elfa/elfacorpus.html) now contains one million words of transcribed speech, and the Varieties of English for Specific Purposes (VESPA) project aims to build a large corpus of texts written by L2 writers (www.uclouvain.be/en-cecl-vespa.html). The Engineering Lecture Corpus (ELC) has been specially created to compare lectures on similar Engineering topics delivered in diverse educational settings; the British, Malaysian and New Zealand components are now available at www.coventry.ac.uk/elc.

The BAWE corpus can be downloaded for research purposes via the Oxford Text Archive (http://ota.ahds.ac.uk/headers/2539.xml), and can also be freely accessed using the open version of the corpus query tool SketchEngine. Details of the functions of SketchEngine with special reference to the BAWE corpus are provided in Nesi and Thompson (2011).

Information about research with the BAWE corpus and links to all these related resources can be found at www.coventry.ac.uk/bawe.

# References

Askehave, I., & Swales, J.M. (2000). Genre identification and communicative purpose: A problem and a possible solution. *Applied Linguistics*, 22(2) 195–212.

Benesch, S. (2001). *Critical English for Academic Purposes: Theory, politics and practice.* New Jersey: Lawrence Erlbaum.

Biber, D. (1988). *Variation across speech and writing.* Cambridge: Cambridge University Press.

Carter, M. (2007). Ways of knowing, doing and writing in the disciplines. *College Composition and Communication*, 58: 385–418.

Charles, M. (2007). Reconciling top-down and bottom-up approaches to graduate writing: Using a corpus to teach rhetorical functions. *Journal of English for Academic Purposes*, 6(4), 289–302.

Clark, R., & Ivanič, R. (1997). *The politics of writing.* London: Routledge.

Coffin, C. (2006). *Historical discourse.* London: Continuum.

Cooper, A., & Bikowski, D. (2007). Writing at the graduate level: What tasks do professors actually require? *Journal of English for Academic Purposes*, 6(3), 206–21.

Fakhra, A. (2009). Relative clauses and cohesive conjunctions in Syrian university students' writing in English. Unpublished PhD Thesis. Warwick, UK: University of Warwick.

Gardezi, S.A., & Nesi, H. (2009). Variation in the writing of economics students in Britain and Pakistan: The case of conjunctive ties. In M. Charles, S. Hunston, & D. Pecorari (Eds.), *Academic writing: At the interface of corpus and discourse*, London: Continuum, 236–50.

Gardner, S. (2009). The influence of genre vs disciplinary context on the choice of lexico-grammatical features in university student writing. Paper presented at 21st European Systemic Functional Linguistics Conference and Workshop, 8–10 July 2009, Cardiff, Wales.

Gillett, A., & Hammond, A. (2009). Mapping the maze of assessment: An investigation into practice. *Active learning in higher education*, 10, 120–37.

Gruber, H. (2006). Rhetorical Structure Theory and quality assessment of students' texts. *Information Design Journal & Document Design*, 14(2), 114–29.

Ha, P.L (2009). Strategic, passionate, but academic: Am I allowed in my writing? *Journal of English for Academic Purposes*, 8(2), 134–46.

Hale, G., Taylor, C., Bridgeman, B., Carson, J., Kroll, B., & Kantor, R. (1996). A study of writing tasks assigned in academic degree programs. Research Report 54. Princeton, NJ: ETS.

Hood, S.E. (2004). Managing attitude in undergraduate academic writing: A focus on the introductions to research reports. In L.J. Ravelli & R.A. Ellis (Eds.), *Analysing academic writing: Contextualized frameworks*, London: Continuum, 24–44.

Jackson, L., Meyer, W., & Parkinson, J. (2006). A study of the writing tasks and reading assigned to undergraduate science students at a South African University. *English for Specific Purposes*, 25(3), 260–81.

John, S. (2009). Using the revision process to help international students understand the linguistic construction of the academic identity. In M. Charles, S. Hunston & D. Pecorari (Eds.), *Academic writing: At the interface of corpus and discourse*. London: Continuum, 272–90.

Johns, T., & King, P. (Eds.) (1991). *Classroom concordancing*. Birmingham University: *English Language Research Journal*, 4.

Lea, M.R., & Street, B.V. (1998). Student writing in higher education: An academic literacies approach. *Studies in Higher Education*, 23(2), 157–71.

Lillis, T. (2008). Ethnography as method, methodology, and "deep theorizing": Closing the gap between text and context in academic writing research. *Written Communication*, 25(3), 353–88.

Loudermilk, B. (2007). Occluded academic genres: An analysis of the MBA thought essay. *Journal of English for Academic Purposes*, 6(2), 190–205.

Martin, J.R. (1992). *English text: System and structure*. Amsterdam: Benjamins.

Melzer, D. (2009). Writing assignments across the curriculum: A national study of college writing. *College Composition and Communication*, 61(2), W240–61.

Moore, T., & Morton, J. (2005). Dimensions of difference: A comparison of university writing and IELTS writing. *Journal of English for Academic Purposes*, 4(1), 43–66.

Myers, G. (1990). *Writing biology: Texts in the social construction of scientific knowledge*. Madison: University of Wisconsin Press.

NCTE (1982, 2008). *CCCC Position Statement on the Preparation and Professional Development of Teachers of Writing*. www.ncte.org/cccc/resources/positions/statementonprep.

Nesi, H., & Gardner, S. (2006). Variation in disciplinary culture: University tutors' views on assessed writing tasks. In R. Kiely, P. Rea-Dickins, H. Woodfield & G. Clibbon (Eds.), *Language, culture and identity in applied linguistics*. British Studies in Applied Linguistics 21, London: Equinox Publishing, 99–117.

Nesi, H., & Thompson, P. (2011). *Using SketchEngine with BAWE*. Available online at http://trac.sketchengine.co.uk/wiki/SharedResources.

North, S. (2005). Different values, different skills? A comparison of essay writing by students from arts and science backgrounds. *Studies in Higher Education*, 30(5), 517–33.

Norton, L. (1990). Essay writing: What really counts. *Higher Education*, 20(4), 411–42.

Nwogu, K., & Bloor, T. (1991). Thematic progression in professional and popular medical texts. In E. Ventola (Ed.), *Functional and systemic linguistics: Approaches and uses*, Berlin: Mouton de Gruyter, 369–84.

Paltridge, B. (2006). *Discourse analysis: An introduction*. London: Continuum.

Pramoolsook, I. (2008). Genre transfer from dissertations to research article among Thai scientists. Unpublished PhD Thesis. University of Warwick.

Rosenfeld, M., Courtney, R., & Fowles, M. (2004). *Identifying the writing tasks important for academic success at the undergraduate and graduate levels*. GRE Board Research Report No. 4, Princeton, NJ: Educational Testing Service.

Scott, M. (1997). PC analysis of key words – and key key words. *System*, 25(2), 233–45.

Sharpling, G. (2010). When BAWE meets WELT: The use of a corpus of student writing to develop items for a proficiency test in grammar and English usage. *Journal of Writing Research*, 2(2), 179–95.

Stapleton, P. (2010). Writing in an electronic age: A case study of L2 composing processes. *Journal of English for Academic Purposes*, 9(4), 295–307.

Starfield, S. (2004). Negotiating success in a first year undergraduate sociology essay. In L. Ravelli & R. Ellis (Eds.), *Analysing academic writing: Contextualized frameworks*. London: Continuum.

Swales, J.M. (1990). *Genre analysis. English in academic and research settings*. Cambridge: Cambridge University Press.

Swales, J.M., & Feak, C. (2000). *English in today's research world: A writing guide*. Ann Arbor: University of Michigan Press.

Swales, J.M., & Feak, C. (2004). *Academic writing for graduate students: Essential tasks and skills*. 2nd edition. Ann Arbor: University of Michigan Press.

Swales, J.M., & Feak, C. (2009). *Abstracts and the writing of abstracts*. Michigan Series in English for Academic and Professional Purposes, Vol 1. Ann Arbor: University of Michigan Press.

Thompson, P. (2005). Points of focus and position: Intertextual reference in PhD theses. *Journal of English for Academic Purposes*, 4(4), 307–23.

Tribble, C. (2009). Writing academic English: A survey review of current published resources. *ELT Journal*, 63(4), 400–17.

Turner, J. (2011). *Language in the academy: Cultural reflexivity and intercultural dynamics*. Bristol: Multilingual Matters.

Wu, S.M. (2007). Investigating the effectiveness of arguments in undergraduate Geography essays from an evaluation perspective. *Journal of English for Academic Purposes*, 6(3), 254–71.

Zhu, W. (2004). Writing in business courses: An analysis of assignment types, their characteristics, and required skills. *English for Specific Purposes* 23(2), 111–35.

# *Appendices*

## Appendix 1.1

Further information about the BAWE corpus holdings

The distribution of assignments written by males and females

| Disciplinary grouping | Males | Females |
|---|---|---|
| AH | 265 | 440 |
| LS | 176 | 507 |
| PS | 399 | 197 |
| SS | 264 | 513 |
| Total | 1104 | 1657 |

A summary of the distribution of assignments written by students whose first language was not English, by level and disciplinary grouping

| Disciplinary grouping | Level 1 | Level 2 | Level 3 | Level 4 | Total |
|---|---|---|---|---|---|
| AH | 15 | 25 | 44 | 30 | 114 |
| LS | 24 | 30 | 30 | 101 | 185 |
| PS | 43 | 31 | 45 | 47 | 166 |
| SS | 82 | 55 | 61 | 142 | 340 |
| Total | 164 | 141 | 180 | 320 | 805 |

Assignments written by students whose first language was not English

| First language | Assignments | Words |
|---|---|---|
| Arabic | 15 | 27564 |
| Bengali | 5 | 18437 |
| Bulgarian | 7 | 23934 |
| Chinese: Cantonese | 66 | 126934 |
| Chinese: Mandarin | 26 | 65338 |
| Chinese unspecified | 153 | 383881 |
| Czech | 5 | 9369 |
| Dutch | 13 | 28395 |
| Finnish | 15 | 30574 |
| French | 60 | 151825 |
| German | 57 | 146691 |
| Gujarati | 46 | 99331 |
| Hindi | 33 | 86137 |
| Hungarian | 3 | 14574 |
| Igbo | 3 | 15850 |
| Italian | 12 | 28377 |
| Japanese | 40 | 85528 |
| Korean | 11 | 30516 |
| Malay | 23 | 41220 |
| Maldivian | 5 | 10298 |
| Mongolian | 2 | 948 |
| Norwegian | 12 | 27603 |
| Panjabi | 1 | 1553 |
| Persian | 11 | 37345 |
| Polish | 34 | 87866 |
| Portuguese | 24 | 58133 |
| Pulaar | 5 | 14771 |
| Romani | 5 | 21156 |
| Serbian | 1 | 7814 |
| Sinhala | 22 | 36349 |
| Slovak | 10 | 25749 |
| Slovenian | 5 | 14224 |
| Spanish | 17 | 51209 |
| Swahili | 5 | 9645 |
| Swedish | 15 | 36475 |
| Tamil | 8 | 16371 |
| Thai | 9 | 19619 |
| Turkish | 6 | 11209 |
| Urdu | 5 | 9984 |
| Welsh | 3 | 32053 |

# Appendix 1.2

Schedule of interviews with students

|  |  | Level 1 | Level 2 | Level 3 |
|---|---|:---:|:---:|:---:|
| Arts and Humanities | English | ✓ | ✓ | ✓ |
|  | History | ✓ | ✓ | ✓ |
|  | Philosophy | ✓ | ✓ | ✓ |
| Life Sciences | Biological Sciences | ✓ | ✓ | ✓ |
|  | Medicine | ✓ | ✓ | ✓ |
|  | Psychology | ✓ | ✓ | ✓ |
| Physical Sciences | Chemistry | ✓ | ✓ | ✓ |
|  | Physics | ✓ | ✓ | ✓ |
|  | Engineering | ✓ | ✓ | ✓ |
| Social Sciences | Business | ✓ | ✓ | ✓ |
|  | Law | ✓ | ✓ | ✓ |
|  | Sociology | ✓ | ✓ | ✓ |

# Appendix 1.3

Summary of Biber's (1988) Factor Analysis (adapted from Biber et al., 2002)

| Feature | Example | Factor loading |
|---|---|---|
| **Dimension 1: Involved versus Informational** | | |
| POSITIVE FEATURES (INVOLVED PRODUCTION) | | |
| private verbs | think, know, believe | 0.96 |
| *that*-deletions | I think [0] he went | 0.91 |
| contractions | can't, she's | 0.90 |
| present tense verbs | is, likes, wants | 0.86 |
| second person pronouns | you | 0.86 |
| *do* as pro-verb | so *did* Sandra | 0.82 |
| analytic negation | that's not likely | 0.78 |
| demonstrative pronouns | this shows… | 0.76 |
| general emphatics | really, a lot | 0.74 |
| first person pronouns | I, we | 0.74 |
| pronoun *it* | I didn't like *it* | 0.71 |
| *be* as main verb | that *was* sad | 0.71 |
| causative subordination | because… | 0.66 |
| discourse particles | well, anyway | 0.66 |
| indefinite pronouns | nothing, someone | 0.62 |
| general hedges | kind of, something like | 0.58 |

| Feature | Example | Factor loading |
|---|---|---|
| amplifiers | absolutely, extremely | 0.56 |
| sentence relatives | Bob didn't study at all, which is usual for him | 0.55 |
| *wh*-questions | Why did you go? | 0.52 |
| Possibility modals | can, could, may, might | 0.50 |
| Nonphrasal coordination | Sally was biking last weekend *and* then she... | 0.48 |
| *wh*-clauses | Jill asked what happened | 0.47 |
| Final prepositions | the candidate that I was thinking of | 0.43 |
| NEGATIVE FEATURES (INFORMATIONAL PRODUCTION) | | |
| nouns | community, case | −0.80 |
| word length | – | −0.58 |
| prepositions | of, in, for | −0.54 |
| type / token ratio | – | −0.54 |
| attributive adjectives | good, possible | −0.47 |

### Dimension 2: Narrative versus non-narrative

| POSITIVE FEATURES (NARRATIVE DISCOURSE)[a] | | |
|---|---|---|
| past tense verbs | considered, described | 0.90 |
| third person pronouns | he, she, they | 0.73 |
| perfect aspect verbs | had been, has shown | 0.48 |
| public verbs | said, explain | 0.43 |
| synthetic negation | no answer is good enough | 0.40 |
| present participial clauses | Having established the direction, we can now... | 0.39 |

### Dimension 3: Situation-dependent versus elaborated[b]

| POSITIVE FEATURES (SITUATION-DEPENDENT REFERENCE) | | |
|---|---|---|
| time adverbials | early, instantly, soon | 0.60 |
| place adverbials | above, beside, outdoors | 0.49 |
| adverbs | always, significantly | 0.46 |
| NEGATIVE FEATURES (ELABORATED REFERENCE) | | |
| *wh*-relative clauses in object positions | something *which everybody can do* | −0.63 |
| pied piping constructions | the way *in which this happens* | −0.61 |
| *wh*-relative clauses in subject positions | those *who retain inhibitions* | −0.45 |
| phrasal coordination | salt and pepper | −0.36 |
| nominalisations | extension, proposition | −0.36 |

| Feature | Example | Factor loading |
|---|---|---|
| **Dimension 4: Overt expression of persuasion** | | |
| POSITIVE FEATURES (OVERT EXPRESSION OF PERSUASION) | | |
| infinitives | hope to go | 0.76 |
| prediction modals | will, would, shall | 0.54 |
| suasive verbs | command, insist, propose | 0.49 |
| conditional subordination | if you want | 0.47 |
| necessity modals | must, should, have to | 0.46 |
| split auxiliaries | should be | 0.44 |
| (possibility modals) | can, could, might | (0.37)[c] |
| **Dimension 5: Non-impersonal versus impersonal[b,d]** | | |
| NEGATIVE FEATURES (IMPERSONAL STYLE) | | |
| conjuncts | however, therefore *really* | −0.48 |
| agentless passives | The same mechanism *was analyzed* on each. | −0.43 |
| Past participial adverbial clauses | Directed by Twilling, the production is delightful. | −0.42 |
| *by* passives | He *was surrounded by a ring of men.* | −0.41 |
| past participial postnominal clauses | the course *chosen by the large majority* | −0.40 |
| other adverbial subordinators | since, while, whereas | −0.39 |

Notes. The table includes only features with loadings larger than ±0.35; features with smaller loadings have not demonstrated strong evidence for their occurrence on the dimension.
[a]no negative features; [b]Polarity reversed; [c]feature was not used in the computation of dimension scores; [d]no positive features.

## Appendix 1.4

Key lemmas in the BAWE corpus with reference to the BNC (excluding dates, numbers and names of people)

| Lemma | Frequency in BAWE | ARF*per million words | Frequency in BNC | ARF*per million words | Keyword score** |
|---|---|---|---|---|---|
| London | 4914 | 400 | 17 | 0.1 | 5 |
| i*** | 13069 | 925.1 | 16960 | 108.8 | 4.9 |
| data | 4981 | 335.1 | 1 | 0 | 4.3 |
| therefore | 7845 | 965.8 | 22983 | 172.2 | 3.9 |
| Oxford | 3255 | 260.1 | 17 | 0.1 | 3.6 |

| Lemma | Frequency in BAWE | ARF*per million words | Frequency in BNC | ARF*per million words | Keyword score** |
|---|---|---|---|---|---|
| ed | 3394 | 253.9 | 857 | 2.9 | 3.4 |
| theory | 6158 | 485.6 | 16367 | 75.7 | 3.3 |
| due | 5488 | 663.2 | 15301 | 134.9 | 3.2 |
| analysis | 4610 | 447.2 | 14113 | 69.4 | 3.2 |
| et | 4125 | 255.7 | 4748 | 16 | 3.1 |
| factor | 4548 | 470.7 | 14939 | 96 | 2.9 |
| however | 12267 | 1742 | 59730 | 535.1 | 2.9 |
| introduction | 2500 | 342.6 | 6865 | 55.4 | 2.8 |
| conclusion | 2410 | 350.6 | 7390 | 58.7 | 2.8 |
| essay | 2019 | 204.7 | 2361 | 10.9 | 2.7 |
| York | 1855 | 171.2 | 11 | 0.1 | 2.7 |
| result | 9490 | 1087.5 | 41971 | 347.6 | 2.7 |
| journal | 2911 | 213.3 | 3375 | 19.2 | 2.6 |
| university | 4324 | 410 | 18945 | 94.5 | 2.6 |
| method | 5083 | 450.8 | 17816 | 112.1 | 2.6 |
| UK | 2447 | 159.9 | 8 | 0.1 | 2.6 |
| value | 7759 | 627.9 | 26720 | 181.2 | 2.6 |
| bibliography | 1119 | 158.2 | 475 | 2.2 | 2.5 |
| al | 2938 | 175.2 | 3293 | 10.6 | 2.5 |
| process | 6316 | 619.5 | 29214 | 192.7 | 2.5 |
| low | 4705 | 482 | 16397 | 138.4 | 2.4 |
| focus | 2749 | 314.3 | 9438 | 70.8 | 2.4 |
| thus | 4496 | 477.2 | 20247 | 138 | 2.4 |
| increase | 6734 | 647 | 30894 | 209.8 | 2.4 |
| Cambridge | 1795 | 136.5 | 2 | 0 | 2.4 |
| reference | 2242 | 307 | 10525 | 73.4 | 2.3 |
| social | 7756 | 608.3 | 41659 | 203.7 | 2.3 |
| structure | 4061 | 384.4 | 18801 | 110.7 | 2.3 |
| define | 2375 | 272.6 | 9426 | 62.8 | 2.3 |
| human | 5336 | 425.5 | 21294 | 130.2 | 2.3 |
| model | 5595 | 355.9 | 19242 | 102.7 | 2.2 |
| compare | 3031 | 354.4 | 12858 | 102.6 | 2.2 |
| appendix | 2370 | 137.2 | 1850 | 8 | 2.2 |
| research | 5179 | 401 | 27529 | 128.5 | 2.2 |
| high | 8206 | 866.5 | 37718 | 340.9 | 2.2 |
| culture | 3202 | 228.8 | 10221 | 51.7 | 2.2 |
| affect | 3116 | 356.5 | 13433 | 112.3 | 2.2 |
| hence | 2097 | 182.9 | 4684 | 32.2 | 2.1 |
| occur | 3170 | 355.8 | 15473 | 113.4 | 2.1 |
| study | 6495 | 606.4 | 41545 | 231.7 | 2.1 |
| argue | 3562 | 337.6 | 14595 | 105.5 | 2.1 |
| function | 3404 | 297.9 | 14462 | 87.5 | 2.1 |
| concept | 2448 | 227.6 | 8995 | 54.3 | 2.1 |

| Lemma | Frequency in BAWE | ARF*per million words | Frequency in BNC | ARF*per million words | Keyword score** |
|---|---|---|---|---|---|
| example | 6385 | 766.5 | 43082 | 308.9 | 2.1 |
| impact | 2265 | 229 | 7712 | 56 | 2.1 |
| decrease | 1513 | 141.7 | 2414 | 14.7 | 2.1 |
| significant | 2683 | 296.3 | 11988 | 88.3 | 2.1 |
| state | 8778 | 841.4 | 53678 | 347.9 | 2.1 |
| create | 4096 | 472.6 | 21207 | 173.5 | 2.1 |
| negative | 1712 | 174.6 | 4932 | 32 | 2.1 |
| press | 4462 | 383.9 | 17218 | 133.4 | 2.1 |
| Europe | 1594 | 106.9 | 32 | 0.2 | 2.1 |
| strategy | 3076 | 205.8 | 8816 | 48.3 | 2.1 |
| product | 5343 | 326.3 | 21608 | 106.9 | 2.1 |
| different | 7870 | 950.7 | 47607 | 412.6 | 2 |
| analyse | 1440 | 160.6 | 4127 | 27.5 | 2 |
| use | 22858 | 2619.6 | 151333 | 1235.6 | 2 |
| determine | 2589 | 295.6 | 11822 | 95.7 | 2 |
| role | 3998 | 404.9 | 20699 | 151.4 | 2 |
| system | 9237 | 789.9 | 61349 | 345.5 | 2 |
| access | 3455 | 244.8 | 11410 | 72.8 | 2 |
| edition | 1734 | 138.5 | 3196 | 20.1 | 2 |
| influence | 2922 | 310.8 | 15061 | 107.3 | 2 |
| individual | 4809 | 463.1 | 26885 | 184.8 | 2 |
| identify | 2626 | 287.9 | 13157 | 96.4 | 2 |
| according | 2419 | 280.3 | 10626 | 93.8 | 2 |
| whilst | 1777 | 161.5 | 5775 | 33.8 | 2 |
| order | 7027 | 822.4 | 44903 | 373.6 | 1.9 |
| interaction | 1393 | 123.2 | 3333 | 14.8 | 1.9 |
| relationship | 3271 | 328.5 | 18592 | 120.7 | 1.9 |
| society | 5040 | 394.3 | 27778 | 155 | 1.9 |
| environment | 2664 | 254.2 | 14360 | 82.8 | 1.9 |
| cause | 5400 | 571 | 29979 | 252.7 | 1.9 |
| cite | 1694 | 123.1 | 2356 | 17.3 | 1.9 |
| characteristic | 1632 | 173.4 | 6760 | 43.8 | 1.9 |
| reduce | 3302 | 345 | 17679 | 134.4 | 1.9 |
| variable | 2058 | 127.5 | 4987 | 19.8 | 1.9 |
| furthermore | 1319 | 124.6 | 2882 | 18.6 | 1.9 |
| nature | 3405 | 354.7 | 17932 | 140.2 | 1.9 |
| base | 4150 | 527.2 | 27772 | 231.6 | 1.9 |
| level | 6115 | 626 | 39188 | 283.9 | 1.9 |
| global | 1933 | 120.3 | 3524 | 17 | 1.9 |
| consider | 4400 | 550.5 | 28518 | 246.4 | 1.9 |
| specific | 1971 | 233.7 | 11234 | 77.8 | 1.9 |
| behaviour | 2671 | 215.9 | 12685 | 68.5 | 1.9 |
| perspective | 1262 | 131.3 | 3729 | 24.1 | 1.9 |
| e.g. | 1497 | 116.6 | 4835 | 16.5 | 1.9 |

| Lemma | Frequency in BAWE | ARF*per million words | Frequency in BNC | ARF*per million words | Keyword score** |
|---|---|---|---|---|---|
| positive | 1848 | 198.2 | 8399 | 60.6 | 1.9 |
| difference | 3353 | 358.2 | 18907 | 147.6 | 1.9 |
| i.e. | 1399 | 124.9 | 4537 | 21.7 | 1.8 |
| comparison | 1298 | 154.2 | 5015 | 37.6 | 1.8 |
| economic | 4290 | 287.8 | 23338 | 110.2 | 1.8 |
| development | 5389 | 497.4 | 37087 | 224.6 | 1.8 |
| review | 2536 | 233.1 | 13028 | 81 | 1.8 |
| source | 3045 | 297.7 | 15628 | 116.3 | 1.8 |
| suggest | 4844 | 534.3 | 28248 | 246.3 | 1.8 |
| America | 1368 | 82.2 | 6 | 0.1 | 1.8 |
| aspect | 1997 | 242.5 | 11495 | 88.7 | 1.8 |
| important | 5485 | 696.7 | 38716 | 339.3 | 1.8 |
| require | 3810 | 456.7 | 28257 | 207.4 | 1.8 |
| highlight | 1260 | 137.1 | 3711 | 31.1 | 1.8 |
| firstly | 863 | 103.6 | 1709 | 13 | 1.8 |
| effect | 5240 | 559.8 | 34649 | 266.8 | 1.8 |
| terms | 1740 | 199.3 | 10066 | 67.2 | 1.8 |
| importance | 1785 | 217 | 9579 | 77.4 | 1.8 |
| gender | 1805 | 90.9 | 2003 | 7 | 1.8 |
| content | 1648 | 163.9 | 6182 | 48.2 | 1.8 |
| potential | 2179 | 233.8 | 11269 | 87.6 | 1.8 |
| cultural | 1763 | 132.1 | 6432 | 30.5 | 1.8 |
| sample | 3182 | 144.2 | 7991 | 38.2 | 1.8 |
| Britain | 1165 | 76.9 | 31 | 0.2 | 1.8 |
| England | 1158 | 76 | 33 | 0.2 | 1.8 |
| understanding | 1521 | 173.1 | 7664 | 55.4 | 1.8 |
| evidence | 3687 | 331.8 | 21411 | 146.7 | 1.8 |

*ARF = Average Reduced Frequency, a variant on a frequency list that 'discounts' multiple occurrences of a word that appear close to each other, e.g. in the same document.

**For an explanation of the statistic used to generate the score see http://trac.sketchengine.co.uk/wiki/SimpleMaths

***11767 occurrences are 1st person singular personal pronouns (*I* or *me*)

# Appendix 1.5

## USAS semantic categories in the BAWE corpus

Figures have been normalised to 10,000 words by dividing the raw frequencies by the total number of words in the corpus (6,506,995), and then multiplying by 10,000.

Raw and normalised frequencies of USAS semantic categories

| USAS Semantic Category | raw frequency | per 10,000 |
|---|---|---|
| GENERAL & ABSTRACT TERMS (A) | 410138 | 630 |
| THE BODY & THE INDIVIDUAL (B) | 21729 | 33 |
| EMOTIONAL ACTIONS, STATES AND PROCESSES (E) | 27988 | 43 |
| FOOD & FARMING (F) | 289 | 0 |
| GOVERNMENT & THE PUBLIC DOMAIN (G) | 719 | 1 |
| ARCHITECTURE, BUILDING, HOUSES & THE HOME (H) | 55 | 0 |
| MONEY & COMMERCE (I) | 2725 | 4 |
| ENTERTAINMENT, SPORTS & GAMES (K) | 254 | 0 |
| LIFE & LIVING THINGS (L) | 12043 | 19 |
| MOVEMENT, LOCATION, TRAVEL & TRANSPORT (M) | 1654 | 3 |
| NUMBERS & MEASUREMENT (N) | 45132 | 69 |
| EDUCATION (P) | 3449 | 5 |
| LINGUISTIC ACTIONS, STATES & PROCESSES (Q) | 931 | 1 |
| SOCIAL ACTIONS, STATES & PROCESSES (S) | 105011 | 161 |
| TIME (T) | 53919 | 83 |
| THE WORLD & OUR ENVIRONMENT (W) | 609 | 1 |
| PSYCHOLOGICAL ACTIONS, STATES & PROCESSES (X) | 61957 | 95 |

Raw and normalised frequencies for some subcategories of General and Abstract Terms (A)

| USAS Semantic Category | raw frequency | per 10,000 |
|---|---|---|
| AFFECT: CAUSE / CONNECTED General / abstract terms denoting causal relationship, or lack of (A2.2) | 71608 | 110 |
| EVALUATION (A5) | 8269 | 13 |
| COMPARING (A6) | 4312 | 7 |
| DEFINITE (+ MODALS) Abstract terms of modality (possibility, necessity, certainty, etc.) (A7) | 3348 | 5 |
| SEEM / APPEAR Abstract terms relating to appearance/impression (A8) | 12344 | 19 |

# Appendix 2

Table A2 shows the percentage of assignment texts from each genre family at each level of study in each disciplinary group. The genre families are presented from least populated (Literature Survey) to most populated (Essay). It shows, for instance, that more than 90% (91.5%) of Level 1 Arts and Humanities assignment texts are Essays, while less than 12% (11.2%) of Level 1 Physical Sciences assignment texts are Essays. The data in Table A2 is shown as a graph in Figure 2.6.

Table A2  Distribution of percentage of genre families over disciplinary groups and levels of study

| | AH1 | AH2 | AH3 | AH4 | SS1 | SS2 | SS3 | SS4 | LS1 | LS2 | LS3 | LS4 | PS1 | PS2 | PS3 | PS4 |
|---|---|---|---|---|---|---|---|---|---|---|---|---|---|---|---|---|
| Es | 91.5 | 85.5 | 80.5 | 61.5 | 60.9 | 60.2 | 57.5 | 50.2 | 22.3 | 17.6 | 19 | 15.7 | 11.2 | 6 | 10.9 | 6.3 |
| MR | 1.3 | 3.9 | 1.8 | 3.8 | 1.8 | 1.5 | 0.6 | 4 | 26.9 | 25.1 | 15.7 | 13.2 | 33.5 | 42.4 | 16 | 19.8 |
| Cr | 4.3 | 5.3 | 7.3 | 20.5 | 15 | 13.9 | 14.4 | 13.9 | 9.7 | 12.1 | 9.9 | 15.7 | 10.1 | 9.3 | 12.8 | 14.3 |
| Exp | 0.4 | 2.6 | 1.2 | 0 | 3.6 | 1 | 1.9 | 2 | 24.6 | 17.1 | 14.9 | 8.6 | 12.8 | 9.3 | 7.1 | 8.7 |
| CS | 0 | 0 | 0 | 0 | 4.5 | 8.5 | 11.3 | 8 | 2.6 | 4.5 | 5.8 | 35 | 5.6 | 2.6 | 6.4 | 12.7 |
| Exc | 1.3 | 1.8 | 3 | 2.6 | 0.9 | 1.5 | 0.6 | 4.5 | 3.4 | 6 | 9.9 | 1.5 | 9.5 | 6 | 8.3 | 10.3 |
| DS | 0 | 0 | 0.6 | 0 | 0 | 0 | 0.6 | 0.5 | 0 | 0 | 0.8 | 0.5 | 13.4 | 12.6 | 20.5 | 10.3 |
| Pr | 0 | 0 | 0 | 1.3 | 1.8 | 1.5 | 2.5 | 9 | 1.7 | 5.5 | 2.5 | 4.1 | 1.7 | 3.3 | 2.6 | 6.3 |
| NR | 0 | 0.4 | 2.4 | 3.8 | 3.2 | 1.5 | 3.1 | 2 | 5.1 | 3.5 | 5.8 | 1 | 0.6 | 5.3 | 3.2 | 4.8 |

| | | | | | | | | | | | | | | | | |
|---|---|---|---|---|---|---|---|---|---|---|---|---|---|---|---|---|
| RRt | 0 | 0.4 | 3 | 2.6 | 0 | 1.5 | 2.5 | 4.5 | 3.4 | 5.5 | 2.5 | 0.5 | 0.6 | 0.7 | 6.4 | 3.2 |
| PQ | 0 | 0 | 0 | 0 | 5.5 | 7.5 | 2.5 | 0.5 | 0 | 1 | 0 | 0 | 0 | 1.3 | 1.3 | 1.6 |
| EW | 0 | 0 | 0 | 0 | 1.4 | 0 | 0.6 | 0 | 1.7 | 0.5 | 8.3 | 2.5 | 0 | 1.3 | 4.5 | 0 |
| LS | 1.3 | 0 | 0 | 3.8 | 1.4 | 1.5 | 1.9 | 1 | 1.1 | 1.5 | 5 | 1.5 | 1.1 | 0 | 0 | 1.6 |
| TOTAL | 100 | 100 | 100 | 100 | 100 | 100 | 100 | 100 | 100 | 100 | 100 | 100 | 100 | 100 | 100 | 100 |

**Key:**

Cr = Critique
Es = Essay
Ex = Explanation
NR = Narrative Recount
RR = Research Report

CS = Case Study
EW = Empathy Writing
LS = Literature Survey
PQ = Problem Question

DS = Design Specification
Ex = Exercise
MR = Methodology Recount
Pr = Proposal

AH1 = Level 1 Arts and Humanities;
SS1 = Level 1 Social Sciences;
LS1 = Level 1 Life Sciences;
PS1 = Level 1 Physical Sciences;

AH2 = Level 2 Arts and Humanities, etc.
SS2 = Level 2 Social Sciences, etc.
LS2 = Level 2 Life Sciences, etc.
PS2 = Level 2 Physical Sciences, etc.

# Appendix 4.1

### Key adjectives in Critique genres

This list of 64 key adjectives in order of keyness in Critiques indicates the range of perspectives from which phenomena are evaluated

| | | | |
|---|---|---|---|
| 1. extra | 17. existing | 33. limited | 49. single |
| 2. beneficial | 18. future | 34. obvious | 50. specific |
| 3. reliable | 19. overall | 35. potential | 51. successful |
| 4. fair | 20. serious | 36. suitable | 52. above |
| 5. accurate | 21. true | 37. able | 53. bad |
| 6. correct | 22. complete | 38. additional | 54. fundamental |
| 7. scientific | 23. constant | 39. cultural | 55. increasing |
| 8. useful | 24. real | 40. easy | 56. legal |
| 9. sufficient | 25. relevant | 41. following | 57. necessary |
| 10. unlikely | 26. stable | 42. increased | 58. open |
| 11. detailed | 27. theoretical | 43. likely | 59. physical |
| 12. environmental | 28. unable | 44. major | 60. wide |
| 13. reasonable | 29. apparent | 45. original | 61. young |
| 14. average | 30. complex | 46. particular | 62. British |
| 15. concerned | 31. external | 47. practical | 63. essential |
| 16. effective | 32. interesting | 48. recent | 64. independent |

# Appendix 4.2

Collocates of *important, significant* and *useful* in Critiques

| Important | | |
|---|---|---|
| 1. aspect | 11. technique | 21. point |
| 2. factor | 12. principle | 22. approach |
| 3. element | 13. thing | 23. decision |
| 4. consideration | 14. feature | 24. analysis |
| 5. implication | 15. part | 25. question |
| 6. role | 16. development | 26. change |
| 7. issue | 17. quality | 27. research |
| 8. tool | 18. information | 28. study |
| 9. objective | 19. stage | 29. process |
| 10. step | 20. area | 30. model |

| Significant | | |
|---|---|---|
| 1. impact | 8. change | 15. evidence |
| 2. reduction | 9. role | 16. result |
| 3. difference | 10. figure | 17. factor |
| 4. growth | 11. development | 18. number |
| 5. effect | 12. influence | 19. cost |
| 6. amount | 13. research | 20. increase |
| 7. benefit | 14. term | |

| Useful | | |
|---|---|---|
| 1. tool | 4. source | 6. analysis |
| 2. information | 5. site | 7. method |
| 3. model | | |

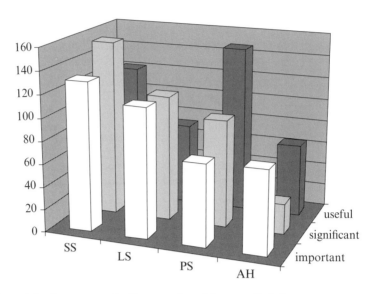

Figure 4.1    *Important, significant* and *useful* across disciplinary groups

# Appendix 5.1

Top 100 keywords in Literature Surveys compared to British National Corpus

| | Word | Freq | LS ARF | BAWE ARF/mill | Freq | BNC ARF | ARF/ mill | Keyness Score |
|---|---|---|---|---|---|---|---|---|
| 1. | 2004 | 102 | 16.5 | 682.3 | 16 | 8.8 | 0.2 | 7.8 |
| 2. | 2002 | 101 | 16.2 | 667.7 | 35 | 17.3 | 0.3 | 7.7 |
| 3. | 2003 | 113 | 15.8 | 653.3 | 56 | 24.4 | 0.4 | 7.5 |
| 4. | & | 131 | 15.2 | 628.2 | 0 | 0 | 0 | 7.3 |
| 5. | 1999 | 89 | 15.2 | 627.3 | 150 | 53.1 | 1 | 7.2 |
| 6. | 1998 | 70 | 15.2 | 627.1 | 147 | 64.7 | 1.2 | 7.2 |
| 7. | 2001 | 103 | 14.3 | 592.1 | 161 | 52.7 | 1 | 6.9 |
| 8. | M. | 124 | 15.8 | 650.6 | 2155 | 616.5 | 11.3 | 6.7 |
| 9. | J. | 116 | 16.3 | 672 | 4197 | 956.4 | 17.6 | 6.6 |
| 10. | Et | 264 | 16.4 | 677.4 | 5168 | 1059.7 | 19.5 | 6.5 |
| 11. | 2005 | 114 | 13.1 | 541.7 | 131 | 39.8 | 0.7 | 6.4 |
| 12. | A. | 107 | 15 | 621.4 | 3283 | 1019.9 | 18.8 | 6.1 |
| 13. | S. | 64 | 13.8 | 568.5 | 2041 | 585.4 | 10.8 | 6 |
| 14. | D. | 54 | 13.5 | 559.1 | 1560 | 526.6 | 9.7 | 6 |
| 15. | Press | 68 | 14.2 | 587.6 | 2373 | 882.9 | 16.3 | 5.9 |
| 16. | Journal | 96 | 12.9 | 532.3 | 1211 | 377.9 | 7 | 5.9 |
| 17. | C. | 78 | 13.8 | 571.1 | 2486 | 810.9 | 14.9 | 5.8 |
| 18. | R. | 90 | 13 | 538.2 | 2034 | 570.6 | 10.5 | 5.8 |
| 19. | 2000 | 64 | 12.6 | 518.4 | 1624 | 582.9 | 10.7 | 5.6 |
| 20. | 1997 | 44 | 10.9 | 450.4 | 424 | 136.8 | 2.5 | 5.4 |
| 21. | K. | 59 | 11.2 | 462.2 | 912 | 288 | 5.3 | 5.3 |
| 22. | B. | 81 | 12 | 493.6 | 2029 | 683.3 | 12.6 | 5.3 |
| 23. | al. | 123 | 10.4 | 427.4 | 1252 | 164.5 | 3 | 5.1 |
| 24. | P. | 47 | 10.8 | 447.5 | 1474 | 436.5 | 8 | 5.1 |
| 25. | 1994 | 45 | 10.8 | 445.6 | 1606 | 429 | 7.9 | 5.1 |
| 26. | Al | 138 | 11.3 | 467.9 | 3516 | 678.5 | 12.5 | 5 |
| 27. | G. | 95 | 10.8 | 446.9 | 1563 | 508.6 | 9.4 | 5 |
| 28. | E. | 66 | 10.3 | 425.6 | 1911 | 596.7 | 11 | 4.7 |
| 29. | University | 102 | 15.2 | 627.5 | 11756 | 3236 | 59.6 | 4.6 |
| 30. | L. | 47 | 9.2 | 381.6 | 945 | 323.2 | 5.9 | 4.5 |
| 31. | selection | 64 | 12.5 | 516.1 | 5690 | 2032.2 | 37.4 | 4.5 |
| 32. | Th | 38 | 9.3 | 384 | 3618 | 458 | 8.4 | 4.5 |
| 33. | 1996 | 31 | 8.5 | 351.3 | 481 | 166.7 | 3.1 | 4.4 |
| 34. | W. | 24 | 8.8 | 363.7 | 1681 | 488.1 | 9 | 4.3 |
| 35. | studies | 79 | 13.2 | 543.6 | 10855 | 2827.7 | 52.1 | 4.2 |
| 36. | ... | 25 | 7.5 | 311.7 | 110 | 32.1 | 0.6 | 4.1 |
| 37. | methods | 52 | 12.3 | 506 | 8148 | 2974.3 | 54.7 | 3.9 |
| 38. | H. | 35 | 7.9 | 325.3 | 1754 | 539.2 | 9.9 | 3.9 |
| 39. | N. | 36 | 7.3 | 302.6 | 736 | 248.4 | 4.6 | 3.9 |
| 40. | Oxford | 56 | 10.1 | 415.9 | 8074 | 1899.5 | 35 | 3.8 |

| | Word | Freq | LS ARF | BAWE ARF/mill | Freq | BNC ARF | ARF/ mill | Keyness Score |
|---|---|---|---|---|---|---|---|---|
| 41. | evolutionary | 65 | 7.1 | 295.1 | 1021 | 225.1 | 4.1 | 3.8 |
| 42. | species | 294 | 9.1 | 373.7 | 8821 | 1373.3 | 25.3 | 3.8 |
| 43. | Review | 23 | 7.5 | 311.4 | 1607 | 529.9 | 9.8 | 3.7 |
| 44. | 1995 | 28 | 7.1 | 292.6 | 882 | 275.9 | 5.1 | 3.7 |
| 45. | genetic | 67 | 7.2 | 298.1 | 1728 | 390.3 | 7.2 | 3.7 |
| 46. | Science | 28 | 7.6 | 313.1 | 2724 | 761.9 | 14 | 3.6 |
| 47. | T. | 52 | 7 | 288.3 | 1330 | 411.9 | 7.6 | 3.6 |
| 48. | J | 21 | 7.5 | 309.2 | 3303 | 826.2 | 15.2 | 3.6 |
| 49. | " | 392 | 26.2 | 1081.7 | 142124 | 12760.4 | 234.9 | 3.5 |
| 50. | suggests | 30 | 10.2 | 420.3 | 6663 | 2727.6 | 50.2 | 3.5 |
| 51. | Pp | 32 | 6.1 | 250.4 | 489 | 79.2 | 1.5 | 3.5 |
| 52. | F. | 16 | 6.4 | 265.8 | 1198 | 409.6 | 7.5 | 3.4 |
| 53. | research | 144 | 13.9 | 572.9 | 20596 | 5328.9 | 98.1 | 3.4 |
| 54. | molecular | 50 | 6.1 | 250.7 | 1165 | 185.1 | 3.4 | 3.4 |
| 55. | Studies | 18 | 6.8 | 282.2 | 2592 | 691.4 | 12.7 | 3.4 |
| 56. | aspects | 24 | 10.1 | 418.2 | 7000 | 2890.2 | 53.2 | 3.4 |
| 57. | I. | 15 | 6.6 | 270.7 | 1293 | 582.9 | 10.7 | 3.3 |
| 58. | Therefore | 18 | 7 | 289.3 | 2368 | 902.7 | 16.6 | 3.3 |
| 59. | environment | 45 | 10.6 | 437.7 | 9808 | 3375.4 | 62.1 | 3.3 |
| 60. | Natural | 16 | 6.2 | 256 | 1049 | 410.3 | 7.6 | 3.3 |
| 61. | variation | 31 | 6.7 | 276.9 | 2597 | 823.8 | 15.2 | 3.3 |
| 62. | study | 164 | 14.9 | 617 | 20726 | 6498.9 | 119.6 | 3.3 |
| 63. | organisms | 32 | 5.7 | 236.3 | 1006 | 209.1 | 3.8 | 3.2 |
| 64. | populations | 23 | 6 | 246.1 | 1455 | 428.3 | 7.9 | 3.2 |
| 65. | 2006 | 22 | 5.3 | 220.5 | 20 | 10.4 | 0.2 | 3.2 |
| 66. | results | 65 | 13.1 | 541 | 14218 | 5600.3 | 103.1 | 3.2 |
| 67. | technique | 21 | 7.2 | 298.1 | 4380 | 1489.2 | 27.4 | 3.1 |
| 68. | significant | 41 | 11.7 | 482.1 | 11828 | 4813.6 | 88.6 | 3.1 |
| 69. | states | 26 | 8.5 | 349.6 | 8513 | 2542.9 | 46.8 | 3.1 |
| 70. | evolution | 37 | 5.8 | 239.2 | 2297 | 612.2 | 11.3 | 3 |
| 71. | analysis | 45 | 9.5 | 393 | 12210 | 3385.8 | 62.3 | 3 |
| 72. | adaptive | 39 | 5 | 207.4 | 295 | 77.5 | 1.4 | 3 |
| 73. | molecules | 21 | 5.2 | 213.6 | 1486 | 190 | 3.5 | 3 |
| 74. | review | 29 | 8.4 | 347.2 | 7808 | 2588 | 47.6 | 3 |
| 75. | investigate | 15 | 6.3 | 261 | 2314 | 1044.3 | 19.2 | 3 |
| 76. | References | 10 | 5 | 206.7 | 179 | 75.3 | 1.4 | 3 |
| 77. | effects | 62 | 10 | 414.7 | 10489 | 3832.6 | 70.5 | 3 |
| 78. | 1992 | 33 | 8.2 | 338.5 | 10249 | 2463.2 | 45.3 | 3 |
| 79. | natural | 47 | 12.1 | 501.7 | 12958 | 5440.3 | 100.1 | 3 |
| 80. | characteristics | 23 | 6.6 | 271.9 | 3682 | 1297.8 | 23.9 | 3 |
| 81. | associated | 28 | 9.4 | 386.8 | 8854 | 3393.2 | 62.5 | 3 |
| 82. | Moreover | 10 | 6.4 | 263.9 | 3482 | 1192.4 | 21.9 | 3 |
| 83. | humans | 27 | 5.5 | 227 | 1854 | 539.3 | 9.9 | 3 |

|      | Word        | Freq | LS ARF | BAWE ARF/mill | Freq  | BNC ARF | ARF/ mill | Keyness Score |
|------|-------------|------|--------|---------------|-------|---------|-----------|---------------|
| 84.  | authors     | 54   | 5.8    | 238.5         | 2353  | 787.2   | 14.5      | 3             |
| 85.  | factors     | 30   | 8.4    | 347.6         | 8474  | 2794.5  | 51.4      | 3             |
| 86.  | individuals | 56   | 8.3    | 342.6         | 7663  | 2717.6  | 50        | 3             |
| 87.  | stated      | 17   | 7.4    | 304.3         | 5101  | 2035.9  | 37.5      | 2.9           |
| 88.  | L           | 10   | 5.5    | 226.7         | 2513  | 642     | 11.8      | 2.9           |
| 89.  | culture     | 25   | 7.4    | 307           | 7582  | 2157.4  | 39.7      | 2.9           |
| 90.  | adapted     | 8    | 5.5    | 225.2         | 1411  | 664.5   | 12.2      | 2.9           |
| 91.  | Due         | 55   | 13.9   | 574.3         | 14927 | 7243.2  | 133.3     | 2.9           |
| 92.  | pp.         | 56   | 5.2    | 216.6         | 5475  | 605.9   | 11.2      | 2.8           |
| 93.  | differences | 39   | 7.7    | 319.9         | 7461  | 2591.2  | 47.7      | 2.8           |
| 94.  | experimental| 32   | 5.3    | 217.8         | 2114  | 666.6   | 12.3      | 2.8           |
| 95.  | organic     | 118  | 5.1    | 209.7         | 1908  | 525.4   | 9.7       | 2.8           |
| 96.  | literature  | 24   | 6.2    | 257.6         | 4616  | 1455.6  | 26.8      | 2.8           |
| 97.  | sample      | 32   | 6      | 247.5         | 4473  | 1271    | 23.4      | 2.8           |
| 98.  | processes   | 21   | 6.3    | 260.9         | 5281  | 1547.6  | 28.5      | 2.8           |
| 99.  | population  | 50   | 8.8    | 364           | 12131 | 3551.1  | 65.4      | 2.8           |
| 100. | diseases    | 11   | 5      | 206.6         | 1675  | 512.3   | 9.4       | 2.8           |

# Appendix 5.2

Top ten keywords in context from comparison of literature searches and BAWE corpus *(al, literature, whose, authors, survey, overview, et, paper, discover, search)*

| Discipline | Context |
|---|---|
| Biological Sciences | thetaiotaomicron, was studied by Xu *et al* . and was found to have interesting features |
| HTLM | lowest paid sector. However, Torrington *et* al (2002) suggested that people may be motivated |
| Agriculture | parents to buy organic food (Davies *et al* , 1995). In another study carried out in |
| Biological Sciences | of the S-gene. This paper (Pandey *et* al 1979) suggests there may be some evidence |
| Classics | produce a broad sweep of the most important literature on *this* topic over time from the late nineteenth |
| Classics | Fortunately I have found evidence within the literature that suggests *this* phenomenon is not merely |
| Health | on thorough academic enquiry, in fact, my literature search on *this* subject shows that very |
| Health | prosecution of parents. (Zhang 2004). A thorough literature review on *this* subject has been carried |
| Health | teacher's which was not relevant to *this* literature review. Having considered the above pieces |
| Health | Data was collected from 30 children whose parents had been prosecuted. Thirteen were |
| English | Introduces the concept of the "frigid heroine" whose reaction to the threat of sexuality is |
| Biological Sciences | . E. faecalis, a Gram-positive bacterium whose natural habitat is the mammalian gastrointestinal |
| Politics | 1851, only minority of males in factories whose working hours increased Even factory workers |
| Engineering | company to Asa Griggs Candler a businessman whose influencer ended up making it one of the |
| Anthropology | the remaining group of its presence, and whose apparently suicidal altruism moved him |

Law     various aspects of Islamic divorce. The **author** alerts the reader to the different themes

Law     . The selection of the cases reflect the **author** 's research skills, and ability to choose

**Biological Sciences** exogenously acquired DNA. According to the **authors** , this is one of the highest proportions

Publishing     stopped from digitising books, so that the **authors** remain in control of how their books are

Publishing     about the difficulty of selecting winning **authors** for the Man Booker Prize and the delight

Anthropology     lack of data does not seem to affect these **authors** from denominate their findings of a new

Anthropology     Journal of Primatology, 21, 537–555.The **authors** , researchers at Universities of Cambridge

**Biological Sciences** wider range of species. I suggest that the **papers** to be reviewed can be sorted into three

**Biological Sciences** close geographical location. The first two **papers** reviewed in this section (Shepardal. 2002

**Biological Sciences** exist within this line of research, but **papers** that have been reviewed all build upon

**Biological Sciences** genetic control of plant morphology. The **papers** reviewed within the morphology section

| Discipline | | |
| --- | --- | --- |
| Law | he has undertaken a detailed research *to discover* | the cases related to his statement; "The |
| Biological Sciences | of these studies is that B. anthracis was *discovered* | *to* have three homologues of sortase transpeptidase |
| Anthropology | tool can act *to* maximise the possibility of *discovering* | new species within a region of interest |
| English | enjoyed. The pulling apart of nonsense *to discover* | its structures may serve us to understand |
| Cybernetics & Electronic Engineering | femtosecond pulse shaping is sensitive *to discover* | and exploit the difference in the investigated |
| Biological Sciences | repeats (VNTRs). Only four differences were *discovered* | between the main chromosomes of the Florida |
| Health | been included in the final analysis. The **search** | was then widened using Caredata and the |
| Health | included. The following data bases were **searched** | in order to collect relevant papers. These |
| Publishing | Google Print is an online book and content, **search** | engine. The Guild want to protect writers |
| Publishing | that it restricts what text is available to **search** | through but believes that having this content |
| English | without rhyme as a parody of Lear, and a short **search** | on the internet throws up dozens of parodies |
| Cybernetics & Electronic Engineering | therefore, more robust than existing directed **search** | methods (Michalewicz, 1999). Evolutionary |
| Cybernetics & Electronic Engineering | incorporated other concurrently running **search** | methods in addition to traditional GA search |

# Appendix 7

Distribution of Narrative Recounts by discipline and level

|    | Disciplines | Level 1 | Level 2 | Level 3 | Level 4 |
|----|-------------|---------|---------|---------|---------|
| AH | Archaeology, Linguistics | | 1 | 4 | 1 |
| LS | Agriculture, Biological Sciences, Health, Medicine | 9 | 7 | 7 | 2 |
| PS | Architecture, Chemistry, Computer Science, Cybernetics, Engineering, Physics | 1 | 9 | 5 | 6 |
| SS | Anthropology, Business, HLTM, Publishing, Sociology, Education | 7 | 3 | 5 | 3 |

Distribution of Empathy Writing by discipline and level

|    | Disciplines | Level 1 | Level 2 | Level 3 | Level 4 |
|----|-------------|---------|---------|---------|---------|
| AH | English | 5 | | | |
| LS | Agriculture, Food Sciences, Health, Medicine, Psychology | 3 | 1 | 10 | 5 |
| PS | Architecture, Computer Science, Maths, Physics | | 1 | 7 | |
| SS | Publishing, HLTM | 2 | | 1 | |

# Index